The Library at Trinity College, designed by Sir Christopher Wren and completed in 1695, is known all over the world for its books, its architecture and its sculpture. Each of these aspects is authoritatively examined in this volume, as David McKitterick, Howard Colvin and Malcolm Baker explore the ways in which seventeenth-century ideas were modified and extended until by the early nineteenth century the Library had achieved the coherent appearance which it has today. Their discussion is accompanied by numerous illustrations, including reproductions of all of Wren's surviving drawings.

The making of the Wren Library

The making of the

Wren Library

Trinity College, Cambridge

Edited by David McKitterick

Fellow and Librarian, Trinity College

CAMBRIDGE
UNIVERSITY PRESS

Published by the Press Syndicate of the University of Cambridge

The Pitt Building, Trumpington Street, Cambridge CB2 IRP

40 West 20th Street, New York, NY 10011-4211, USA

10 Stamford Road, Oakleigh, Melbourne 3166, Australia

© Cambridge University Press 1995

First published 1995

Printed in Great Britain at the University Press, Cambridge

A catalogue record for this book is available from the British Library

Library of Congress cataloguing in publication data

The making of the Wren Library, Trinity College, Cambridge/edited
by David McKitterick.

p. cm.

Includes bibliographical references and index.

ISBN 0 521 44305 9 (hardback)

1. Trinity College (University of Cambridge). Library–History.
2. Academic libraries–England–Cambridge–History. 3. Library
buildings–England–Cambridge–History. 4. Wren, Christopher, Sir,
1632–1723. 5. Cambridge (England)–Buildings, structures, etc.
1. McKitterick, David.

Z792.T75W74 1995

027.7426'59–dc20   94–33387 CIP

ISBN 0521 44305 9 hardback

Contents

Illustrations   (Between pages 27 and 28)

Acknowledgements

Three hundred years after the completion of the Wren Library in 1695, this book is designed to examine its planning, construction and use during the first century and a half of its existence, as its appearance and collections gradually assumed the form familiar today. In many respects, this is thus a continuation of Philip Gaskell's *Trinity College Library: the first 150 years*, published in 1980. But on this occasion, thanks to the survival of many of Wren's drawings, it has proved possible to reproduce, more fully than ever before, the material evidence of the way the building was conceived. Thanks are due first to the Warden and Fellows of All Souls College, Oxford, for permission to reproduce the drawings in their possession. In particular, the authors wish to thank the Librarian, Mr Peter Lewis, and the Sub-Librarian, Miss Norma Potter.

In Trinity College, this book would be considerably poorer but for the knowledge and generosity with which it was discreetly guided by the late Robert Robson. His death in January 1995, a few days before the first proofs were received, has taken from us a generous friend and one who found constant delight and inspiration in Wren's library. His own account of it forms a central chapter in *The library of Trinity College, Cambridge*, written jointly with the then Librarian, Philip Gaskell, and published by the College in 1971, shortly after the building was restored.

In conversation or in correspondence others have provided help at crucial moments, including Mark Blackburn, Robert Dunton, Peter Gathercole, Peter Hoare, Neil Hopkinson, David E. Johnston, Ronald Milne, Stephen Parkes, David Scrase, Frank Stubbings and Mark Wilkinson. Peter Locke, who oversaw the restoration a quarter of a century ago, has been constantly ready to answer questions as they have occurred to the contributors, while James Campbell provided timely help in examining the structure of the building even as this book was being written. Others are acknowledged at appropriate places later in this volume.

Most of the photographs are by the photographic staffs of the Bodleian Library and of Cambridge University Library, but particular thanks are due to Les Goodey, to whom has fallen most of the work at Cambridge.

D. McK. *March 1995*

Abbreviations

Bernard, *Catalogi*
> Edward Bernard, *Catalogi librorum manuscriptorum Angliae et Hiberniae* (Oxford, 1697)

Cambridge under Queen Anne
> J. E. B. Mayor (ed.), *Cambridge under Queen Anne* (Cambridge Antiquarian Society, 1911)

Clark, *Endowments*
> J. W. Clark, *Endowments of the University of Cambridge* (Cambridge, 1904)

DNB
> *Dictionary of national biography*

Fenlon, *Cambridge music manuscripts*
> Iain Fenlon (ed.), *Cambridge music manuscripts, 900–1700, published to coincide with an exhibition held at the Fitzwilliam Museum* (Cambridge, 1982)

Gaskell, *Trinity College Library*
> Philip Gaskell, *Trinity College Library: the first 150 years* (Cambridge, 1980)

Gaskell and Robson
> Philip Gaskell and Robert Robson, *The library of Trinity College, Cambridge: a short history* (Cambridge, 1971)

Hearne, *Remarks and collections*
> Thomas Hearne, *Remarks and collections*, ed. C. E. Doble *et al.*, 11 vols. (Oxford Historical Society, 1885–1921)

Historical register
> J. R. Tanner (ed.), *The historical register of the University of Cambridge to the year 1910* (Cambridge, 1910)

James, *Western manuscripts*
> M. R. James, *The western manuscripts in the library of Trinity College, Cambridge*, 4 vols. (Cambridge, 1900–4)

Jolly, *Histoire*

    Claude Jolly (ed.), *Histoire des bibliothèques françaises: les bibliothèques sous l'ancien régime, 1530–1789* (Paris, 1988)

McKenzie, *Cambridge University Press*

    D. F. McKenzie, *The Cambridge University Press, 1696–1712: a bibliographical study*, 2 vols. (Cambridge, 1966)

McKitterick, *Cambridge University Library*

    David McKitterick, *Cambridge University Library: a history. The eighteenth and nineteenth centuries* (Cambridge, 1986)

Monk, *Life of Bentley*

    J. H. Monk, *The life of Richard Bentley, DD*, 2nd edn, 2 vols. (1833)

Nichols, *Illustrations*

    J. and J. B. Nichols, *Illustrations of the literary history of the eighteenth century*, 8 vols. (1817–58)

Nichols, *Literary anecdotes*

    J. Nichols, *Literary anecdotes of the eighteenth century*, 9 vols. (1812–16)

Oates, *Cambridge University Library*

    J. C. T. Oates, *Cambridge University Library: a history. From the beginning to the Copyright Act of Queen Anne* (Cambridge, 1986)

RCHM, *Cambridge*

    Royal Commission on Historical Monuments, *An inventory of the historical monuments in the City of Cambridge*, 2 vols. + maps (1959)

RIB

    R. G. Collingwood and R. P. Wright, *The Roman inscriptions of Britain.* 1. *Inscriptions on stone* (Oxford, 1965)

Sinker, *Biographical notes*

    Robert Sinker, *Biographical notes on the librarians of Trinity College, Cambridge* (Cambridge Antiquarian Society, 1897)

Stukeley, *Family memoirs*

    William Stukeley, *Family memoirs*, 3 vols. (Surtees Society, 1882–7)

Sutherland and Mitchell, *Oxford*

    L. S. Sutherland and L. G. Mitchell (ed.), *The history of the University of Oxford.* 5. *The eighteenth century* (Oxford, 1986)

TCBS

    Transactions of the Cambridge Bibliographical Society

TC Mun.

    Trinity College muniments

Willis and Clark

    Robert Willis and J. W. Clark, *The architectural history of the University of Cambridge, and of the colleges of Cambridge and Eton,* 3 vols. (Cambridge, 1886)

Wren Soc. 5

    Wren Society, vol. 5. *Designs of Sir Chr. Wren for Oxford, Cambridge, London, Windsor, etc.* (Oxford: Wren Society, 1928)

Unless stated otherwise, the place of publication is London.

CHAPTER ONE

INTRODUCTION
David McKitterick

The eighteenth century is hardly far enough removed from us to be canonized among the 'good old times' and the tradition of abuses which have since been reformed or partially reformed, is sufficiently strong an advocatus diaboli to deter us even from beatifying it.[1]

The University of Cambridge in the eighteenth century has been convicted of violating its statutes, misusing its endowments, and neglecting its obligations. It is impossible to dispute the essential justice of this verdict.[2]

Both verdicts, delivered sixty years apart, were by members of Trinity College. But both judges also discovered some virtues at least to belie the poor reputation of the eighteenth century. In any period, reformers must necessarily paint the status quo in a poor light. In the hands of those who sought university reform in the nineteenth century, as well as in the eyes of a more remote twentieth century, the eighteenth century easily lent itself to criticism.

Inevitably, in a great measure the libraries of the University and colleges expressed these contradictions. In 1715, King George I presented to the University the library of John Moore, Bishop of Ely. It was munificent in every way, one of the largest private collections not only in England, but even in Europe, in a generation that also witnessed the beginnings of the Harleian Library, whose manuscripts were in 1753 to form one of the foundation collections of the British Museum. But in Cambridge, this royal munificence (inspired by political as much as University needs) was followed by decades in which the books lay unsorted on the floors of the Old Schools, uncatalogued and pilfered. For some members of the University it was an embarrassment that so unprecedented a gift should be so neglected.[3] In retrospect, it seems yet more shameful, in that Moore's library has proved to be the core collection for many of the aspects of the University Library that are now most valued. Moreover, it arrived within a few years of legislation that was to have

1 Christopher Wordsworth, *Scholae academiae* (Cambridge, 1877), p. 1.
2 D. A. Winstanley, *Unreformed Cambridge* (Cambridge, 1935), p. 3.
3 McKitterick, *Cambridge University Library*, pp. 47–152, 153–66.

an even more profound effect. In 1710, the Copyright Act of Queen Anne, in its provisions for copyright deposit, seemed to secure for the University Library copies of all new books as they were published. But here, too, hopes were temporarily disappointed, and books did not arrive as some had expected. The failures of legislation to provide what the legislators had apparently intended was not set to rights for more than a century.[4]

In the eighteenth century, as in most of the nineteenth, the colleges were more important than the University, wielding political, social and financial power, and maintaining their dominance in teaching as well as the loyalties of their members. In Trinity, as in the University, it is difficult to discover much consistency. The new Wren Library, by far the largest public building to be erected in Cambridge since King's College Chapel, remained universally admired. As events were to prove, its purposes, and the assumptions of those who envisaged it and built it, could easily be neglected. A succession of private libraries given to the College in the late seventeenth and early eighteenth centuries brought rapid transformation and expansion, widening the scope of the collection already existing in the College Library, increasing the depth of coverage in subjects already represented, and providing much-needed recent books. Like most institutional libraries in this period, the college library depended on private generosity. But such dependence easily led to imbalance, and even inadequacies. The surge of interest and accessions in the decades immediately following the completion of Wren's building ceased for a generation in the later part of the century. The shelves seemed full (in fact there was plenty of room, albeit in the cupboards); and the prolonged discussions that eventually led to long-overdue sales of duplicates were a distraction from what others might perceive as a need to keep abreast of modern books. As the book trade in Britain as a whole expanded in the last two decades of the eighteenth century, and the numbers of new publications increased as never before, accessions to the College Library decreased – in the first decade of the nineteenth century almost to vanishing point.

Meanwhile, the Wren Library's reputation as a museum grew, distracting from its function and potential as a library. For casual visitors especially, it remained in large part a museum until the first years of the twentieth century.

Though they were financially independent, the fortunes of the colleges were in many other respects bound up with those of the University of which they formed part. In detail they were subject to many variations. In the 1830s,

4 *Ibid.*, pp. 27–44.

those who sought university or college reform found much of which to complain. But the changes in the fortunes of the Wren Library were by then well established, for the better. A new focus on the principal Greek authors was nowhere more obvious than in the publications of a reinvigorated University Press and on the shelves of the Library. In 1829, C. H. Hartshorne, a young graduate of St John's College, published his *Book rarities in the University of Cambridge*, a work that, for all its inaccuracies and its lamentable stylistic imitation of Thomas Frognall Dibdin, did more than any other single volume in the nineteenth century to publicise some of the riches among the early printed books in Cambridge libraries.[5] Hartshorne was not interested in manuscripts, and so ignored some of the College's greatest treasures; but he did list the Caxtons in Trinity and, most importantly, the collection formed by Edward Capell, editor of Shakespeare.[6] By Hartshorne's day, much of the future importance of the Wren Library had become clear. Capell's books in 1779, and the bequest of Jonathan Raine in 1831, identified the Library as a resort not simply of early printing, but of early printed editions that had an antiquarian, literary and bibliographical value over and above the fashions of bibliophily. This had been assumed in the medieval manuscripts since the days of Whitgift and Nevile in the sixteenth and early seventeenth centuries. For all their heterogeneous nature, the Gale manuscripts, mostly given in the eighteenth century, offered a working collection, which both Thomas and Roger Gale had already quarried.[7] But these earlier collections were themselves now enriched.

So, in the generations of post-Napoleonic Europe, and to the accompaniment of a new determination among members of the College to ensure that modern books were bought regularly, the Wren Library became identified also as one of the country's principal repositories of early printed books as well as manuscripts. Unfashionable as is Hartshorne's style, there lay beneath his linguistic veneer a view of the Library that was widely shared:

> The whole appearance is strikingly beautiful, and yields to no interior view whatever in the kingdom, whether the perfect proportions of the architecture are considered, or the exquisite tracing and minuteness of the carvings, or the living marble of the statuaries, or the varied and precious mass of learning upon the surrounding shelves. The casual observer may be satisfied with a sight of the antiquities brought from the Sandwich Isles by Captain Cook, or the dried man from the Madeiras;

5 Arnold Hunt, 'A study in bibliomania: Charles Henry Hartshorne and Richard Heber', *The Book Collector* 42 (1993), pp. 24–43, 185–212.
6 See below, pp. 78–82.
7 See below, pp. 63–4.

but our book-lover will long to handle some of the thirty thousand volumes, to fix his eyes upon manuscripts written by the immortal Newton, and Milton, and Barrow. Here may he find them all, bending under venerable dust, and slumbering in an almost unbroken repose; seldom disturbed, unless by rare and ardent spirits like his own, who touch with consecrated enthusiasm their hallowed pages.[8]

It is difficult to reconcile the dust, on the books and also hanging in the haze of Hartshorne's prose, with undergraduates at the beginning of term, intent on seizing the necessary books from the Library. A member of the College, J.M.F.Wright, depicted this latter scene vividly – and perhaps a little fancifully – in his *Alma mater*, published only two years before Hartshorne's work.[9] Both authors made exaggerated claims to captivate their readers' imagination. But while both, in very different ways, caught a little of the Library, neither caught the characteristics that had established it as a collection unique of its kind, of international importance and reputation – characteristics that were, within a generation, to prove it one of the principal resources for some of the triumphs of Victorian literary and historical scholarship.

In the years covered by this volume, a period in which the Wren Library was gradually filled with books until the original shelves were no longer adequate, and new ones had to be built, Trinity College saw its position and influence in the University transformed in several respects; but in none more dramatically than in numbers of undergraduates. In the late seventeenth century, the population of students in the University was in decline. St John's College, then the largest, often had as many as twice the number of undergraduates as its neighbour Trinity, the next largest; but both were more populous than the other colleges, at each of which fewer than ten matriculations a year were usual until a general rise set in by about 1810. During the eighteenth century, the two largest colleges shared a similar pattern in their fortunes in this respect, after a decline in the St John's intake from the late 1720s, Trinity overtaking its neighbour briefly at the end of the 1750s and the two running more or less parallel until Trinity leapt ahead after about 1820. Trinity reached about a hundred matriculations in the first years of the 1820s, and St John's the same at the end of the 1860s. As always, these numbers are reflected in residential building. Between the construction of Bishop's Hostel in the early 1670s, and the commencement of New Court (or King's Court as it

8 C. H. Hartshorne, *The book rarities in the University of Cambridge* (1829), pp. 277–8.
9 See further below, pp. 87–8.

was first known) in 1823, no new residential buildings for undergraduates were erected at Trinity. St John's built Third Court in 1669–71, and nothing further for the purpose until Rickman's New Court in 1827–31.[10]

According to tradition, the inspiration for the new library at Trinity came from Isaac Barrow, Master from 1673 to 1677 (fig. 88). It is not clear how many details are strictly true in the often-quoted tale of the circumstances of its beginning. It was one thing for the Master to be convinced; the Fellows had to be convinced also. But the elements of the story are probably sufficiently accurate in that as Vice-Chancellor in 1675–6 Barrow led discussions on the University's need for buildings, and for a library in particular:[11]

They say that Dr. Barrow pressed the heads of the university to build a theatre; it being a profanation and scandal that the speeches should be had in the university church, and that also be deformed with scaffolds and defiled with rude crowds and outcries. This matter was formally considered at a council of the heads; and arguments of difficulty and want of supplies went strong against it. Dr. Barrow assured them that if they made a sorry building they might fail of contributions; but if they made it very magnificent and stately, and at least exceeding that at Oxford, all gentlemen of their interest would generously contribute; it being what they desired and little less than required of them; and money would not be wanted as the building went up and occasion called for it. But sage caution prevailed, and the matter at that time was wholly laid aside. Dr. Barrow was piqued at this pusillanimity, and declared that he would go straight to his college and lay out the foundations of a building to enlarge his back court and close it with a stately library, which should be more magnificent and costly than what he had proposed to them; and doubted not but upon the interest of his college in a short time to bring it to perfection. And he was as good as his word; for that very afternoon he, with his gardeners and servants, staked out the very foundation upon which the building now stands.[12]

The ensuing events, and the course of Wren's design, are explored in more detail by Howard Colvin later in this volume. The Sheldonian Theatre at Oxford, a youthful and ingenious design by Wren, had been in use since 1669. At Cambridge, the University had begun to proceed towards a similar

10 Figures for matriculation are taken from J. A. Venn, *The entries at the various colleges in the University of Cambridge, 1544–1906, based on an average extending over ten years about any given year* (Cambridge, 1908). For the arguments over building New Court, see Winstanley, *Early Victorian Cambridge* (Cambridge, 1955), pp. 60–5.

11 Isaac Barrow, 'Oratio habita in Comitiis' [1676], repr. in his *Theological works*, ed. A. Napier, 9 vols. (Cambridge, 1859), 9, pp. XLI–XLII and 221–2.

12 Roger North, *The lives of the Norths*, ed. A. Jessopp, 3 vols. (1890), 2, p. 326.

building, roughly on the site of the present Senate House, in 1673, and at first all had gone well.[13] But North's allusion to thought of a new senate house, or theatre, designed to rival the Sheldonian, is a distraction in the context of libraries. As Wren's drawing of 1675–6 for the proposed senate house at Cambridge makes clear (fig. 18), by then the University was considering a single building to contain both a 'theatre' (or, as became the normal use at Cambridge, senate house) and the University Library, both on the first floor. North's suggestion – that Barrow's mind moved from theatre to library – omits the crucially important dual purpose of this building, of which Barrow now seized on one part.[14]

For most Cambridge residents, the more obvious parallel with the building that gradually appeared at the back of Trinity was the library abutting the river only a little way downstream. At St John's, the new library had been completed only about fifty years previously. It, too, had been of an adventurous design in its own way, in taking its windows up to a high ceiling. As befitted so large a college, it was at the time of its planning and erection easily the biggest library building in the University, on a larger scale than the University Library itself. And unlike part of the latter, which by the mid seventeenth century had spread to a second side of the medieval court then comprising the Schools, it could claim to have been built especially as a library. In 1654, John Evelyn had considered St John's College and its library 'the fairest of that Universitie', and the University Library 'but mean': the library of Trinity, hidden away upstairs in the north range of Great Court, was not worth notice.[15] Foreign writers likewise saw little remarkable in Trinity when compared with either the University Library, home of the fifth-century manuscript of the Gospels and Acts of the Apostles known as the Codex Bezae, or (as was the case for Johann Hottinger in 1664, and his follower Johannes Lomeier in 1669) the library at Corpus.[16] In 1662, the Dutch artist William Schellinks visited Cambridge. Like others, he admired the library at St John's, and (since it was then in the side-chapels of the one building essential to every visitor to Cambridge) remarked on that at King's; but though he appreciated some of the architectural beauties of Trinity, his guide ignored the library, instead showing him the tennis courts and introducing him to the College beer.[17]

In 1675, Trinity was in no position to embark on an ambitious building of the kind Barrow had in mind. Agriculture was depressed.[18] In 1672, William Lynnett, then Junior Bursar, had written with unusual, but not necessarily much exaggerated, gratitude in acknowledgement of a gift of venison:

13 Willis and Clark, 3, pp. 40–3.
14 Wren's drawings of the proposed senate house are also reproduced in Wren Soc. 5, p. 31 and plates XIII–XIV.
15 John Evelyn, *Diary*, ed. E. S. de Beer, 6 vols. (Oxford, 1955), 3, p. 136.
16 J. Lomeier, *A seventeenth-century view of European libraries: Lomeier's De bibliothecis, chapter x*, trans. with an introduction and notes by J. W. Montgomery (Berkeley, 1962), pp. 53–4.
17 *The journal of William Schellinks' travels in England, 1661–1663*, trans. and ed. Maurice Exwood and H. L. Lehmann (Camden Society, 5th ser. 1, 1993), p. 152.
18 Joan Thirsk, 'Agricultural policy: public debate and legislation', in Joan Thirsk (ed.), *The agrarian history of England* (Cambridge, 1985), 5.2, at pp. 325–88. See also H. F. Howard, *An account of the finances of the College of St John the Evangelist in the University of Cambridge, 1511–1926* (Cambridge, 1935).

When my Lords Venison is eaten we must resolve either to break up house or run on tick till ye next rent-day, to such miserable poverty are we reduced that we haue not a farthing left in ye College to buy commons; but I pray let not every body know so much, for we live by our credit.[19]

In the financial year 1672–3, the Senior Bursar's final accounts recorded a loss. Rather than borrow, the College could only raise the money for a major new building either from a private benefactor or by public appeal. The latter was the path that was chosen. In January 1675/6, a printed notice was issued, signed by Barrow, drawing attention to the needs and opportunities in a manner calculated to appeal to several interests:

Whereas the Right Reverend Father in God, Dr *John Hacket*, late Lord Bishop of *Lichfield* and *Coventrey*... out of his great kindness to *Trinity College*, (of which Society he some time was a most worthy Member and Ornament), did inlarge the same with a fair Building, the Yearly Rents whereof, he did out of his great Wisdom, Assign to be imployed in Buying Books for the Library of the said College: And whereas the present Library, notwithstanding much cost laid out in Supporting and Repairing it, is found too weak a Fabrick for the great weight of Frames and Books, already contained in it; so, that its failing for a time hath been feared, that fear growing with frequent accessions of New Books thereto; However, assuredly it cannot either for Strength or capacity be fit to receive the Addition of Books intended by our Noble Benefactour, (whose Intentions we resolve exactly to perform) and by other Donations constantly accruing to it. We the Master and fellows of the said College have entertained a design of Erecting a new Library in a place very convenient for use, and for the grace of the College, intending to inlarge the *New Court*, called *Nevil's Court*; and by adjoyning the Library, to make it up a fair Quadrangle: The accomplishment of which design, beside the advantages from it to this Society, will as we conceive, yield much Ornament to the *University*, and some honour to the Nation. Wherefore, as we our selves have not been wanting by a free Contribution of Money, according to the Abilities of each one, to set it on foot; so we do earnestly recommend the furtherance of it to all Generous Persons, Favourers of Learning, and Friends to the *Universities*, especially to those, who have had any part of their Education in this College; Humbly requesting, and

19 Lynnett to John Thornton, at Woburn, 7 August 1672: Bodleian Library MS Rawlinson Letters 109, f. 70.

hoping from them, That now, upon so needful and worthy an occasion, they will express their Affections to Learning, and to this Royal Nursery thereof: Whereby, as they will at present injoy the satisfaction of having in so noble a way benefited the Publick and Obliged Posterity; so they shall certainly perpetuate their own Memory with Honour, by so conspicuous and durable a Monument of their Benefaction. To which end, we promise that our most careful endeavour shall concur, in recording their Names with the best advantage, as in the Duty of Gratitude we are bound.[20]

John Hacket (fig. 3), whose gift of money had enabled the College to erect Bishop's Hostel by the end of 1671, had from his first entry to Trinity as an undergraduate during Thomas Nevile's term as Master been among those who took a leading part in shaping the libraries of seventeenth-century Cambridge. He had been elected a Fellow of the College in 1614, and had enjoyed the patronage of John Williams, Lord Keeper, first as his chaplain and then in being presented to livings in London and Surrey. He was chaplain at the very time that Williams was most involved in the conception and commencement of the new library at St John's College in the 1620s. Richard Holdsworth, Master of Emmanuel (d. 1649), whose books transformed the University Library after the Restoration, had been among his friends. As Bishop, Hacket had been principally responsible for restoring the fabric of Lichfield Cathedral, following damage in the Civil War. Apart from Trinity, both Clare College and St John's benefited from his generosity. On his death in 1670, he bequeathed his own books (which his biographer estimated to have cost him £1,500) to the University Library, the Library to sell those books that it already possessed.[21]

The appeal for the new library, supported by an engraving by David Loggan of the proposed building (fig. 35),[22] was launched first among the fellowship and members of the College. At the head of the donors was James Duport, formerly Vice-Master and now Dean of Peterborough and Master of Magdalene, followed by Barrow.[23] Barrow has been given the credit for the Wren Library in popular tradition. But the influence of Duport may have been almost as great. Although his appointments, first in 1668 as Dean of Peterborough, had taken him away from the College, his recognition of the importance of libraries provided a stimulus as strong in its way as Barrow's own determination. For him, books offered not only reading, but also the

20 MS 0.11a.4 (9). A misdated transcript is in MS Add.a.106, f. 106, taken from Thomas Abingdon, *The antiquities of the Cathedral Church of Worcester* (1717), part 2 (Lichfield), pp. 52–4. Feingold ('Isaac Barrow: divine, scholar, mathematician', in M. Feingold (ed.), *Before Newton: the life and times of Isaac Barrow* (Cambridge, 1990), pp. 1–104, at p. 89) is mistaken in dating Barrow's appeal to June 1676: the printed paper is dated 3 January 1675/6.
21 John Hacket, *A century of sermons*, ed. Thomas Plume (London, 1675); Oates, *Cambridge University Library*, pp. 398–401.
22 'To Mr Loggan for ye plate Cutting in 730 Cutts 24 00 6' (MS 0.4.47, p. 165).
23 The donors are recorded in MS 0.4.46a.

means to learn what others dare not always speak out loud, offering in their silence a formal neutrality on which political, theological or scholarly debate could be founded:

mortui loquentur,
Muti & Consiliarii docebunt,
Quae nec forte alii sciunt, nec audent.[24]

Duport's lines, published in 1676, the same year that the College began its new library, offered a timely reminder of the value of libraries in a context of political turmoil: Duport himself, a committed royalist, well knew the dangers of a university and college divided by political and religious loyalties. The 1640s and 1650s had brought destruction, interruption and threats for the second time in little more than a century. The movement throughout England to refound or restore libraries was commensurately reinforced. By 1694, the historian John Strype was to note with gratitude the change from destruction to preservation and 'gleaning' by historians such as himself. Duport's belief similarly accorded libraries an unchallenged central importance.

By the end of the seventeenth century, uneasiness at England's lack of major libraries (and for most that meant in London) had warmed into a debate that was only to be halted with the foundation of the British Museum in 1753. But in the aftermath of the Restoration, the established cathedral libraries proved an especial focus of attention. Neglected, and even damaged, during the Interregnum, they attracted the attention of a new generation of deans and bishops determined on the restoration of buildings, the liturgy and cathedral libraries. John Hacket, one of Trinity's most imaginative benefactors, concentrated on restoring the building and proper services at Lichfield. At Ely, the Dean, Robert Mapletoft (who was also Master of Pembroke College) left his books to the cathedral on his death in 1677;[25] and by also providing for the library to be fitted up, he in effect refounded the cathedral library. At Peterborough, James Duport was instrumental in founding a new cathedral library in 1672.[26] Quite apart from any inspiration for the new library at Trinity, his direct influence is to be seen in the many books bearing a bookplate recording his gift to the College; in the rich library presented by one of his pupils, Sir Henry Puckering (fig. 4); and in Barrow himself, the pupil who he hoped would succeed him in the chair of Greek. While Duport at Peterborough, Mapletoft at Ely and (further away) Hacket at Lichfield all retained strong connections

24 James Duport, 'In bibliothecam bene instructam', in *Musae subsecivae* (Cambridge, 1676), pp. 54–5.
25 Mapletoft's will is in Cambridge University Archives, VC Court Wills IV, p.158. See also Dorothy M. Owen, *The library and muniments of Ely Cathedral* (Ely, 1973).
26 Peterborough Cathedral MS 37 (Benefactors' book), on deposit at Cambridge University Library.

9

27 Junior Bursar's accounts, 1665–6; Willis and Clark 2, p. 531. The Fire of London was example enough in 1666; but even in 1699, Martin Lister was to wax eloquent on the superiority of stone building (in Paris) to wooden constructions (in England) for the safety of libraries: 'And having said so much of the *Publick Libraries*, I cannot but congratulate their Happiness, to have them so well secured from Fire; it being one of the Perfections of this City to be so built and furnish'd, as not to have suffered by it these many Ages; and, indeed, I cannot see how Malice it self could destroy them, for the Houses here are all built of Stone, Wall, Floors, Stair-cases and all, some few Rooms excepted; no Wainscot, Woollen or Silk Hangings, which cannot be fired without giving notice by the intolerable stench, and the supply of much Fuel. 'Tis well for us in *London*, that there are very few publick Libraries, and those small and inconsiderable, and that the great number of Books are distributed into a thousand Hands, (no Country in *Europe* can compare to us for private Libraries) for if they were together in such vast quantities as in *Paris*, learning would run the hazard of daily suffering. Here with us, methinks, every Man that goes to Bed, when asleep, lies like a dead *Roman* upon a Funeral Pile, dreading some unexpected *Apotheosis*; for all is combustible about him, and the Paint of the Deal Boards may serve for Incense, the quicker to burn him to Ashes' (Martin Lister, *A journey to Paris in the year 1698* (1699), pp. 138–9).
28 On his death, Babington's books were sold at auction, in the College, in July 1692; a copy of the catalogue is in Emmanuel College Library, recording a collection overwhelmingly theological, with a smattering of English history and poetry.
29 'How many Donors names do I behold/ Names in vermilion dy'd, & grav'd with Gold!' (Barnes's own translation). Emmanuel College MS 169. For further remarks on the appeal, and other sources of money, see below, pp. 38–9.
30 M. Feingold, 'Isaac Barrow's library', in Feingold (ed.), *Before Newton*, pp. 333–72.

with Trinity, it was also possible in the mid 1670s to point to Honywood at Lincoln and Compton at St Paul's, and in the following decade to the refitting of the libraries at Durham and (with Morley's books to hand) at Winchester. In a fellowship whose members looked to ecclesiastical preferment, links between the College and dioceses across the country created a web of information and opinions of which it was impossible to be unaware.

The fire that damaged the roof of the old library on the top floor of the north range of Great Court in 1665–6 was an eloquent reminder of dangers of another kind, and of the advantages of a stone building rather than one so much composed of wood.[27]

Both Duport and Barrow gave £100 (Barrow following it with the same amount again in 1679), as did Humphrey Babington, Senior Bursar,[28] and George Chamberlaine, Vice-Master, and Anthony Marshal, Clement Nevile, William Lynnett, senior Fellows, and Sir John Barrington. Among the rest of the Fellows, past and present, Isaac Newton gave £40 and John Ray £10. In London (where donations were collected by the College's agent Thomas Boughey of Token House Yard, Lothbury), Sir John Ottway, Chancellor of Durham, the Earl of Kent, and Richard Sterne, Archbishop of York, all gave £100. By the end of 1676, the appeal had produced £2,805. 10s. Although no trace of it now remains, there seems to have been a board, or perhaps even a stone inscription, on which the names of benefactors were recorded. 'Quot Benefactorum miniatis nomina signis / Splendent aurato nomina sculpta stylo', exclaimed Joshua Barnes, of Emmanuel College, in a poem to which we shall return.[29] It is not clear, on this evidence alone, whether such a record existed, or Barnes was at this point drawing on his mind's eye.

It was an encouraging beginning, and by spring 1677 the building was well advanced. But on 4 May 1677, only sixteen months after issuing his public appeal, Barrow died, intestate. Had he lived longer, and made a will, the College might have received both his books (to add to what he had already given in the previous few years) and more money than the initial gifts he had made towards the building of the new library. Instead, the books were sold, and his property passed to his father.[30]

Barrow's successor was John North, a man of very different temperament but who now found himself obliged to take the lead at a critical point in the appeal for money. With work on the new building now well under way, a further printed appeal was issued in July 1677, signed now by North, intended to invigorate those who had not yet been generous to the project, or who might give further sums.[31] Nothing had been said in the original appeal of the design of the new building, its size, or even very precisely of its location. With these matters now settled, North was able to be particular. Now that the end of Nevile's Court had been decided on, he explained, other matters followed as a consequence:

> Because it was necessary, that it should bear proportion with the Greatness of the Hall standing at the other End, and that the whole *Court* should comprehend a decent and beautiful Space, they [i.e. the Master and Fellows] thought it would be best to carry on the Sides of *Nevils Court* eight Arches farther; All which would not only answer the Necessity and Convenience of this *College*, but also be a great Ornament to the *University*.[32]

By now, he explained, the building had been raised to the top of the ground-floor arches, and the floor of the Library itself was almost laid. Apart from this printed appeal, North, like Barrow, followed up possible benefactors with more personal letters. On 25 July 1678 he wrote to Sir Thomas Browne, explaining that the new library was expected to cost twelve or fourteen thousand pounds. Browne's son responded with £20 in 1682.[33] A few months later, with building either already suspended or in danger of being so, North wrote to his own elder brother Francis (later Lord Chancellor, Baron Guilford) seeking now not a gift, but a loan. He applied again two years later, this time in the hope that, Lord Culpeper apparently having fallen behind with money already promised, sufficient would be forthcoming to build the rooms to extend the south range of Nevile's Court, to match those already paid for by Sir Thomas Sclater on the opposite side.[34] In the event, the southern extension was paid for partly by Humphrey Babington, senior Fellow, and partly by subscription.

But although the first three years of the appeal raised £6,632 (much of it in gifts of £10 or less), the next three produced under £2,000; in the following years the income slipped still further. In October 1679, it was agreed that immediate costs should be temporarily met from the College's funds, until appeal monies were received.[35] In November, approval was given for the sale of duplicates from Duport's library.[36] But as expenditure on building each year was usually tied to the income, the pace of construction was inevitably affected. Loans from members of the College enabled work to continue, and were generous in themselves; but it was an unsatisfactory way in which to

31 North's character is described at some length in Roger North, *The lives of the Norths*, vol. 2.
32 MS O.11a.4 (9). Another more personal letter seeking funds to extend the south range of Nevile's Court, in manuscript and written slightly later, is preserved in British Library MS Harley 7001, f. 420r: see also Hartshorne, *The book rarities in the University of Cambridge*, p. 274. Notwithstanding its inclusion in Barrow's *Theological works*, 1, pp. LXV–LXVII, its content suggests it was written after Barrow's death.
33 North to Sir Thomas Browne, St James's Day 1678: Bodleian Library MS Rawlinson D.391, ff. 15, 17, 21. Trinity College MS O.4.46a, p. 19.
34 John North to Francis North, 31 March 1679, 12 June [1681]: Bodleian Library MS North c. 5, ff. 71, 93. Francis North gave £10 in 1678. For Sclater, see below, p. 46.
35 Conclusion Book, 14 October 1679.
36 *Ibid.*, 18 November 1679.

proceed. The decision not to build a staircase pavilion at the south end, as indicated by Wren's plans (fig. 35), must have been taken early, since the stonework shows no sign of the alteration that would have been a consequence. When in 1683 John North died, having been Master for only six years, the arrival of his successor brought some succour, since John Montagu, son of the Earl of Sandwich, applied to members of his family for assistance; but even so, in the year 1684–5 less than £250 was received. Moreover, in almost every year between 1685–6 and the end of the century, the College's more general audited accounts showed a deficit, sometimes substantial.[37] The College could not afford to provide what subscriptions failed to raise. In this persistent shortage of money, the gift by the Chancellor of the University from 1689, the Duke of Somerset, was not merely encouraging; it also, in effect, revitalised the programme of work. Shortly afterwards, in March 1691/2, seven further individuals each provided a *classis*, or group of shelves, sure indication that the building was at last advancing towards completion. The books were moved in from the old library in Great Court in 1695.[38]

It is impossible today to be certain to what extent the design of the Library followed any instructions from Barrow, his successor John North, or the Fellows. In the provision for entry to the new library at first-floor level from the westernmost rooms in the north and south ranges, it is perhaps possible to see a College requirement or suggestion, rather than the architect's invention. Yet this decision, to permit access at first-floor level from these new rooms, and thus in practice to align the floor of the interior of the Library with the already-existing floor of Nevile's Court, fundamentally affected both the inside and the outside of the new building. Whatever the meeting of minds here, the decision to take up as much space as was available at the end of Nevile's Court affected the appearance of the court in several ways that may not have been expected, in that Wren's great pavilion, lit from the east and west by a procession of vast windows running from end to end, sat uneasily against the smaller and older buildings. It also committed the College to expenditure on a scale that in the difficult years of the late seventeenth century required not a little courage.

The modern arrangement of the court has obscured part of Wren's and the College's conception, and in particular some of the visual links between the older buildings and the new. Loggan's view of Nevile's Court (fig. 5) shows the grass plots arranged so that a wide path linked Wren's tribunal on the west

37 Senior Bursar's accounts, 1685–6, 1686–7, 1687–8, 1688–9, 1689–90, 1691–2, 1692–3, 1693–4, 1695–6, 1696–7, 1697–8, 1698–9, 1699–1700. In several years the deficit was over 15 per cent of the total income.

38 'To the Porters for Remouing the Books into the New Library 3.6.0' (Junior Bursar's accounts, 1694–5).

wall of the Hall directly with the central arch of the new library, this crucial visual point being established by the bas-relief by Caius Gabriel Cibber, who was also responsible for the large statues on the roof. This sculpture (fig. 6), depicting the translators of the Septuagint presenting their work to Ptolemy in the library at Alexandria, was carefully chosen. It was a reminder of the College Library as the means of preserving and sharing the written (and printed) word. It was also a means of claiming the ambitious plans for the new building as a modern version of the greatest library of antiquity. In his letter to the College,[39] Wren had written of not wishing to emphasise the centre of the east face of his building; yet by April 1679 this carving had been prepared[40] – a sculptural rather than an architectural statement to make its own visual as well as intellectual contribution.

For further inspiration in the design of the building as a whole, as well as for architectural parallels, one must look abroad.[41] Wren never visited Italy. His overseas travels were limited to a few months in Paris in 1665–6, when he also travelled a little outside the capital. In Paris, the growing collection of the abbey of Saint-Germain-des-Prés, under the eye of its librarian Luc d'Achery, was attracting increasing attention. But by far the most important library building then in course of construction was at the new Collège des Quatre Nations, including provision for the library of Cardinal Mazarin, who had died in 1661.[42] In their conception, in their arrangements and in their wide-ranging contents, such libraries were directly relevant to the needs of a new college library in Cambridge.

But while precedents and comparisons can be proposed for the design of the building, these do not explain the decision of the College to build on such a scale. The architectural conception for such a purpose was unparalleled in Britain. No college library hitherto had been conceived in such intellectual terms: a large building, but one that was expected to expand both in numbers of books and in subject-matter. There would seem to be much truth in North's account of the disappointment that inspired Barrow to embark on such a project. The circumstantial detail of his proceeding with his gardeners to stake out the plan of the present building may be fanciful; but it seems not improbable that Barrow had for some time been meditating on how, and on what scale, the College should replace its existing library. In London, the gift to the Royal Society in 1667 of most of the library in Arundel House raised a similar agenda, still unfinished in 1676, respecting housing and subject

39 See p. 142 below.
40 MS 0.4.47, p. 97.
41 See further below, pp. 35–6.
For a wider discussion of the European background, see Regina Becker, 'Theorie und Praxis – zur Typologie in der Bibliotheksarchitektur des 17. und 18. Jahrhunderts', in C.-P. Warncke (ed.), *Ikonographie der Bibliotheken, Wolfenbütteler Schriften zur Geschichte des Buchwesens* 17 (Wiesbaden, 1992), pp. 235–69.
42 Alfred Franklin, *Histoire de la Bibliothèque Mazarine*, 3rd edn (Paris, 1931); Pierre Gasnault, 'De la Bibliothèque de Mazarin à la Bibliothèque Mazarine', in Jolly, *Histoire*, pp. 135–45.

coverage.[43] But in Cambridge, thwarted in one grand design, he turned to the other that had been occupying his mind.

Barrow's own experience of libraries was certainly more broadly based than Wren's. In the course of his overseas travels in 1655–9, he had spent time in Paris, had briefly visited Venice, and had passed several months engaged in the study of coins in the Biblioteca Laurenziana in Florence. He also spent a prolonged period in Turkey, and passed briefly through Germany and the Netherlands on his return journey.[44] Although he has left no impressions of his opinions, and little clue as to which libraries he may simply have visited, the time abroad provided ample opportunities for gaining a perspective quite outside the traditional experience of the libraries of Cambridge.

Perhaps the tale of Barrow's promptness after his disappointment at the failure to agree on a new senate house grew in the telling. But in itself it does little to explain how University discussions concerning a meeting place should be turned in his mind into determination to build a library for his college – and, moreover, one larger than the University was to need for almost fifty years. In order to explore the background that inspired such a transition it is, again, necessary to look beyond Cambridge, and to libraries in other parts of the country. For Barrow, Wren and their circle, the libraries at Paris, and the buildings that contained them, were most familiar of all. Wren himself found the 'masculine furniture' of the Palais Mazarin much to his taste.[45] At the abbey of Ste Geneviève, a splendid new gallery for the library was to be completed in 1675. At Reims, the Jesuits' new library was built three years later, incidentally making use of the rather restricted available wall space for extra shelving as Wren did so magisterially at Trinity.[46] In 1689, after a difficult period and having been closed for twenty-eight years, the Bibliothèque Mazarine was to reopen to the public, in a new building and on a new site, designed by Louis Le Vau and François d'Orbay.[47]

But an abundance of books on libraries and on their management required no foreign travel. In 1676, the year in which the decision was taken to build the Wren Library, John Battely gave to the College Library a copy of one of the most authoritative of all works on the subject then available: Claude Clément's *Musei, sive bibliothecae extructio, instructio, cura, visus, libri IV* (Lyon, 1635). It may have been a happy accident; but it was a firm reminder of the context in which the new library would be viewed. The choice of books; the means of acquiring them (including hints on searching them out, not

43 Marie Boas Hall, *The library and archives of the Royal Society, 1660–1990* (1992), pp. 2–3.

44 Isaac Barrow, *Theological works*, 9, pp. 111–27, 444–80; P. O. Osmond, *Isaac Barrow: his life and times* (1944); Feingold, 'Isaac Barrow: divine, scholar, mathematician', pp. 47–53.

45 Stephen Wren, *Parentalia* (1750), p. 261.

46 Claude Jolly, 'Bâtiments, mobilier, décors', in Jolly, *Histoire*, pp. 361–71; J. W. Clark, *The care of books* (Cambridge, 1902), pp. 265–90.

47 Gasnault, 'De la Bibliothèque de Mazarin à la Bibliothèque Mazarine', in Jolly, *Histoire*, pp. 135–45; Alfred Franklin, *Les Anciennes Bibliothèques de Paris*, 3 vols. (Paris, 1867–73), 3, pp. 101–14.

necessarily in the most obvious bookshops); the need to ensure that manuscripts and pamphlets were collected as well as more substantial volumes; their classification and arrangement; and the kinds of decoration and furnishings appropriate to a library: all came under the scrutiny of polymaths or librarians, theoreticians or practitioners, especially in France and Germany. Naudé (1627), Claude Clément (1635) and Louis Jacob (1644) provided the beginnings of a literature that after 1640 was to escalate. Philippe Labbé's *Bibliotheca bibliothecarum* (1664) reached its fourth edition in 1682. The literature on the management of libraries was to prove eclectic as, with the abandonment of many of the traditional principles, there was little agreement on questions of classification until the eighteenth century. Johannes Lomeier's more general *De bibliothecis*, first published at Zutphen and Amsterdam in 1669, and again at Utrecht in 1680, was honoured by plagiary in Pierre le Gallois's *Traitté historique des plus belles bibliothèques de l'Europe* (Paris, 1680, 1689, Amsterdam, 1697). Most comprehensive of all was Daniel Morhof's *Polyhistor* (Lübeck, 1688–92), partly the fruit of experience in the university library at Kiel: by 1714 it extended to three volumes. Morhof had seen some English libraries at first hand; but apart from Evelyn's translation of Naudé in 1661, this late seventeenth-century literature was remarkable for the absence of English authors.[48]

The new library proved to be the most ambitious and most magnificent to be constructed in England in the seventeenth century. It was not to be emulated until others were built at Oxford in the eighteenth century – notably at The Queen's and All Souls Colleges, at Christ Church and in Hawksmoor's Radcliffe Camera. In Cambridge, no remotely similar library project was to be attempted until the enlargement of the Old Schools for the University Library in the mid eighteenth century.[49] At Magdalene College, Samuel Pepys's much smaller collection was housed in a building adapted from one already under construction, and perhaps finished, by the time of his bequest in 1703.[50] No Cambridge college was to erect a specialist library building after 1700 until the nineteenth century. One that might have proved the exception was St Catharine's, where a proposal was put forward in the 1670s for the completion of the new court by an east range that would contain a library. In the end, nothing came of either library or range, and it remained for Thomas Sherlock (Master from 1714 to 1719) to oversee the new fitting out of the library room in the north range.[51] Each college had its own reasons for making do with what was already provided; but one result of this caution was that few major benefactors are to be

48 For a French view, see Claude Jolly, 'Naissance de la "science" des bibliothèques', in Jolly, *Histoire*, pp. 380–5.
49 McKitterick, *Cambridge University Library*, pp. 162–4, 255–67.
50 Willis and Clark, 2, pp. 366–73. Pepys's books were moved to Cambridge in 1724.
51 Willis and Clark, 3, pp. 468–9. W. H. S. Jones, *A history of St Catharine's College, once Catharine Hall, Cambridge* (Cambridge, 1936), p. 375.

found amongst the eighteenth-century libraries of Cambridge. The exceptions, such as Thomas Baker at St John's (1740), or Sherlock at St Catharine's (1761), caused refitting, but did not cause either college to extend its library much, still less to rebuild.[52] By contrast, Trinity's new library, built on a scale far larger than the College could conceivably need in the 1670s, required, and inspired, donations on a scale commensurate with the space to be filled. Even as it was being erected, its scale and magnificence proved to be the best possible means of attracting benefactions of books. Although in 1689 Samuel Sewall, visiting England from Massachusetts, had no means of estimating how much the College was building beyond its immediate needs, he was quick to make a similar point about the University Library. There, much of the extra provision made for the books from Lambeth Palace after 1649 had been made redundant with the Restoration, and the consequent return of the books to the Archbishops: the library of Richard Holdsworth, Master of Emmanuel, was only a partial recompense in this respect. So, Sewall noted that one of the two galleries was still not filled, and that vacant shelves remained 'to bespeak Benefactors'.[53] It was an example that Trinity took almost to excess. But in the collections that arrived at the Wren in the century or so after its inception are to be found many of the manuscripts and printed books for which it is most valued and renowned today.

Not surprisingly, so large a building attracted comment from the start. But the first poem that it inspired was an attempt to remind those who looked only to their own that they were in danger of neglecting a greater good for the University, *alma mater*, as a whole. The College's public appeal was clearly not universally welcomed. At Emmanuel, the young Joshua Barnes, later to make his name (if not an unblemished reputation) with his editions of Euripides and Homer, was moved to verse as members of the whole University, and not simply of Trinity, were entreated to meet the cost. Wren's new chapel at Emmanuel, begun in 1668, was consecrated only in September 1677, its building having been interrupted for four years as subscriptions were gathered. At the time of its consecration there were still outstanding bills. In the following November, the Master, Thomas Holbech, was still seeking to persuade William Sancroft, former Master, to meet the remaining costs.[54] For this College at least, the existence of an appeal from another college, for another building by Wren before their own had been finished, must have been unwelcome. Barnes, however, with the confidence of youth, took a longer view of the

52 Frans Korsten, *A catalogue of the library of Thomas Baker* (Cambridge, 1990); *Bibliotheca Aulae Divae Catharinae* (Cambridge, 1771).
53 Samuel Sewall, *Diary*, ed. M. Haley Thomas, 2 vols. (New York, 1973), 1, p. 221.
54 Willis and Clark, 2, pp. 707–8.

University as *alma mater*, and of Trinity's plans. His opinion of the College was also, perhaps, coloured by admiration for Duport, whose skills as a Latin versifier had set him an example of another kind. So, in parallel Latin and English, Barnes hymned the new library, and concluded:

> Nor is it strange, this work's advanced by all;
> When fame and profitt will be generall.
> Cambridge epitomied is Trinitie,
> All others center in this Librarie.
> And when should Doctors joyntly lend ther aid,
> But when ye Muses Palace should be made?
> This or no custome, as ye fates intend,
> O Mildmay's Colledge, must thy Chappel end
> Each Colledge is the Mothers aequal care,
> Then let each Colledge joynt affections share.[55]

Nevertheless, in 1678 Sancroft gave £100 towards the Wren Library: by then he had been consecrated Archbishop of Canterbury, in succession to Gilbert Sheldon. In other colleges, Ralph Cudworth, Master of Christ's, and John Gostlin, Fellow of Caius, were among the first to contribute, to be followed later by the heads of Pembroke, St John's, Queens' and Clare, and a handful of Fellows.

Even during its construction, the Library became a tourist sight. One of the earliest accounts to have been preserved is by an undergraduate at Trinity in 1677, who wrote a series of letters in Latin to his patrons in a style and on subjects clearly intended to make the best possible impression. As in most such exercises, it is not clear how far it may be read as literal truth; but the letter does clearly attest to the impression that the new building was already creating in the minds of those members of the College who witnessed its then daily advance. Charles Lewis wrote of its lofty columns, its decorative shields, its carved stonework; that it was built not simply for use, but also for splendour ('non tantum ad usum sed ad luxum'). In Lewis's view, and no doubt he reflected contemporary gossip, it was a worthy and fitting monument to Barrow, 'primi huius authoris et fundatoris'.[56]

Others, not members of the College, were no less impressed. Samuel Sewall, in 1689, brought the curiosity of a tourist, and responded to the building in a manner that was to become commonplace in succeeding centuries. He began his survey of Cambridge, naturally enough, with Emmanuel College

55 Emmanuel College MS 169. Barnes took his BA in 1675–6, and was elected a Fellow of his college in 1679. Sir Walter Mildmay founded Emmanuel College in 1584.

56 Notebook with transcripts of exercises and correspondence kept by Charles Lewis. I am grateful to Mr David Johnston for help in this matter, and particularly for permission to quote from this notebook.

and its new chapel, before visiting St John's (and being shown the same putrefied cheese that was to be produced for Uffenbach twenty-one years later) and then passing to Trinity's still unfitted Library:

> Trinity College is very large, and the new Case for the Library very magnificent, paved with marble checkered black and white; under, stately walk on brave stone.[57]

In January 1692/3, Abraham de la Pryme, then an undergraduate at St John's College, found much of the building completed. He was misinformed about the stone from which the building is constructed; but like many others he was quick to concern himself with gossip about the cost of the new building:

> I went lately to take a view of the new library of Trinity College in this University, and it is indeed a most magnificent piece of work within, and it is very well built without. 'Tis raised from the foundations wholy of Portland stone, and has cost finishing thus farr above three thousand pounds. 'Tis ... yards long, ... broad, and ... high. It is bore up by three rows of pillars each ... foot about. The starecase up into the library is excellently carved, and the steps are all of them of marble, which staircase alone cost above fifteen hundred pounds.[58]

Two years later, the antiquary Ralph Thoresby followed a programme common to visitors to the University, taking in the University Library and that at St John's, though he omitted that of King's, and proceeded to Trinity's 'stately library, which is the noblest *case* of any, but not yet furnished'.[59]

When the building was at last finished, it became a regular feature for visitors. In 1697, Celia Fiennes recorded her impressions of Trinity College first, before moving on to other colleges, and like so many others was drawn into making comparisons with Oxford: the College was 'the finest yet not so large as Christ-Church College', while

> the Library farre exceeds that of Oxford, the Staires are wanscoated and very large and easye ascent all of Cedar wood, the room spacious and lofty paved with black and white marble, the sides are wanscoated and decked with all curious books off Learning their Catalogue and their Benefactors; there is two large Globes at each end with teliscopes and

57 Sewall, *Diary*, 1, p. 220.
58 Abraham de la Pryme, *Diary* (Surtees Society, 1870), p. 27. The omissions are Pryme's.
59 Ralph Thoresby, *Diary*, ed. Joseph Hunter, 2 vols. (London, 1830), 1, p. 294.

microscopes and the finest Carving in wood in flowers birds leaves figures of all sorts as I ever saw; there is a large Balcony opens at the end that answers to the Staires.[60]

In 1701, Sir John Percival and his travelling companion William Byrd II likewise found much to admire, in a library that was nevertheless 'not over well Stock'd with books'.[61] And even though he found plenty of which to disapprove in Cambridge, including the organisation of the Wren Library, the irritable but formidably learned bibliophile Zacharias Conrad von Uffenbach, from Frankfurt, was typical of visitors in commenting on the building: 'It could not be handsomer or more convenient for a library. It is very light, long and well-lighted, and also highly decorated.'[62]

Not for nothing had the appeals spoken of honour to the nation, as well as ornament to the University. The adjective used most often by visitors was 'magnificent'; but it was more than that. Indeed, the building was more remarked on than the contents – a distinction that was the opposite of that accorded to the University Library or the college libraries of St John's or Corpus. Moreover, within the space of twenty years, between 1695 and 1715, Cambridge found itself possessed of two new splendours: on the one hand a library building to outshine any other in the country, and for which parallels could only be found overseas; and on the other, in King George I's gift of John Moore's books to the University Library, a collection of unquestionable national importance. Although these two large libraries, one college and one university, developed in very different ways over the next century, they did so amidst local and national influences that often had much in common.

The anxieties of colleges, jealous to preserve their customs, rights and independence in the face of suggestions for university-wide reform, contributed indirectly to some of the major benefactions that came to Trinity in the eighteenth century, such as the Gale manuscripts, Beaupré Bell's coins, the Cotton inscriptions, or the Capell Shakespeariana.[63] But beyond this debate lay further, national concerns about the means whereby the country should preserve its literary heritage. In 1694, Richard Bentley (fig. 93) was appointed Royal Librarian. He remained in this post after he became Master of Trinity College six years later, dividing his time between Cambridge and London. Displaying the same irritation, in the face of what he perceived as poor practices, that was to mark his term as Master, he showed himself alert to the inadequacies of

60 Celia Fiennes, *Journeys*, ed. Christopher Morris (1949), pp. 64–5.
61 *The English travels of Sir John Percival and William Byrd II: the Percival diary of 1701*, ed. Mark R. Wenger (Columbia, Mo., 1989), pp. 72–3.
62 *Cambridge under Queen Anne*, p. 125, trans. from von Uffenbach, *Merkwürdige Reisen durch Niedersachsen, Holland und Engelland*, 3 vols. (Frankfurt, Leipzig, Ulm, 1753–4), 3, p. 3.
63 See below, pp. 61–4, 78–82, 100–3.

national librarianship. As librarian of the royal collection, he attempted (with limited success) to increase the numbers of newly published books deposited, by law, in the Royal Library. With an eye to a national library, in 1697 he put forward a series of proposals for building, equipping and maintaining the Royal Library on a new footing, the present one having 'gradually gone to decay, to the great dishonour of the Crown and the whole Nation'.[64] Within a few years there was talk of uniting the Royal Library with the Cotton Library and that of the Royal Society.[65] As Royal Librarian, he saw Moore's books given by King George I to his own university, only months after Moore had sat in judgment on him as Bishop of Ely and Visitor of his college. And as both Royal Librarian and Master of Trinity he saw his most vociferous adversary, Conyers Middleton, triumphantly appointed to the specially created post of *Protobibliothecarius* to look after what the University quickly learned to call its own Royal Library.[66] It is all the more unfortunate that the rapid increase in the library of his own college during his mastership should have been over-shadowed by College feuds, and by the demonstrable inadequacies of his own nephew as College Librarian.[67]

Yet there could be little doubt of the Wren Library's national importance. Before it was finished, John Evelyn, surveying the country's great book collections, regretted the paucity of major libraries even in the largest towns. In particular, the library of Isaac Vossius, offered to the Bodleian Library in Oxford (allegedly at a high price), had been refused. Amidst rumours that it was being considered at Wolfenbüttel, and in the face of Bentley's hope that it could be secured for an English library,[68] the books had been taken back to the Low Countries, 'where', Evelyn remarked, 'they expect a quicker mercate'. 'I wish'd with all my heart some brave and noble Maecenas would have made a present of them to Trinity Colledge in Cambridge, where that sumptuous structure (design'd for a library) would have been the fittest repository for such a treasure.'[69] Evelyn's hopes for Trinity came to nothing; but his more national hopes were to be taken up again in a slightly different vein in Bentley's proposals of 1697 – proposals that found little welcome at the time, and that were only to take on a practical, if unforeseen, form with the foundation of the British Museum in 1753. Meanwhile, in 1710 the death in France of Charles Maurice Le Tellier, Archbishop of Reims, and the subsequent passing of his books to the library of Sainte-Geneviève brought yet another reminder that, notwithstanding many appeals and much anguish, Britain had yet to produce a

64 A.T. Bartholomew, *Richard Bentley, D.D.: a bibliography* (Cambridge, 1908), pp. 75, 93–6.

65 Sir Hans Sloane to Arthur Charlett, 26 April 1707, *Letters written by eminent persons*, 2 vols. (1813), 1, p. 166.

66 McKitterick, *Cambridge University Library*, pp. 17–18, 168–9.

67 Sinker, *Biographical notes*, pp. 39–53.

68 Bentley, *Correspondence*, 1, pp. 6–10; TC Mun. box 29, no. 646. The books went to Leiden, whose interest in the collection Bentley seriously underestimated.

69 Evelyn to Samuel Pepys, 12 August 1689: John Evelyn, *Diary*, ed. William Bray, rev. Henry B. Wheatley, 4 vols. (London, 1906), 3, p. 450.

benefactor on a major scale, and that it still lacked a comparable public library in London.[70] The royal gift of books to the University of Cambridge in 1715 was born partly of such sentiments, though any assumption concerning the importance of London was countered by setting the argument in a mixture of political and firmly traditional academic circles.

Among the colleges, Trinity was not alone in addressing its library accommodation in the latter part of the seventeenth century. Indeed, the existence of a library in Great Court constructed as recently as 1600–4 may even, for some, have discouraged further consideration. At Jesus College, the library was refitted under the aegis of Edmund Boldero, Master of the College from 1663 to 1679.[71] At Gonville and Caius College, the library (then in Gonville Court) was refitted in 1675 with cases closely modelled on those made for the University Library to receive the books from Lambeth Palace in 1649.[72] A few years later, and with the new library at Trinity already under way, the old chapel at Emmanuel College was fitted up as a library – again with bookcases inspired by this same work in the University Library, now thirty years old.[73] Pembroke College Chapel, apparently disused since the completion of Wren's new one in 1665, was to be similarly equipped as a library, in the early 1690s.[74]

These alterations, making use of redundant buildings and involving the erection of new bookcases to a design that was familiar to all senior resident members of the University thanks to the example of the University Library, involved little new building for specialist library purposes. In contrast, the new library at Trinity provided the opportunity for a wholly fresh conception, in which ideas could be drawn equally from elsewhere in England or continental Europe. But Wren also took some of the most familiar features of older college libraries (including some from the old library in Great Court), and either amended or incorporated them into his new design. Most importantly, he achieved extra wall space by lifting the windows above the line of the tops of the bookcases, and so created a series of bays, or studies, more roomy than was familiar in older libraries. This arrangement appealed especially to Uffenbach, who was best acquainted with German libraries: 'an excellent device, because in the first place you can stow away many more books, on both sides and on the walls; and in the next place it is good for those who study there, as they are not put out by seeing others facing them'.[75] In the most recent large library building in Cambridge, at St John's (completed in 1628),

70 'It were to be wish'd, that some Lovers of learning in *Great Britain*, who have large Libraries, would imitate the Archbishop of *Reims*, and consecrate them to the Publick Use, when Death deprives 'em of those Teasures. A large and universal Library, for the Benefit of the Publick, is an ornament wanting to this Great and Wealthy City.' *Memoirs of Literature*, 1 May 1710, p. 32.

71 Willis and Clark, 2, p. 165; 3, pp. 460–1.

72 *Ibid.*, 1, p. 200; 3, p. 463; John Venn, *Biographical history of Gonville and Caius College*, 3 (Cambridge, 1901), p. 189. For the University Library cases, see Oates, *Cambridge University Library*, pp. 251–3.

73 Willis and Clark, 2, p. 760; 3, pp. 463–4. T. S. Hele and H. S. Bennett, 'Recent discoveries at Emmanuel College, Cambridge', *Proc. Cambridge Antiquarian Soc.* 34 (1934), pp. 84–7.

74 Willis and Clark, 1, pp. 136, 149; 3, p. 465.

75 *Cambridge under Queen Anne*, p. 125; Uffenbach, *Merkwürdige Reisen*, 3, p. 4.

the windows had still been situated conventionally between each projecting stack, though in that library they are much larger than in earlier libraries of otherwise similar design, such as at Queens' or Jesus. Now, at Trinity, Wren combined the old with the more recent innovation of wall-cases, an innovation long familiar in the Arts End of the Bodleian Library but that had also been adopted for the remodelled cases in the Mazarine in Paris. At the ends of his projecting bookcases (fig. 7), he continued a tradition already proved to be a practical means of locating books when they stood more anonymously, with fewer labels, than they do today. Here, small doors conceal lists of books contained on the adjoining shelves; such doors also survive, for example, in Cambridge at St John's, and similar lists had been used at the Bodleian since the days of its founder.

Indeed, the whole of Wren's disposition of the interior was designed to be as practical as possible. His emphasis on light not only meant that the room was agreeable to visit; it also allowed work to continue longer in dull or gloomy conditions, in poor weather or at the end of the day. The stone floor, hardwearing and a less noisy surface for walking than a wooden one, contrasted with the wooden floors in between the cases, where it was necessary to have a surface that could be more easily cleaned. Even in its provision for reading, the new library broke fresh ground. Where in former college libraries readers had been expected to sit or stand, facing either a lectern (as originally in the old library in Great Court at Trinity)[76] or, in the more recent stall system, the books on the shelves a few inches across a fixed desk that itself formed a part of the adjoining shelves, Wren introduced loose furniture. Readers were no longer obliged to work facing the shelves. They were now provided with stools at a table; and in the centre of each table a four-sided revolving lectern allowed easy reference among several books if necessary. Wren's drawing (fig. 42) makes clear his appreciation of readers' needs. It may be presumed that such features were discussed with the College, whether they were Wren's conception or no. But the College will certainly have specified that there should be parts of the Library where manuscripts and other books of particular value could be locked away: as he explained, Wren created such space in what are now classes B, O, R and VI, near the four corners of the room. Similarly, the cupboards at the foot of each case, designated for manuscripts in one of Wren's drawings, may have been a College requirement, though they never seem to have been used for this particular purpose.

---

76 Gaskell, *Trinity College Library*, pp. 70–1.

Although it was from the first assumed that the building would have some figurative ornament, many of the decorative elements in the Library were conceived rather later. The early drawings show both the statues on the roof and full-length statues on the ends of each of the bookcases; but the work of Grinling Gibbons was certainly not among the original proposals.[77] It is probable that either the intervention, or the encouragement, or the example of the Duke of Somerset was responsible for this departure. Somerset became Chancellor of the University in 1689, when building (though not the fitting out) was all but finished. As Chancellor, the University found it difficult to ignore this 'proud duke'; and although he gave generously to the fund for building the Wren, his generosity was acknowledged with a statue of himself, by Gibbons, added to the Library in one of two niches specially cut after the main work had been completed (fig. 58).[78] Limewood ciphers and coats of arms (figs. 8 and 9) were added on the ends of the cases, recording some of the principal benefactors – Somerset and his family taking up the west side, and the rest east.[79] The second niche in the south wall, opposite that housing Gibbons' statue of Somerset, has never been filled.

No pictures could be hung in the new library until building work was complete. Accordingly, it was only in 1699 that the College began to organise the first paintings. It already possessed a portrait of John Hacket (fig. 3), given by Andrew Hacket in 1680 and therefore well before the Library was finished.[80] This was now sent to London to be framed under the eye of Sir Godfrey Kneller. On its return it was joined by another full-length portrait, bought in 1691, of Somerset's predecessor as Chancellor, the Duke of Albemarle, also a member of the College, who had given £100 towards the building.[81] To these in turn was added a painting described in the accounts simply as 'Mʳ Montagu's', that is, a full-length portrait of Charles Montagu, Earl of Halifax, given by Thomas Bainbridge, Vice-Master.[82] So, with the close of the accounts at the end of 1699 it was possible to refer to three paintings in the Library, the beginning of a collection that was to be much extended in the following century.

The portrait of Sir Henry Puckering (fig. 4), by far the most notable donor to the new library, was not a gift, but a purchase, bought by the College in 1702 from 'Mʳ Gibson limner in Covent garden' for £21. 10s.[83] Thomas Nevile and Isaac Barrow followed in 1715, the gift of the antiquary and member of the College Samuel Knight. Of all these various large pictures, placed above the bookcases, five remain in place today. The sixth, of the Earl of Halifax, has

77 See further below, pp. 44–45, and Margaret Whinney, *Grinling Gibbons in Cambridge* (privately pr., Cambridge, 1948).

78 See below, p. 112.

79 MS O.4.46, p. 70. These are listed in Willis and Clark, 2, pp. 685–6. The carving commemorating Robert Drake (at the south end of the east side) is by the local Cambridge carver Cornelius Austin, who charged £5. 0s. 0d. (Junior Bursar's accounts, July–December 1695).

80 MS R.17.6, f. 4r; Senior Bursar's accounts, 1679–80.

81 Senior Bursar's accounts, 1690–1.

82 MS Add.a.106, f. 213. Bainbridge died in 1703.

83 Junior Bursar's accounts, 1701–2. See also below, pp. 56–8.

been displaced by Jeremiah Radcliffe, Vice-Master from 1597 to 1611 and one of the team of translators of the Authorised Version of the Bible: it was presented in 1761, and was originally intended for the Hall – presumably as part of Smith's programme for the College.

Further, smaller paintings were added later in the eighteenth century. Ackermann's view of the interior, dating from 1814, shows the full-length paintings of Barrow and Nevile, as well as what are most probably the paintings of Abraham Cowley (whose origin has been forgotten) and of Sir Robert Cotton (given by Sir John Cotton in 1754), today still in their positions at the south end of the Library. Opposite the last two, in equivalent positions at the north end, there are now portraits of Thomas and Roger Gale (figs. 11 and 12), the first given by his son Roger and the second bought from Samuel Knight in 1739. Thus, though the history of where some of these paintings have been hung in the College since their acquisition is obscure, it is clear that the iconographical embellishment of the Library was well advanced before the death of Richard Bentley in 1742. However, during the following years the College moved away from emphasising benefactors to introducing both other members of the College and figures from the past – recent as well as ancient – more generally: those 'whose immortall spirits doe speake still and ever shall, in those places where their books are'.[84] The two busts of Anacreon and Ben Jonson, which may have stood as somewhat isolated figures for half a century following their arrival, were joined by others in a programme described by Malcolm Baker below.[85]

Under Bentley's successor Robert Smith (fig. 80), the interior of the Library was notably altered in other ways, with the introduction of portrait busts by Roubiliac – initially of Francis Bacon, Isaac Newton, Francis Willoughby and John Ray (figs. 67–70) – and of the series of further busts on the tops of the bookcases. The College had become accustomed to alterations, and by no means only in the Wren Library. The restoration and refacing of Nevile's Court in 1755–8 under James Essex, the new bridge, also by Essex, in 1764–5, the rebuilding of the Combination Room in Great Court in 1770–5 and, by no means least dramatically, the planting of the Backs all changed the appearance of the College within the space of a generation. Under Smith, Master from 1742 to 1768, a dedicated Newtonian ever active in promoting his memory and his work in College and University alike, the College had also accumulated a new wealth of portraits both of its members and of those who could be said to have

84 Pliny, *Historia naturalis* xxv. 2, Philemon Holland's translation.
85 See pp. 116–19. The long tradition of library ornamentation of this kind has most recently been addressed in an English context by M. R. A. Bullard, 'Talking heads: the Bodleian frieze, its inspiration, sources, design and significance', *Bodleian Library Record* 14 (1994), pp. 461–500.

had some intellectual bearing on their work. These are explored later in this volume.[86] It is thanks to Smith's generosity that the College now possesses Vanderbank's portrait of Newton in his old age, and the portrait of Galileo, adapted by Allan Ramsay from that by Justus Sutterman now in the Uffizi, that now hangs in the drawing room of the Master's Lodge.[87] For some years, the hall of the Lodge was graced by a plaster of Paris statue of Edward VI, also presented by Smith.[88]

Smith died in 1768, and his work of ornamentation was continued out of his bequest. The great south window (figs. 13–15) designed by Giovanni Battista Cipriani now dominates the initial view of the Library as one enters from the north. Wren had in the 1670s been especially particular in designing a building full of light; and although in 1682–3 Samuel Price, a London goldsmith, caused the introduction of the coat of arms of King Charles II (since modified to those of Queen Anne), this first conception had not hitherto been seriously compromised. It has now been forgotten who suggested the window in the Library: it was not impossible that it was Smith himself. But the subject is certainly one that would have met with his approval. It depicts the presentation of Newton to King George III, in the presence of Sir Francis Bacon. Behind the King is the British Minerva, or Britannia. The figure presenting Newton, clad in deep yellow and dominating the centre of the scene, has been variously described as Fame and (more convincingly and much earlier) as the Muse of the College. Cipriani seems to have prepared a sketch, perhaps for approval by the College, slightly different from the design finally completed (see fig. 14).[89] For the execution of the window, there was but one serious choice, in that William Peckitt dominated his profession. His work at York Minister, at Lincoln and, in academic circles, in New College Chapel in Oxford, was all of recent memory.[90] Using a mixture of stained and enamelled glass, he achieved an exceptional brilliancy of tone. The window was an obvious intrusion, and partly as a consequence it has by turn been admired and denigrated even to the point where, in the mid nineteenth century, it was covered over by a thick curtain. In 1776, the anonymous author of a local guidebook was politic in his phrasing, distancing his personal opinion from those whose sensibilities might be offended by criticism; the window was 'allowed by the best Judges to be highly finished, in an entire new Style', though he did add that it had 'an admirable Effect'. But by the second decade of the nineteenth century there was no need for such evasiveness, and another

86 See below, pp. 121–31.

87 Alastair Smart, *Allan Ramsay: painter, essayist and man of the Enlightenment* (New Haven, 1992), pp. 127, 134, figs. 122–3. Ramsay's version dates from 1757.

88 *A guide through the University of Cambridge* (Cambridge, 1811), p. 105. The statue has not survived.

89 This sketch (fig. 14) was presented to the Fitzwilliam Museum by Charles Fairfax Murray in 1912; the Library contains both a small version (fig. 15) and a full-size cartoon for the later design.

90 R. Robson, 'Cipriani window', *Trinity Review* (1974), p. 14. Peckitt charged the college £315 for his work (commission book in City Art Gallery, York). On Peckitt, see among recent work Trevor Brighton and Brian Sprakes, 'Medieval and Georgian stained glass in Oxford and Yorkshire: the work of Thomas of Oxford (1385–1427) and William Peckitt of York (1731–93) in New College Chapel, York Minster and St James, High Melton', *The Antiquaries Journal* 70 (1990), pp. 380–415 (the familiar window by Reynolds in New College Chapel is by Thomas Jarvis, and dates from 1778–85); J. T. Brighton, 'William Peckitt's commission book', *Walpole Soc.* 54 (1988), pp. 334–453, at pp. 395–6. In 1786–7, Peckitt was further responsible at Trinity for the arms set up in the windows of the Hall.

guidebook, buoyed up with jingoism in the Napoleonic wars, now cast caution to the winds:

> It must be allowed the incongruity of the design is as absurd as could well be imagined; but the artist being a foreigner, may in some degree stand excused for that ignorance of English history, displayed by the introduction of three characters, who never were contemporaries, into one picture.[91]

This remained received opinion, a subsequent guidebook dismissing the window also as 'indifferently executed'.[92] In 1813, Maria Edgeworth visited Cambridge, and came to Trinity after the University Library ('not nearly so fine as the Dublin College Library'). In the Wren, she was entranced:

> Beautiful! I liked the glass doors opening to the gardens at the end, and trees in full leaf. The proportions of this room are excellent, and everything but the ceiling, which is too plain. The busts of Bacon and Newton excellent; but that of Bacon looks more like a courtier than a philosopher: his ruff is elegantly plaited in white marble. By Cipriani's painted window, with its glorious anachronisms, we were much amused; and I regret that it is not recorded in Irish Bulls.[93]

She and her party were amused. Others disliked the window for the incongruity of its composition, and yet others for the incongruity of its intruding a design of a century later into a library that had been conceived as one devoid of stained glass. Yet it is hard not to plead some sympathy for a design that so manifestly evokes the spirit, and develops the themes, of those to be found in baroque painting and book illustration.

With the installation of Cipriani's window, the design of the Wren Library may be said to have reached the last point in its modifications where it was always possible to look back to the founding generation, whether to Wren's conception or to individual members of the College in the late seventeenth century. The Library was certainly not complete, even as a building; for the coffered ceiling envisaged by Wren (albeit to a slightly different design) was not added until the mid nineteenth century (fig. 16). But more importantly, the nature of the College's library had been transformed within a century

91 *The new Cambridge guide*, 2nd edn (Cambridge, 1812), p. 71.
92 *A new guide to the University and town of Cambridge* (Cambridge, 1831), p. 126.
93 Augustus J. C. Hare (ed.), *The life and letters of Maria Edgeworth*, 2 vols. (1894), 1, p. 200. Maria Edgeworth is mistaken, however, in reporting that the head of George III replaced that of Henry VIII in the design. Perhaps she was muddled by the fact that in the full-size cartoon George III's crown is drawn on a piece of paper pasted over an earlier idea. In view of the unwieldy size of the cartoon, it seems unlikely that she saw this for herself.

of Barrow's initial steps. The following chapters explore how the building was created, and how the collections of books, sculpture and other objects were formed in the century and a half after its completion.

1 The Wren Library from the east, viewed across Nevile's Court.

2 The Wren Library from the west, viewed across the river.

3 John Hacket, Bishop of Coventry and Lichfield (1592–1670). From a painting in the Library.

4 Sir Henry Puckering (1618–1701).
From a painting in the Library.

5 Nevile's Court in the late seventeenth century. From David Loggan, *Cantabrigia illustrata* (1690).

6 The translators of the Septuagint presenting their work to Ptolemy II in the Alexandrian Library. Sculpture in the central tympanum of the east side of the Wren Library, attributed to Caius Gabriel Cibber.

7 A bay of the Wren Library, showing the furniture and bookcases designed by Wren, including a small cupboard at the end of the case listing adjacent books. The bust is of Isaac Barrow. See also fig. 32.

8   The arms of William Lynnett. By Grinling Gibbons.

9   The arms of Isaac Barrow. By Grinling Gibbons.

10 The interior of the Wren Library in the early nineteenth century. From [William Combe]
A history of the University of Cambridge, published by Rudolph Ackermann (1815).

11 Thomas Gale (1635?–1702). From a painting in the Library.

12 Roger Gale (1672–1744). From a painting in the Library.

13 The south window of the Library,
designed by Giovanni Battista Cipriani
and made by William Peckitt, 1774.

14 Design by Cipriani for the south window. Fitzwilliam Museum.

15 Drawing of the south window, said to have
been formerly in the possession of Robert Smith,
Master, d. 1768.

16 The interior of the Wren Library today, viewed from the north.

CHAPTER TWO

THE BUILDING

Howard Colvin

With their courts and gatehouses, their halls and chapels, even (in several cases) their long galleries, the bigger Cambridge colleges looked, in the sixteenth and early seventeenth centuries, very like great country mansions such as Haddon or Knole, Apethorpe or Audley End. Architecturally it was only the size of the chapel and the presence of a library that made it clear that it was an academic rather than an aristocratic community for which one of these great complexes of buildings was designed. The chapels were generally more prominent than the libraries, for daily attendance at divine service was a duty incumbent on every Fellow and student, whereas the modest libraries of the fifteenth and early sixteenth centuries could be housed in relatively small spaces that did not invite architectural display. The earliest academic libraries had, indeed, consisted only of a few dozen or at most a few hundred manuscript volumes. These were kept in chests or cupboards, and were loaned to Fellows for months at a time. When, from the end of the fourteenth century onwards, libraries began to be built as places for the study, as well as for the safe-keeping, of books, they were distinguishable from the residential buildings of which they formed part only by their characteristic fenestration, consisting of a row of one- or two-light windows lighting the spaces between the lecterns beneath which the books were stored and upon the sloping tops of which they were read.

By the sixteenth century the transmission of knowledge had been transformed by the invention of printing, and a well-stocked library might now contain many hundred volumes. In England the impact of printing on academic libraries was, however, delayed by the Reformation, which resulted in the loss of many books for doctrinal and other reasons, and it was not until the end of the sixteenth century that most colleges were confronted with the perennial problem of library accommodation that has exercised governing bodies ever since. No longer could the increasing volume of polemical religious literature, not to mention other subjects, be easily housed in modest rooms within existing quadrangles. The solution, both in Cambridge and in Oxford, was the erection of expensive new buildings, often planned as semi-detached blocks projecting from older courts or quadrangles. Such, in Cambridge, were the libraries of Trinity Hall (*c.* 1600) and St John's College (1623–4); at Oxford those of St John's College (1596–8) and Brasenose (1658–62). All these new Elizabethan or Jacobean libraries formed the upper or principal floors of buildings whose ground floors were usually occupied by rooms for students. Although this arrangement exposed the libraries to the risk of fire originating in the rooms below, it ensured that the books were well out of the reach of damp rising up walls innocent of damp-courses and made it possible for the rooms in which they were housed to be well lit and handsomely proportioned.

At Trinity College the building of such a library had been contemplated as early as 1555, and one was eventually built in 1599–1600 in the north-west corner of Great Court (fig. 17). Although capable of housing several thousand volumes, it was rather awkwardly situated on the top floor of a three-storey range between the Chapel and the Master's Lodge, a place where its architectural impact was slight. In the winter of 1665 its roof was badly damaged by a fire which very probably started in one of the chimneys serving the rooms below, and at the same time its walls were showing signs of distress as a result of the increasing weight of books. Despite 'much cost laid out in Supporting and Repairing it' – *inter alia* by adding buttresses on the north side – this third-floor library was 'found too weak a Fabrick for the great weight of Frames and Books'.[1] Hence the decision, in 1675, to build a completely new library in Nevile's Court.

Of that decision there is no formal record. It will have been taken by the Master and senior Fellows who then constituted the governing body of the College. At their head was Dr Isaac Barrow, a man distinguished both as a theologian and as a mathematician and a keen advocate of the new 'experimental philosophy' associated with the Royal Society, of which he was one of the original Fellows. An anecdote told by Roger North (brother of Dr John North, Barrow's successor as Master of Trinity) emphasises Barrow's role in getting the new library built.[2] He had recently been a member of a committee appointed to build a senate house together with a university library. As at Oxford, the public assemblies of the University had long been held in the University church, an arrangement that was neither convenient nor consonant with

1 Gaskell, *Trinity College Library*, p. 137.
2 Roger North, *The lives of the Norths*, ed. A. Jessopp, 3 vols. (1890), 2, p. 326. See also above, p. 5.

seventeenth-century notions of religious propriety. At Oxford the problem had just been solved by the munificence of Archbishop Sheldon in building the Sheldonian Theatre to the designs of Dr Christopher Wren, and Barrow was active in urging the need for a similar building at Cambridge.[3] In 1675 a legacy from Benjamin Laney, Bishop of Ely, provided £500 as the basis for a building fund. Wren was approached and produced designs that would also meet the need for a university library larger than the existing one in the Old Schools quadrangle. His drawings show a building with a long arcaded front facing Great St Mary's Church and a shorter two-storeyed colonnade (somewhat like that of Palladio's Palazzo Chiericati in Vicenza) looking into the Schools quadrangle, whose east range was to be demolished. Behind the colonnade there was to be a galleried assembly-room, and above the arcade the library, a long narrow room lined with bookshelves (fig. 18). Though somewhat gauche as an architectural composition, Wren's scheme would have served its dual purpose well enough. The cost would, of course, greatly have exceeded the bishop's legacy, but Barrow (according to North) urged his colleagues to pursue the scheme, insisting that money would not be wanting for so 'magnificent and stately' a building rivalling the one at Oxford. However, 'sage caution prevailed, and the matter ... was wholly laid aside'. Barrow, 'piqued at this pusillanimity', 'declared that he would go straight to his college and lay out the foundations of a building to enlarge his back court and close it with a stately library ... he was as good as his word; for that very afternoon he, with his gardeners and servants, staked out the very found-ation upon which the building now stands'. This can hardly be literally true, but Barrow was no doubt the moving force immediately behind the decision to build the new library at Trinity, and his determination to press on with the College building may well have been strengthened by his disappointment at the faint-heartedness of his University colleagues.[4]

For the choice of Wren as architect of the library, as of the projected senate house, Barrow was probably personally responsible. Like himself a Fellow of the Royal Society, Wren belonged to the same intellectual circle that was transforming academic thought and laying the foundations of modern science. The two men must often have found themselves together, and Barrow's admiration for Wren as Savilian Professor of Astronomy, publicly expressed in a lecture in 1662,[5] no doubt extended to Wren as the Surveyor General of the King's Works (1669) and the chosen architect of the new St Paul's Cathedral.

3 *The theological works of Isaac Barrow*, ed. A. Napier, 9 vols. (Cambridge, 1859), 9, p. 222 (text of speech at the Commencement ceremony in June 1676).

4 See further above, p. 5.

5 *Theological works*, 9, p. 176.

Wren, for his part, would regard the design of a major new library in the heart of Cambridge as a congenial task that would add to the credit he had already gained as the architect of the college chapels of Pembroke and Emmanuel. Nothing, as he assured the Master of St John's College some years later, was 'more acceptable to me than to promote what in me lies any public Ornament, and more especially in the Universities'.[6]

The site proposed, on the west side of Nevile's Court, implied a building of considerable size and consequence. In the public oration in which Barrow advocated the building of an assembly hall to rival the Sheldonian Theatre at Oxford, he spoke enthusiastically about the architectural splendours of Oxford and Cambridge, which he compared to the churches and public buildings of other countries. 'Where else', he asked, 'are the Muses treated so handsomely or housed so magnificently?'[7] So at Trinity the need for a new library was at the same time an opportunity to erect a building that would be an embellishment to the College and an addition to the architectural glories of the University. In whatever discussions Wren may have had with the Master and senior Fellows, it would be understood that this was his brief.

It went without saying that the new library would be classical in style and that no existing library in either university could provide a suitable architectural model. At Cambridge all the most recently built libraries – those of Trinity Hall (c. 1600), St John's (1623–4) and Peterhouse (1590–5 and 1633) – had been built in a traditional Gothic style; indeed at St John's there was a strongly held view that 'the old fashion of church windows' should be followed, as indeed it was.[8] At St John's College, Oxford, features derived from Flemish baroque had been a feature of the extension of the library built by Archbishop Laud in 1631–6, and at Brasenose the new library begun in 1658 exhibited an intriguing mixture of Gothic and classical motifs that was clearly deliberate.[9] But neither of these would have been viewed with favour by informed architectural opinion in the 1670s, least of all by Wren, who, though far from a purist in practice, kept classical antiquity constantly before his eyes as a standard of reference and had an intellectual's distaste for the wilder flights of baroque or mannerist fancy. As for Barrow, his architectural taste would doubtless have been guided by Wren's. But four years' foreign travel between 1655 and 1659 had given him the opportunity to see many famous buildings for himself, including in Florence the Laurentian Library, in which he is known to have worked, and in Venice the Biblioteca Marciana. Wren's only

6 *Wren Society*, 19 (1942), p. 103.
7 *Theological works*, 9, pp. 221–2.
8 Letter of 1623 printed in *The Eagle* (St John's College periodical) 17 (1893), p. 343.
9 H. Colvin, *The Canterbury Quadrangle, St. John's College, Oxford* (1988), pp. 19, 52.

foreign excursion, in 1665, had taken him no farther than Paris, where there were at that time several important libraries, but none housed in monumental buildings of recent erection.

Two alternative schemes for the library exist among Wren's drawings at All Souls College, Oxford, one for a circular domed building within a square shell, the other for the long rectangular one that was actually built. These two schemes differed not only in form, but also in siting: the circular library was to have stood in the middle of the open end of Nevile's Court as it then existed, whereas the rectangular one was to stand some 80 feet further to the west and the two sides of Nevile's Court were to be prolonged to meet it. As Nevile's Court was slightly wider than it was long, its prolongation was calculated to improve its proportions as well as substantially to increase the accommodation in it. Whether the two schemes were submitted simultaneously or successively we do not know, but one sketch among Wren's drawings shows him experimenting with both a circular and a rectangular one in the same position (fig. 24).

For a circular library there was no precedent, ancient or modern, but plans of a centralised character made a strong appeal to Wren, as they had done to so many European architects from the Renaissance onwards, and his recent 'Great Model' design for St Paul's Cathedral had been of this sort. What Wren envisaged for Trinity would have looked externally somewhat like Palladio's Villa Rotonda near Vicenza, but with only one portico, and that an attached, not a free-standing, one (fig. 30). At ground level the building was to be linked to the two slightly diverging wings of Nevile's Court by iron railings, and it was to be entered by a central doorway facing into the court. The interior was to be articulated by a ring of tall Corinthian pilasters which supported the dome and divided the bookshelves into eleven segments (figs. 29, 31). Each segment was to contain three tiers of five shelves each. None of these could be reached from the floor, and access to them was not by the usual means of galleries, but from a series of poorly lit outer ring corridors, from which alone the books could be taken down or replaced. Whether it was the spines or the fore-edges that Wren envisaged facing inwards towards the central reading-room is not recorded, but in either case his drawing shows no device to prevent a careless reader or librarian from accidentally sending a book crashing to the floor 15 or 20 feet below. Externally the relationship between court and library would have been somewhat awkward, and although there would have been ample space for all the books that Trinity then possessed, or was likely to acquire for many years, the means of access to the shelves was decidedly inconvenient, while the circle of curved seats that Wren envisaged for readers might not have appealed to those who were used to the studious privacy of benches placed between projecting presses. What reception this scheme had at Trinity we do not know, but it is likely that minds that were quite prepared for a strictly classical building would nevertheless have questioned the practicality of the domed solution.

To the longitudinal alternative, on the other hand, there could be no serious objection. It would form a logical conclusion to a rectangular court, with convenient access to the upper storey at either end and a covered way beneath connecting the two existing cloisters. The dignity both of the elevations and of the interior would strike anyone who studied Wren's elegant and easily understood drawings (figs. 32–7). The capacity of the shelving was more than sufficient for the foreseeable future, and the seating arrangements (to be described later) were an ingenious combination of the traditional and the modern.

What were the sources of this grand but thoroughly practical design? It has often been claimed that Sansovino's Biblioteca Marciana in Venice, completed in 1591, was Wren's model. Although no accurate engraved plans or elevations of this celebrated building were available at the time, Barrow had passed through Venice on his return to England in 1659, and he may have brought with him some engraved views showing the library in its setting in the Piazza San Marco. Its north side formed part of a long arcaded elevation articulated by Doric and Ionic columns, and to that extent it was no doubt a precedent that would have been in Wren's mind. But the library represented in Wren's drawings bore only a generic resemblance to the Venetian one. It would be truer to say that both libraries derived their principal elevations from antique buildings illustrated by Palladio (fig. 19), Wren's version, with its unfluted Ionic order and its plain wall-surfaces, being considerably closer to the original than Sansovino's. Moreover there were two libraries in England which need to be borne in mind when considering possible models for a new collegiate library in Cambridge, with one of which, only just completed, Wren himself had been concerned. This was Dean Honywood's Library at Lincoln Cathedral. Michael Honywood was a former Fellow of Christ's who but for the Civil War would almost certainly have been elected

Master of that college. Instead, he became Dean of Lincoln at the Restoration. In 1674–5 he built, at his own expense, a new cathedral library on the north side of the cloister, and the contract specified that it should be constructed 'according to Sir Christopher Wren's directions, and Mr. Tompson's model'. Whoever Mr Tompson may have been (the most likely candidate is a London master-mason of that name), Wren was involved in the design of the library, and the detailing of the classical doorcase and perhaps of other features could well have been provided by his office. The Lincoln library was, however, a relatively minor commission for whose design Wren was probably not wholly responsible, and with its old-fashioned Tuscan arcade it would hardly have been regarded by him as a basis from which to develop the design for a great academic library.[10]

Much more important as a model was the library of the Royal College of Physicians in the City of London. Built in 1651–3 to the designs of Inigo Jones's pupil John Webb, it had been destroyed in the Great Fire of 1666, but as former Professors at Gresham College both Wren and Barrow would have known it well.[11] Webb's drawings show a two-storeyed building of seven bays, with a library and a 'repository', or museum, on the upper floor and an open loggia below. This loggia is formed of arches springing from piers in the Roman or Palladian manner, and the façade is articulated by two superimposed orders of pilasters, one Doric (applied to the piers), the other with unusual reeded capitals (between the windows) (fig. 20). Four bays of the upper floor are occupied by the 'repository', the remaining three by the library. The drawings may not represent the building exactly as executed, but John Aubrey's description of it as 'a noble building of Roman architecture (of Rustique work with Corinthian pillasters)' shows that the classical formula was maintained, probably with a lower storey of channelled masonry and an orthodox Corinthian order at the upper level. For this pioneer design Webb probably had no ready-made model, but he had, at Inigo Jones's behest, drawn many schemes for palaces with two-storeyed galleries of similar architectural character, and mannerist versions of this kind of building were to be seen in England as early as the reign of King James I, for instance at Hatfield House (1609–11) and at the New Exchange in the Strand (1608–9).[12]

Although the recently destroyed Physicians' library must have been at the back of Wren's mind in 1675, the drawings that he gave to Isaac Barrow and his colleagues represented a much grander building. It was thirteen bays

10 The dossier of papers relating to the building of the Honywood Library is among the records of the Dean and Chapter of Lincoln in the Lincolnshire Archives Office (c iij 31/1/1). It includes a note about 'Rates of Gilding' and 'Rates of Painting' signed by Wren. See also N. Linnell, 'Michael Honywood and Lincoln Cathedral Library', *The Library*, 6th ser., 5 (1983) and *Wren Society* 17 (1940), pp. 76–7.

11 Wren was Professor of Astronomy at Gresham College from 1657 to 1661, Barrow Professor of Geometry from 1662 to 1663. Gresham College was in Bishopsgate Street, only a few minutes' walk from the College of Physicians at Amen Court, near St Paul's Cathedral.

12 For Webb's design for the College of Physicians see John Bold, *John Webb* (Oxford, 1989), pp. 165–6. For designs by Webb and others for classical galleries above arcades as components of palace designs see Margaret Whinney, 'John Webb's drawings for Whitehall Palace', *Walpole Society* 31 (1942–3), especially pls. XVI, XXIII, XXV.

long instead of only seven, and the principal façade was ornamented with three-quarter columns, Doric below and Ionic above, instead of with mere pilasters. Moreover, in the descriptive letter that he sent to Barrow (of which a copy (see pp. 142–5 below) survives with the original drawings at All Souls) he shows that he had considered other alternatives. One was for a giant order such as Dr George Clarke was to apply to the façade of the library that he designed for Christ Church, Oxford, in 1716–17. Another was for a central 'frontispiece' like the one that emphasises the middle bays of the library at The Queen's College, Oxford, built in 1692–5. The first he rejected on the ground that it would either have to be 'mutilated in its members', that is, curtailed in dimensions or ornament, in the interests of economy, or else be 'very expensive'; the latter because a central feature would not be logical in a building that was to be entered only at the ends. A central feature could, he said, be provided by making 'the three middle arches with three-quarter columns, and the rest with pilasters of a third of their diameter', but he considered that statues standing on the parapet would provide sufficient emphasis. As for the front facing the Backs, he designed it 'after a plainer manner to be performed most with Ashler, the three portalls one against each cloister and one in the middle, and the pavillions for the Staires give it grace enough for the viewes that way'. His thinking here was probably that, as the bridge over the river Cam was not in line with the centre of Nevile's Court, an emphatic central feature was again uncalled for. In his drawings the central 'portall' is distinguished from the other two by a segmental pediment, but in the end all three doorways were made to an identical design (fig. 33).

On the east side, the lower storey would be arcaded to match the rest of Nevile's Court, but on a larger scale, and with columns and arches of a kind derived from Roman antiquity rather than from the Italian Renaissance (fig. 38). However, there was one feature that had no warrant in antiquity: the filling in of the arches in order to lower the floor to the level of the imposts. This was mainly to gain greater height within the Library. But the exact level was determined by that of the upper floor in Nevile's Court, to which there was to be direct access from either end of the Library, as shown in Wren's drawings (fig. 32). This had presumably been desired by the College, though in the end the communicating doorways were never made. As for the filling in of the arches, this was an expedient of which Wren had, he said, 'seen the effect abroad in good building', thinking no doubt of two buildings in Paris, Le Muet's Palais

Mazarin and Le Vau's Collège des Quatre Nations, whose architects had resorted to the same device in order to accommodate mezzanine floors. The arches, though occluded, were not false: they discharged the weight of the walls on to the piers below, the stone fillings or tympana being supported by voussoirs forming a flat lintel. As the width of the Library was 40 feet, a central support was required in addition to the outer walls. This could take the form either of a longitudinal wall or of a row of columns. Although a wall might have afforded a less draughty communication between the two sides of the court, Wren preferred the columns, whose use in such a context was described by Vitruvius and illustrated by Palladio. 'I have chosen middle pillars ... rather than a middle wall', he wrote, 'as being the same expence, more gracefull, and according to the manner of the auncients who made double walkes (with three rowes of pillars, or two rowes and a wall) about the forum.'

It was when one examined Wren's design for the interior that the advantage of the lowered floor became apparent in the arrangement of the bookshelves. Towards the end of the sixteenth century the lecterns of the medieval library had been generally superseded by rows of projecting book-presses, with seating in the intervening bays. These in turn had in the course of the seventeenth century been replaced in some major libraries by continuous wall-shelving. The bay-system provided convenient spaces for private study, but demanded windows which took up the wall-space between each pair of presses: in a library with wall-shelving, on the other hand, the windows were elsewhere and the readers worked at centrally placed desks or tables. Wren would have seen such wall-shelving both in the Mazarin Library in Paris and in the Bodleian Library in Oxford, where it was used in the Arts and Selden Ends added to Duke Humfrey's Library early in the seventeenth century.[13] At Trinity, with 37 feet at his disposal between floor and ceiling, he was able to combine both systems. Continuous wall-shelving ranged with the projecting bookpresses to provide space for at least 30,000 volumes, while eleven bays on either side created comfortable recesses for readers that were adequately lit from the large windows above. The 'middle ally' was to be paved with marble, the 'celles' (as Wren called the bays) with boards. The walls above the shelving were to be ornamented with pilasters, shown in Wren's drawings as of the Corinthian order, and the plaster ceiling was to be divided into 'three rows of large square pannells answering the pilasters', an arrangement which 'in a long roome ... gives the most agreeable perspective'. Below, a perspective

13 For the architectural history of academic libraries in England see Willis and Clark, 3, pp. 387–471; J. W. Clark, *The care of books* (Cambridge, 1901); J. N. L. Myres, 'Oxford libraries in the seventeenth and eighteenth centuries', in *The English library before 1700*, ed. F. Wormald and C. E. Wright (1958); N. R. Ker, 'Oxford college libraries in the sixteenth century', *Bodleian Library Record* 6 (1959); and David Sturdy, 'Bodley's bookcases', *John Donne Journal* 5, nos. 1–2 (1986).

of another kind would be provided by statues standing on the ends of the presses. These, Wren wrote, 'will be a noble ornament. They are supposed of plaster, there are Flemish artists that doe them cheape.' What (if any) iconographical programme Wren had in mind is not recorded, but to devise an appropriate one for as many as twenty-eight statues might not have been easy.

External access to the Library was to be by means of a rectangular staircase rising from either end of the colonnaded space beneath it. These twin staircases were to read as domed pavilions with leaded roofs visible only from the west, north or south, but not from the interior of Nevile's Court. In the event only the northern one was built, an external iron balcony (since removed) being substituted for the southern one.[14]

That this design, for which Wren made no charge,[15] met with a favourable reception at Trinity may be inferred from the fact that in the course of the next twenty years it was to be carried out with very few alterations. How much the building was to be expected to cost is not recorded. The College evidently had a figure in mind, for at the end of his explanatory letter Wren says that he has 'made a Cursory estimate and it is not that at which you will stumble as not exceeding the charge proposed'. If the designs were approved he would 'give you a careful estimate of the charge'. In England in the seventeenth century the calculation of building costs was apt to be far from exact, and Wren's 'careful estimate' may well have erred on the side of optimism. However, it was obvious that a large sum of money would be needed, and by 1678 the College was thinking in terms of £12,000–£14,000.[16] Although the corporate revenue, administered by the two Bursars, could on occasion be drawn on for ready money, it could not finance a great new work like the proposed library. There was only one way of doing this, and that was by subscription.[17] Then, as now, past and present members of a college could be relied on to subscribe generously to any well-conceived building project.

An appeal was accordingly launched, in the form of a printed letter signed by the Master and dated 3 January 1675/6. It was addressed 'to all Generous Persons, Favourers of Learning, and Friends to the Universities, especially to those, who have had any part of their Education in this College'. The recipients were informed that the Master and Fellows had 'entertained a design of Erecting a new Library in a place very convenient for use, and for the grace of the College, intending to inlarge the New Court, called Nevil's

14 This balcony was removed, presumably when New Court was built in 1821–3, but traces of it can be seen in the masonry at the south end of the Library.

15 In the inscription beneath his plate of the Library (fig. 5), David Loggan explicitly states that Wren's design was given 'spontane et gratuito'. The College must have given Wren a present of some sort in return, but of this there appears to be no record.

16 This is the figure mentioned in letters of 1678 appealing for contributions (Bodleian Library, Oxford, MS Rawl. D.391, f. 15 and British Library, Harleian MS 7001, f. 420).

17 See also above, p. 7.

Court; and by adjoining the Library, to make it up a fair Quadrangle: The accomplishment of which design, beside the advantages from it to this Society, will as we conceive, yield much Ornament to the University, and some honour to the Nation'. No reference was made to Wren, but the engraver David Loggan was employed to make two sheets of engravings from his drawings, and copies of these engravings were presumably sent out with the appeal, or made available to anyone interested. Seven hundred and thirty sheets were printed, but only one copy of the engravings is known to survive, bound up with a copy of Loggan's *Cantabrigia Illustrata* acquired by Trinity in 1727 (fig. 35).[18]

The printed appeal was followed up by private letters to individuals who might contribute or persuade others to do so. On 10 February 1675/6, for instance, Isaac Barrow wrote to John Thornton, a former sizar of the College who was now tutor and chaplain in the family of the Earl of Bedford, to ask him to 'use your interest (which must surely be great in your noble family …) to the procuring contributions toward carrying on our designe'.[19] The result was a gift of £100 from the earl and £50 from his son. The pressure was kept up. When John North succeeded Barrow as Master in 1677, he reissued the printed appeal, and several manuscript letters of later date begging for funds survive.[20]

The response was gratifying. Over a period of twenty years the College raised £11,879 by way of gift towards expenditure which eventually totalled £16,425. At Trinity everyone from the Master to the two manciples subscribed, even the College barber giving £5. Fellows past and present contributed nearly £4,000, former students of the College, £3,250. The Master and senior Fellows gave up to £100 each, other Fellows £10 to £50, often in yearly instalments. Instead of the customary gift of plate, newly elected noblemen and Fellow-Commoners were encouraged to make an equivalent donation in money, an expedient that yielded some £400. Masters and Fellows of other Cambridge colleges contributed just over £600, and local gentry added their quota. Uniquely munificent, the Duke of Somerset (a Trinity man) gave £500 soon after his election as Chancellor of the University in 1689.[21]

As might be expected, most of the donors were directly or indirectly connected with the College or the University: often they were relations of the Master or of a Fellow, or parents of scholars or Fellow-Commoners in residence while the Library was being built. Seven bishops (including both Archbishops) were among the subscribers, and money came in from rectories and vicarages all over the country whose incumbents were Trinity men. It was an impressive

18 Printed copy of Barrow's letter in Trinity College Library, 0.11a 4⁹: see pp. 7–8 above. The payment to Loggan for engraving is in the building accounts (0.4.46, p. 6, 0.4.47, p. 165).

19 Bodleian Library, MS Rawl. Letters 109, f. 2.

20 Bodleian Library, MS Rawl. D.391, ff. 15, 17, 21 (1678, etc.); MS North c. 5, f. 93 (1681).

21 His predecessor, the Duke of Albemarle, had given £100 some years before he became Chancellor in 1682, the Duke of Monmouth (Chancellor 1674–82), nothing.

demonstration of academic loyalty that transcended political, religious and intellectual differences. The balance of some £4,500 was made up partly by the College out of its corporate revenues, partly by loans which were gradually paid off in subsequent years, and partly by the sale of plate (£699) and duplicate books (£302).[22]

Work began in February 1675/6, with the digging of foundations and the demolition of a tennis-court which stood between the site of the Library and the river. A committee of fifteen Fellows was appointed 'to oversee the workmen and promote the work', and three of them (Dr Humphrey Babington, Thomas Bainbridge and John Ekins) were 'empowered to bargain for and buy materials' on behalf of the Master and Fellows.[23] In seventeenth-century England neither architects nor builders normally fulfilled the comprehensive supervisory and organising functions of their modern counterparts. Wren himself could not be expected to do more than visit the building very occasionally (as we know he did in October 1676[24]), so a considerable amount of responsibility will, at least initially, have fallen on the members of the committee. One of their first actions was to appoint a master-mason in the person of Robert Grumbold. An experienced mason whose family had long-established interests in the Northamptonshire quarries, he was the leading master-builder in Cambridge and the obvious man to be entrusted with the execution of Wren's designs.[25] At Trinity his role was partly that of a supervisor, for which he received one guinea a week, and partly that of a master-craftsman, for which he was paid specific sums for specific tasks. To have contracted for the entire masonry shell of the building would probably have been beyond his capital resources, and was in any case apt to be a risky procedure. As Wren explained to the Dean of Christ Church a few years later, there was a danger either that the client would be 'overreached' or that the contractors might underestimate the task 'and shuffle and slight the work to save themselves'.[26] Without quantity surveyors to calculate the materials needed these were very real dangers, and Wren advocated working 'by measure', that is at an agreed rate per yard, foot or pound.

At Trinity, as often elsewhere, much of the work was done on this basis, but much was also done by masons and others paid by the day, and some by specialist craftsmen paid by agreement for a specific item – carving, plasterwork, joinery, etc.[27] Although Grumbold's primary responsibility was for the mason's work, it is evident from the building accounts that he acted in a general supervisory

22 The contributions from 1676 to 1693 are recorded in an MS register (Trinity College Library, O.4.46A). For some other financial transactions relating to the building of the library, see the Conclusion Book for 1646–1811, pp. 119, 148, 149, 161, 177, 184. At St John's College a similar appeal to build the Third Court (1669–71) had raised approximately £2,000 towards a total cost of about £5,200 (St John's College archives, C.1.14 and C.11.3).
23 Willis and Clark, 2, pp. 537–8.
24 The Diary of Robert Hooke, ed. H.W. Robinson and W. Adams (1935), p. 252: 5 October 1676, 'Sir Ch. Wren [and] Dr. Holder ... both to Cambridge'.
25 For his career see H. Colvin, A biographical dictionary of British architects 1600–1840 (1995), pp. 434–5.
26 W. D. Caröe, Wren and Tom Tower (Oxford, 1923), p. 27.
27 The expenditure is recorded in two volumes, one (O.4.46) an annual journal of receipts and expenditure from February 1675/6 to 1699, kept by the Junior Bursar, the other (O.4.47) an itemised account of expenditure only from February 1675/6 to 1690, written in a less literate hand and probably to be identified as the account kept by Robert Grumbold. Both accounts refer to numbered bills that were not preserved.

capacity. It was he who from time to time went up to London 'to see Sir Chr. Wren', it was he who kept an 'account-book of all the charges', and he with whom the Bursars and other members of the building committee would have conferred about workmen, building materials and other matters. In Wren's office he gained the reputation of being an 'honest and skilfull artificer',[28] and his subsequent career in Cambridge suggests that he was considered to have conducted himself well as the principal master-builder of the Wren Library.

At the height of the work in the summer of 1677 some thirty masons were employed under Grumbold, including several members of his own family, and others with names well known in the masonry trade in Northamptonshire and Rutland, such as John Ashley, John and Robert Lovin, Joseph Thorp and Arnold Wilkinson. The master-joiner, Cornelius Austin, was a local man, and so were the principal carpenter, Thomas Silk, and the stone-carver Francis Percy. But the master-plasterers Henry Doogood and John Grove, and the master-smith, William Partridge, were leaders in their respective trades from London, and the master-bricklayer, Matthew Fitch, may have been related to the well-known London bricklayers Thomas and John Fitch.[29]

For his guidance Grumbold had not only Wren's general drawings, but also more detailed ones giving the mouldings to a larger scale. In the seventeenth century it was not unusual for features such as architraves and cornices to be left to the masons to execute in accordance with their normal practice, but at Trinity (as at St Paul's and other major works) Wren was determined to exercise full control over every aspect of the design. 'I would', he informed the Fellows, 'willingly take a farther paines to give all the mouldings in great, wee are scrupulous in small matters and you must pardon us, the Architects are as great pedants as Criticks or Heralds'. Three such drawings survive, with features numbered from I to X (figs. 38–40). Numbers I–VIII provide plans, sections and elevations of the east and west walls to a scale of 1 inch to 8 feet, and numbers IX and X large-scale profiles of the mouldings of the Doric and Ionic orders and of the arcade. By the end of the eighteenth century such drawings would be taken for granted, but in the seventeenth century they were still a symptom of a new professionalism in English architecture of which Wren's office was the centre.

One feature for which no drawings survive, and whose existence was unsuspected until 1970, was the use of inverted brick arches in the foundations of the arcade supporting the east side of the Library (fig. 22). Placed only 40

28 *Wren Society* 19 (1942), p. 105: Hawksmoor to the Master of St John's College, 9 June 1698.

29 For the London craftsmen see G. Beard, *Craftsmen and interior decoration in England 1660–1820* (Edinburgh, 1981) and the index to the *Wren Society* in vol. 20 (1943).

yards from the river, and overlaying the course of the former 'King's Ditch' (a subsidiary waterway made in 1423 and only recently completely filled in), the new library was to stand on treacherous ground. In 1681 the Dean of Christ Church, Oxford, received a long and highly technical letter from Wren about the foundations of Tom Tower.[30] At Trinity, no such letter survives to explain Wren's thinking about the foundations of the Library, but the function of the inverted arches was to distribute the load of super-incumbent masonry evenly instead of concentrating it beneath each of a series of piers, any one of which might be liable to subsidence. Although horizontal arches were employed by the Romans to resist the thrust of piled-up earth in buildings such as fortifications and mausoleums, there appears to be no evidence of the use of inverted arches in antiquity. Their use is, however, prescribed by Alberti in his well-known treatise on the art of building (*De re aedificatoria*), published in 1486, with which Wren would have been familiar.[31] Only excavation could determine how far Alberti's advice was followed by other Renaissance architects, but in England inverted arches were used by Wren's colleague Robert Hooke, who, according to Moxon's *Mechanick Exercises* (3rd edn 1700), 'made use of this Artifice ... in building the Lord Montagu's brave house in Bloomsbury, in the county of Middlesex'. Montagu House was built to Hooke's designs in 1675–9. As the builders of Bedford Square were to discover, the subsoil in Bloomsbury is 'made-up' ground, so here again there was a danger of differential settlement.[32] The foundations of Montagu House were laid in July 1675, a few months before those of the Wren Library, but in the almost simultaneous application of this piece of technical virtuosity, so characteristic of minds in which architecture and science were of equal importance, Wren and Hooke were no doubt giving effect to an idea that they had discussed together on more than one occasion. At Cambridge the positioning of the inverted arches was not carried out with perfect precision. Having been set out from the middle of the site, they proved to be progressively more and more out of step with the piers that were to be built upon them, those at the north and south ends barely coinciding.[33] They were built off a bed of clunch, a hard chalk, 1,394 loads of which were brought from Cherry Hinton to the south-east of Cambridge, and more from Barrington to the south-west. There is no reference to the inverted arches in the building accounts, but their construction is covered by payments to 'Bricklayers and other Laborers working in the Foundations'.

30 Caröe, *Wren*, p. 25.
31 L. B. Alberti, *On the art of building*, trans. J. Rykwert *et al.* (Cambridge, Mass., 1988), p. 68.
32 A. Byrne, *Bedford Square* (1990), pp. 59–60.
33 Information kindly provided by Peter Locke of Donald W. Insall and Associates, 1991.

41

The main structure was built of a combination of Ketton freestone, brick and clunch. The Ketton stone was used for the exterior facing and for the piers and columns, the brick for the inner face of the walls, and the clunch for infilling the core, at least in areas where no major loads were to be carried, where it would be prudent to have solid masonry. The Ketton quarry near Stamford was one of several sources of good-quality oolite free-stone that had been used in Cambridge in the past. Some forty miles north-west of Cambridge, it was accessible by water or main road, but the cost of transport was high, and masons and masonry constituted by far the biggest item of expenditure, amounting altogether to £5,300, of which £2,313 represented the cost of the stone delivered on site, £1,704 the cost of freemasons working by the day, and £1,228 that of work done 'by the great'. It was doubtless as a measure of economy that the staircase was built entirely of brick. Bricks were easily procurable from local brickmakers at prices ranging from 14s. 6d. to 19s. 6d. a thousand.

The building of the walls took four or five years. Work would have been suspended each winter, and its seasonal cessation is marked in the accounts by the purchase of straw to protect the unfinished stonework in November 1676, September–October 1677, October 1678, October 1679 and November 1680. According to Roger North the walls were up to three-quarters of their height when his brother John succeeded Barrow as Master in May 1677, and in the appeal which was sent out in North's name in July of that year, the floor is said to be 'now almost laid'.[34] It was not until 1680 that the roof was covered with lead,[35] and an undulating horizontal joint observed from scaffolding in 1970 above the windows on the west side may mark a pause to allow for settlement before the completion of the cornice and balustraded parapet. Despite all Wren's precautions some movement of masonry did occur, resulting in the slight dropping of the voussoirs of some of the flat arches supporting the tympana of the arcade and the opening of the joints of some of the window heads.

When he made his presentation drawings in 1675 Wren had clearly not fully thought out the carpentry either of the roof or of the floor. For the simple king-post roof shown in his sectional drawing (fig. 34) he eventually substituted a more complex one consisting of king-posts standing on scarfed tie-beams held together by iron bolts and straps and strengthened by subsidiary queen-posts and angle struts (fig. 22). Trusses identical in design to those he had

34 North, *The lives of the Norths*; Trinity College o.11a.4⁹.

35 Lead was ordered from Derbyshire in 1680, and in May 1681 the agreement with Dr Humphrey Babington (see below, p. 46) states that the new library has 'the roofe thereof now covered' (Willis and Clark, 2 p. 523).

originally designed for Trinity were later used by Wren over the choir of St Paul's Cathedral, where the span was some 2 feet wider.[36] For these, however, massive timbers had to be obtained from woods in Nottingham belonging to the Duke of Newcastle, and it was probably the difficulty of procuring timber of sufficient scantling that led Wren to design for the Library roof a more complex truss that could be constructed from smaller component timbers.

The carpentry of the floor presented a more difficult problem, because it had to carry the weight of the bookcases, which project 8 feet 6 inches from the walls on either side. Although they were placed in line with the columns which support the floor at mid-point, there was still a span of 20 feet from wall to column, with the superincumbent weight of the bookcases pressing down on it. In November 1685 Matthew Banckes, the Master Carpenter of the Office of the King's Works, was sent down by Wren to deal with the problem. Payments to him 'by order of a meeting for surveying the fflore' and 'ffor ordring the workmanship of the Library ffloore' indicate a consultation on the site, and the 'moddell' for whose carriage from London 2s. was paid in December of the same year may well have been to demonstrate the revised method of construction worked out in Wren's office. As carried out, this consisted of main girders 16 inches square that were supported at either end on cantilevers (thus reducing the effective span to about 12 feet 6 inches), and assisted by diagonal struts which made the whole system into a sort of truss (fig. 23). In addition the weight of the bookpresses was relieved by a series of diagonal iron bars built into the walls and bolted to a longitudinal girder running beneath the ends of the presses. This ingenious system of structural engineering did not prove to be wholly effective in preventing the main transverse beams from sagging, and in the present century they have had to be stiffened by the addition of pairs of inverted steel tensional trusses fixed on either side.[37] These difficulties could have been avoided had Wren been prepared for a slightly different interpretation of what in his descriptive letter of 1675 he called 'the manner of the ancients who made double walkes (with three rowes of pillars, or two rowes and a wall), about the forum', for with an extra row of columns, or alternatively a longitudinal wall, a support could have been placed much closer to the end of every bookcase.

By 1681 the roof had been completed and the fitting up of the interior could begin. The original design was closely followed, but the order of the pilasters was changed from Corinthian to Composite, and the omission of

36 A. F. E. Poley, *St Paul's Cathedral* (1927), pl. XII.
37 H. M. Fletcher, 'Sir Christopher Wren's carpentry at Trinity College Library', *R.I.B.A. Journal*, 3rd ser., 30 (1923); D. W. Insall and Associates, *The Wren Library, Trinity College, Cambridge: a Report* (1968), p. 11. For a further discussion of the carpentry both of the floor and of the roof see James Campbell, 'Constructing the Trinity Library: an investigation into the role of constructional technology of Sir Christopher Wren', unpublished postgraduate dissertation, Cambridge School of Architecture, 1993.

the projected doorways to the adjoining rooms in Nevile's Court resulted in adjustments to the internal arrangements of the two end bays. For the compartmented ceiling envisaged by Wren a plain one was substituted, perhaps with the idea of covering it with painted decoration, but if so this was never carried out, and in 1850–1 the existing compartments were inserted under the direction of the then Master, William Whewell, thus approximately fulfilling Wren's intentions.[38] Only in the coved ceiling of the staircase were the plasterers Doogood and Grove allowed a lavish display of their art with boldly projecting scrolls of foliage framing the arms of four successive Masters who were also benefactors to the Library – Pearson, Barrow, North and Montagu.[39]

All the internal woodwork was made by the Cambridge joiner Cornelius Austin. Payments to him for a 'journie to London', and 'another journie to Sir Christopher Wren' in 1691/2 and 'for his Jorney to London and one Guinea to [Wren's assistant] Mr. Hawkesmore' in 1692/3 show that, like Grumbold, he kept in close touch with Wren's office. A sketch for the 'classes' or book-presses in Hawksmoor's hand (fig. 43) is further evidence that nothing was done in Cambridge without authority from Scotland Yard. Each 'classis' cost £28, and several of them were paid for by individual donors.[40] The ends of those on the east side were decorated with the arms or crests of these and other benefactors to the Library, those on the west side being all decorated with the arms, crest or garter badge of the Duke of Somerset several times repeated. At either end larger achievements of the royal arms of King William III were set up over the doorways. All but one of these heraldic tributes were carved by Grinling Gibbons. By 1691, when the first payment was made to Gibbons, he was well established as the outstanding British decorative carver in wood, and Wren had already employed him in the royal works. He had also been employed at Petworth House in Sussex by the Library's greatest benefactor, the Duke of Somerset, so it was entirely appropriate that at Trinity he should not only carve the heraldic emblems that commemorated the duke's generosity on the bookpresses, but also supply the marble statue of the duke in Roman dress that stands in one of a pair of niches at the south end of the Library. These niches, not envisaged in Wren's original designs, were made by Grumbold in 1691 at a cost of £24 1s. 0d.

The coats of arms and other heraldic decorations were carved by Gibbons in a light-coloured lime-wood which stands out against the darker wood of which the presses were made. Like all his carvings of this sort, they are cut

38 The work was done by D. Bradwell and Sons at a total cost of £1,553 6s. 7d. (TC Mun., box 31, no. 14). The beams inserted in 1850–1 are, however, somewhat smaller than those intended by Wren.

39 Pearson, as Bishop of Chester, gave £200, and Barrow, North and Montagu £100 each.

40 Bishop Pearson, Dr John Montagu, Sir Thomas Sclater, Dr George Chamberlain, Dr Humphrey Babington, Dr William Lynnett and Robert Drake, steward of the College's manors, are listed as donors of 'classes' in the Register of Subscriptions under the date 23 March 1691/2 (0.4.46a, p. 34).

out of laminated blocks made by gluing together planks about 2½ inches thick, and are miracles of undercutting and sculptural delicacy. This technical virtuosity is combined with great felicity in the design of the naturalistically rendered foliage with which the heraldic shields are framed.[41] Altogether Gibbons was paid £305 for his workmanship in the Library between 1691 and 1693: £200 'for the Duke of Somerset's Statute – Coats of Arms and Cifers and Bustos', £20 for four coats of arms paid for by the College (those of Bishop Hacket, Isaac Barrow, John Montagu and Sir Robert Hildyard), £25 for coats of arms paid for by their owners or others (Sir Thomas Sclater, Dr George Chamberlain, Dr Humphrey Babington, Dr William Lynnett and John Pearson, Bishop of Chester), and finally £60 'more in full for the rest of the things in the Library'. The last item presumably includes the two representations of the royal arms and the decorative carving of the wooden alcoves in the four corners of the Library. For only one coat of arms was Gibbons not responsible: that of Robert Drake, the steward of the Trinity manors, who had been the donor of a 'classis'. For this Cornelius Austin was paid £5 in 1695. By then Gibbons had completed his work for the Library, but Austin imitated his style so well that Drake's shield would be readily attributed to him but for the evidence of the accounts.[42] Austin was also responsible for the openwork carving of the wooden gates which, at either end of the Library, closed off spaces reserved for the safe-keeping of 'archives'.

Wren's original scheme for plaster statues standing on the ends of the presses was not adopted, and the existing series of plaster busts representing 'Ancient' and 'Modern' authors dates from the eighteenth century. However, 'bustos' are included in Grinling Gibbons's account, and there is a payment of £1 in 1691 'To Mr. Gibbons's men who sett up the Busto's'. Two of the existing busts – those of Ben Jonson and Anacreon – are of wood instead of plaster and may have been those supplied by Gibbons.

Externally, sculptural decoration is confined to the east face of the Library. At the lower level the tympana of all but the central arch are occupied by cartouches flanked by garlands, and at the upper level the keystones of the arches are emphasised by human masks. For this conventional architectural decoration and for the twelve Ionic capitals, the local carver Francis Percy or Piercy was responsible. The central tympanum was, however, reserved for a relief of 'King Ptolemy receiving the Septuagint from the Translators'. This was evidently 'the Midle pees in the Midle Arch', for which 'the Carver at

41 Gibbons's work at Trinity was the subject of a small monograph by Margaret Whinney, *Grinling Gibbons in Cambridge* (privately printed, Cambridge, 1948).
42 The three carvings of the arms, crest and cipher of Sir Henry Newton Puckering (1618–1701), of The Priory, Warwick, who gave the bulk of his library to Trinity, were an even later addition, for the accounts record a payment of 2s. 6d. 'to Cremer for carriage of S[r]. H Puckering's arms etc.' among disbursements between 23 December 1695 and 23 December 1698. They can hardly be the work of anyone but Gibbons, and Puckering may have commissioned them himself, since there is no record of any payment for them by the College.

London', identified below as Caius Gabriel Cibber,[43] was paid £38 12s. 4d. in 1679. The subject, obviously appropriate for a foundation so strongly clerical in character, was here given added point by its setting in the Alexandrian Library (fig. 6). On the parapet stand four stone statues representing Divinity, Law, Medicine and Mathematics. Each is a female figure accompanied by her emblem (an eagle, books, a cock and a globe) and is making an appropriate gesture (Mathematics counting on her fingers, Medicine holding an Aesculapian staff, Law a scroll inscribed 'IUBET ET PROHIBET', and Divinity a book). These figures (figs. 52–5) were also made by the Danish sculptor Caius Gabriel Cibber, who was paid £80 'for cutting four statues' in 1681. They personified traditional subjects of academic study, but (like the similar figures over the gateway of Trinity College, Oxford) in style and placing they were baroque and up-to-date.[44]

Meanwhile, the two sides of Nevile's Court had been prolonged to meet the Library. As built in 1605–12, each side of the court stood over an arcade consisting of twelve arches in three groups of four, separated by a pier. In order to fill the gap between the ends of these two ranges and the Library, eight further arches were required on either side. The north side was undertaken first. The first four arches were paid for by Sir Thomas Sclater, a former Fellow of Trinity who had a successful career in medicine, and was by this time a baronet with a landed estate at Linton near Cambridge. In 1676 he undertook to build this section of the court at his own expense, on condition that members of his family who were students of the College would have the right to occupy the two new chambers free of charge and that in the event of there being no such relatives in residence the rent from letting the rooms should be devoted to the purchase of books for the Library. The building was completed by the end of 1679 at a cost of £896 13s. 0½d. As Sclater employed the workmen himself the building records have not been preserved in the College archives, but a payment by the College in 1676 to 'Hutton Sir Thomas Slater's cheif worke-man for his pains in buying scaffolding for us' preserves the name of his master-builder.[45] The remaining four arches on the north side were built soon afterwards, 'by the benefactions of many worthy persons', whose names are not recorded.[46]

The corresponding chambers on the south side were built in 1681–2, the easternmost half at the expense of Dr Humphrey Babington, senior Fellow of Trinity, on similar conditions to those laid down by Sclater. The western

43 See below, p. 111.

44 Cf. A. Masson, *Le Décor des bibliothèques du moyen âge à la Renaissance* (Geneva, 1972), p. 113.

45 Sclater's estate memorandum book in the Cambridgeshire Record Office (R.59.5.3/1) shows that Thomas Hinton was a bricklayer whom he employed at Catley House, his Cambridgeshire seat.

46 Willis and Clark, 2, pp. 519–22, 526.

portion was built at the College's expense, and the accounts show that the craftsmen employed were Robert Grumbold, mason, Matthew Fitch, bricklayer, Thomas Silk, carpenter, and Cornelius Austin, joiner. The cost was £656 6s. 4d.[47] The two ranges thus completed were externally indistinguishable from the remainder of the court, the mannerist detailing of the early seventeenth century being exactly copied. In 1755–6, however, the elevations of both sides of the court were remodelled under the direction of the Cambridge architect James Essex, the gabled parapet being replaced by a balustraded one which conforms more or less with that of the Library (fig. 1). The original appearance of the court is preserved in one of the engravings published by David Loggan in his *Cantabrigia Illustrata* of 1690 (fig. 5), and shows it as it would have been seen by King William III when he visited Trinity in 1689 and was 'presented with a copy of English verses in the new built library, the structure whereof his Majesty was very well pleased with'.[48]

In the foreground of Loggan's view can be seen the plan of a further embellishment to the quadrangle: the 'Tribunal'. This purely ornamental structure was clearly designed to counteract the asymmetry of the Hall by introducing a central feature in a classical style corresponding to the Library. The accounts show that it was built in 1682–5 by Grumbold. No drawings survive, but Grumbold made three journeys to London in 1683 and must have discussed the building with Wren. The design is in every way characteristic of Wren, and the Tribunal may confidently be attributed to him.

On its completion the Wren Library was by far the grandest building of its kind in Britain. In Cambridge no other college library was ever to rival it. In Oxford the Queen's College built in 1693–6 a library that struck a contemporary observer as 'emulating that of [Trinity College] in Cambridge'.[49] But the unknown designer of the Queen's library did not imitate any specific feature of Wren's library, and the internal arrangements were (though elegant in design) wholly traditional in character. The Queen's library did, however, follow the same long, rectangular plan, as did the otherwise very different libraries designed by Nicholas Hawksmoor for All Souls College (begun 1716) and by Thomas Burgh for Trinity College, Dublin (1712–32). It was a tradition that in the early nineteenth century was to be continued in the two great neoclassical libraries of Edinburgh, the Upper Signet Library (1812–16) and that of the University (1824–7),[50] and in Cambridge itself in the upper room of C. R. Cockerell's University Library (1837–40). As for the interior of the Wren

47 *Ibid.*, pp. 522–6.
48 C. H. Cooper, *Annals of Cambridge*, 5 vols. (Cambridge, 1842–1908), 4, p. 10.
49 *The journeys of Celia Fiennes*, ed. C. Morris (1949), p. 36.
50 By William Stark and W. H. Playfair, respectively. Playfair visited the principal libraries of London, Oxford and Cambridge before submitting his plans (Andrew G. Fraser, *The building of Old College* (Edinburgh, 1989), p. 250).

Library, it remained unique in its ingenious combination of wall-shelving with projecting presses. In some seventeenth- and eighteenth-century libraries the display of elaborate leather bindings was envisaged as an element in the design, but it is doubtful whether this was the case in any English academic library of the Stuart or early Georgian period.[51] It was certainly not in Wren's mind at Trinity, for the sketch he provided of a typical bay (fig. 43) clearly shows books with their fore-edges, not their spines, outwards. Although the mass of light-coloured fore-edges would have looked well enough in Cornelius Austin's dark oak presses, it was, of course, Grinling Gibbons's carvings that were designed to catch the eye, rather than the books themselves, few of which in the 1690s would have been notable examples of the binder's art.

Where, finally, does the Wren Library stand in European architectural history? Until the Renaissance few libraries in northern Europe were other than utilitarian in design. But in the sixteenth century their interiors often began to be ornamented with paintings and carving,[52] and from the seventeenth century onwards their forms were varied at the whim of architects concerned as much with the manipulation of space as with the storage and consultation of books. Oval, circular and tripartite libraries were built at Wolfenbüttel (1706–10), Oxford (1737–49) and Vienna (1722–36), and the shelving was subjected to every vagary of baroque or later of neoclassical taste. Seen in this perspective, Wren's circular design for Trinity Library is notable as the earliest known essay of its kind in European architecture, whereas his executed design is simply a splendidly classical version of the long rectangular space whose use for library purposes went back to the later Middle Ages. In its orthodox use of the orders the east front of the Library is comparable to Wren's 'Great Model' design for St Paul's, and belongs to what has been called the 'High Renaissance' phase of an architect whose style 'passed, in a manner of speaking, from Brunelleschi to Carlo Fontana in one life-time'.[53] Only a year or two earlier, he had been involved, at Lincoln Cathedral, in the design of a library which stands on an arcade of the type Brunelleschi had invented at Florence over two hundred years earlier, and within a decade of the completion of the Trinity Library he was designing palaces and other public buildings in the grand manner of Bernini. The east front of the Wren Library shows the fuller understanding of Roman antiquity that was characteristic of the High Renaissance, without any of those deliberate distortions that the

51 A. Hobson, 'English library bindings of the 17th and 18th century', *Wolfenbütteler Forschungen* 2 (1977), p. 68. In his book on books and libraries, translated by John Evelyn as *Instructions concerning the erecting of a library* (1661), the Frenchman Gabriel Naudé deprecates expensive bindings, saying that 'it were better to reserve that money for the purchasing of all the books of the fairest and best editions that are to be found'.

52 Masson, *Décor*.

53 K. Downes, *The architecture of Wren* (1982), p. 29.

baroque would encourage. For Wren the filling in of the arches to drop the floor was a practical expedient that had no ulterior aesthetic motive and that did little to disturb the stately progression of the orders across a façade in which Roman *gravitas* gave dignity to a great academic library.

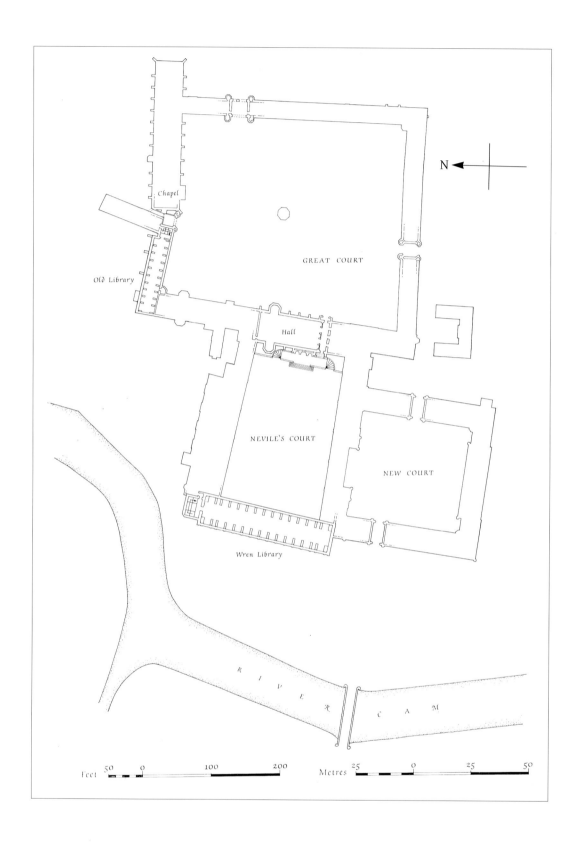

N

Chapel

Old Library

GREAT COURT

Hall

NEVILE'S COURT

NEW COURT

Wren Library

R I V E R   C A M

Feet 50 0 100 200 Metres 25 0 25 50

17 Plan of Trinity College, showing the old library of 1599–1600 and the Wren Library.

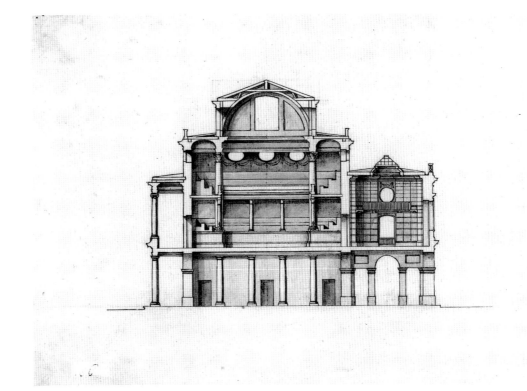

18 Wren's design for an assembly-room and library for the University of Cambridge, 1675–6. The library is seen in section above and in elevation below, with the larger senate house behind it (All Souls, 1, 53, 55).

19 Andrea Palladio, *I quattro libri dell'architettura* (Venice, 1581), book II, p. 32: superimposed orders in an ancient Roman building according to Palladio.

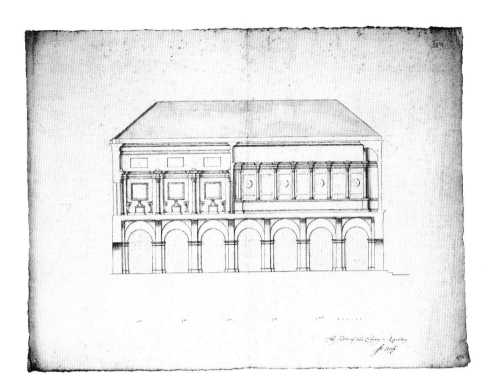

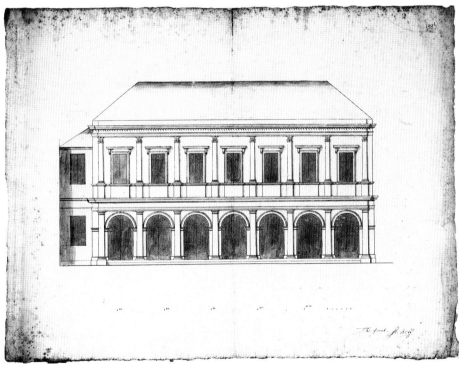

20 The Royal College of Physicians, London: designs by John Webb for the library and 'repository' built in 1651–3 and destroyed in the Great Fire of 1666 (Worcester College, Oxford, I, 58 L and M).

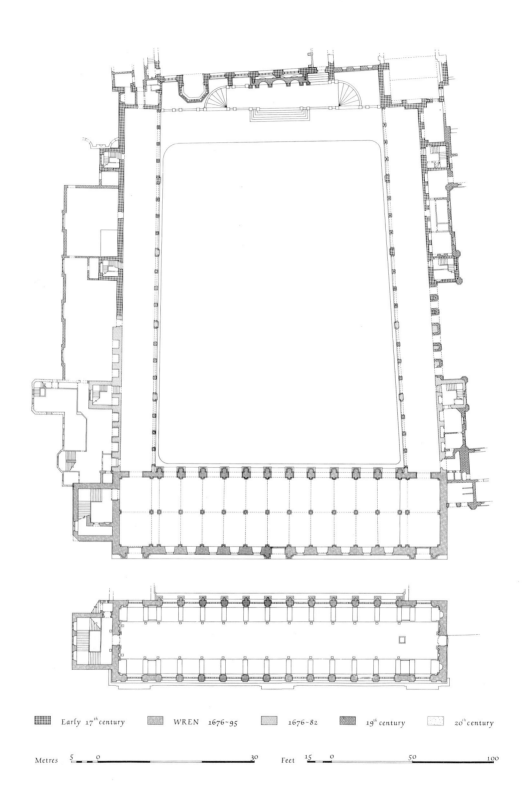

▦ Early 17ᵗʰ century   ▨ WREN 1676~95   ▨ 1676~82   ▨ 19ᵗʰ century   ▨ 20ᵗʰ century

Metres   5   0   30   Feet 15 0   50   100

21   Plan of the Wren Library and Nevile's Court in 1994 (Edward Impey).

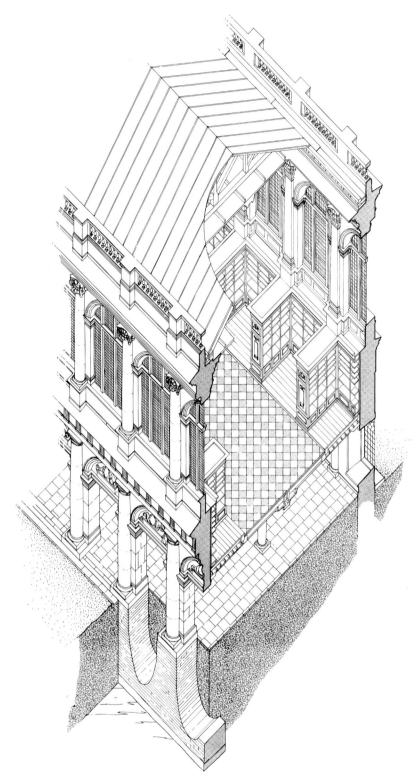

22 Axonometric drawing of the Wren Library, showing the inverted arches forming the foundation for the piers of the east wall and features of the interior (Edward Impey after Donald Insall and Partners).

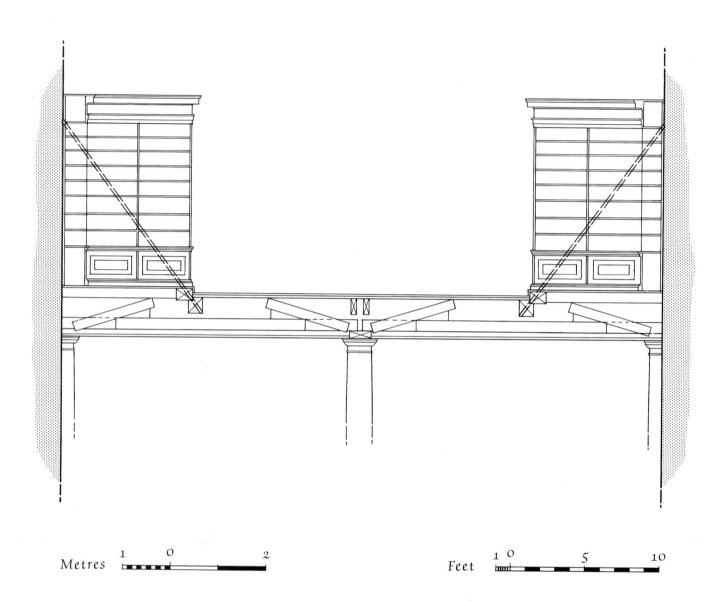

Metres 1 0 2

Feet 1 0 5 10

23 Section showing Wren's method of supporting the bookpresses (Edward Impey).

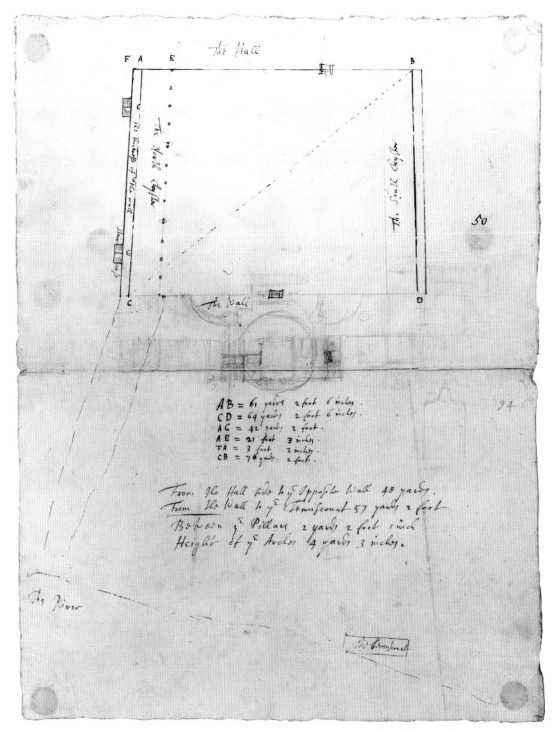

The Hall

F A E   B

The North Cloyster

The South Cloyster

The Wall

50

C   D

94

AB = 61 yards 2 foot 6 inches.
CD = 64 yards 2 foot 6 inches.
AC = 42 yards 2 foot.
AE = 21 foot 3 inches.
FA = 3 foot 2 inches.
CB = 76 yards 2 foot.

From the Hall side to ye Opposite Wall 48 yards.
From the Wall to ye Tenniscourt 57 yards 2 foot
Between ye Pillars 2 yards 2 foot 1 inch
Height of ye Arches 4 yards 3 inches.

The River

The Tenniscourt

24 Site plan of Nevile's Court as it existed in 1675, showing the wall across the open western end and the tennis-court between it and the river. The pencil sketches, presumably by Wren, show as alternative possibilities a circular library or a longitudinal one with a rectangular entrance hall in the middle. The dimensions are inaccurate (All Souls, IV, 50).

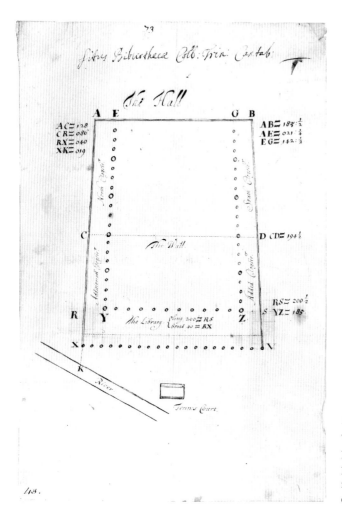

25 Site plan showing Nevile's Court extended westwards, with a library indicated in its ultimate position. The dimensions are inaccurate, and the plan must presumably have been made locally for Wren's use. Inscribed 'Situs Bibliothecae Coll: Trin: Cantab.' (All Souls, I, 43).

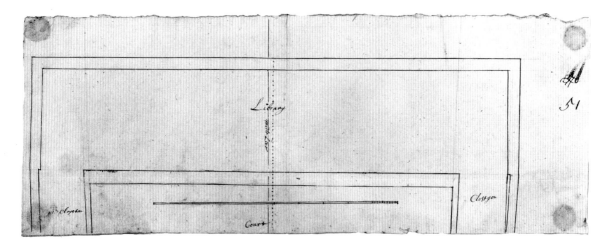

26 Site plan showing 'Library', presumably in its ultimate position (All Souls, IV, 51).

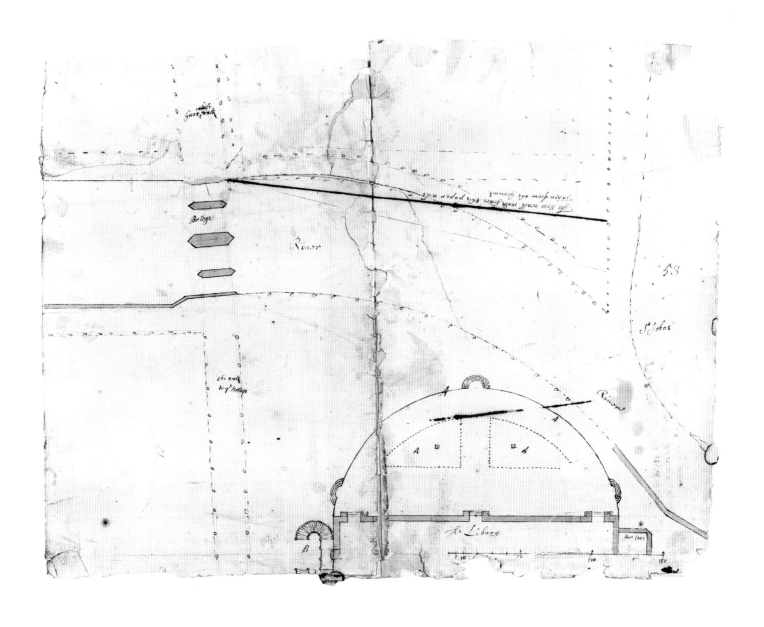

27 Site plan showing the Library essentially as built, but with a projected double-flight curving staircase at its southern end, marked B, and a semi-circular raised garden between its west front and the river. Endorsed: 'This for Mr. Havcksmore at Sr Christopher Wren's Lodging in Scotland Yeard London this present' (All Souls, IV, 53).

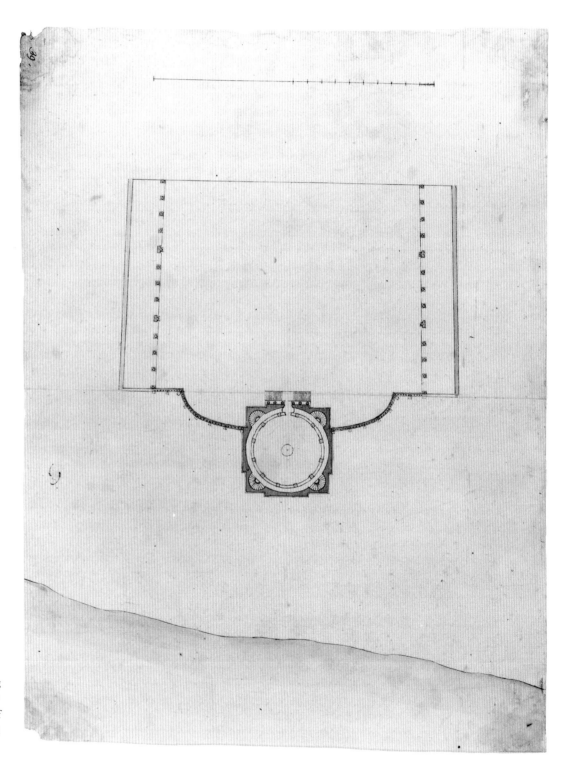

28 Plan by Wren showing
a projected circular library
attached to the west end of
Nevile's Court as it existed
in 1675 (All Souls, 1, 39).

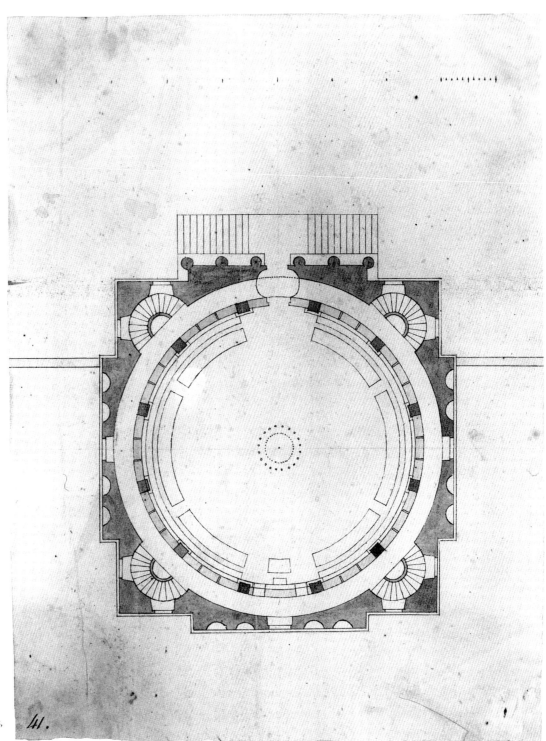

29 Plan by Wren of the projected circular library, showing the bookshelves and the seating (All Souls, I, 41).

41.

42.

30 Elevation by Wren of
the proposed circular library,
showing the attached Ionic
portico facing east towards
Nevile's Court (All Souls, I, 42).

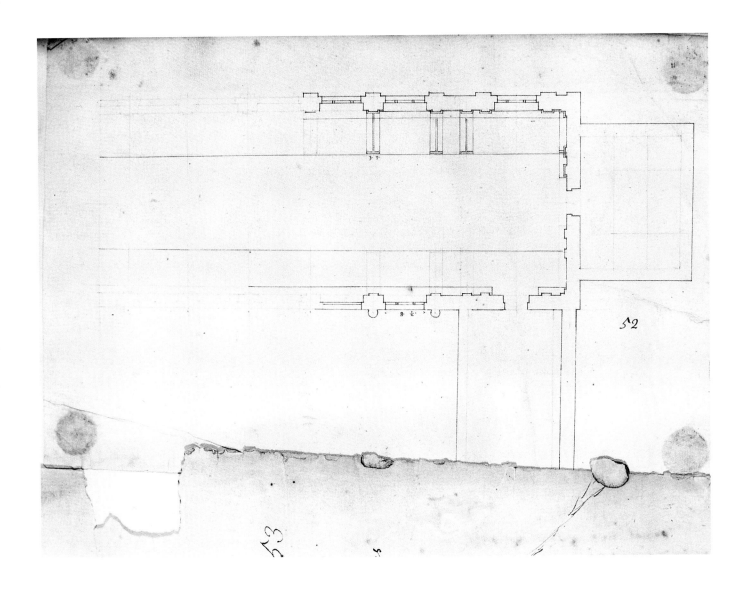

37 Plan at upper level of the north end of the Library, as in fig. 32 (All Souls, IV, 52).

38 Elevation and section of the east front of the Library, showing the architectural details: marked Figs. I, II, III, IV (All Souls, I, 50).

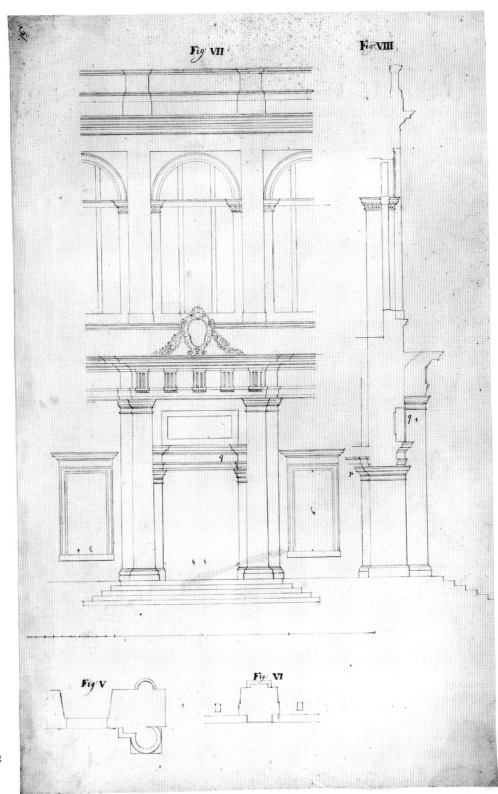

39 Elevation and section of the west front of the Library, showing the architectural details: marked Figs. V, VI, VII, VIII (All Souls, I, 51).

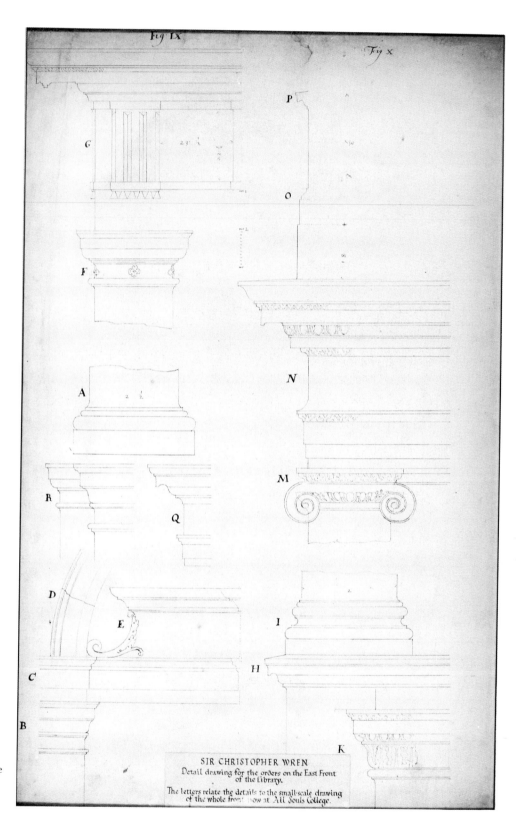

Fig IX

Fig X

SIR CHRISTOPHER WREN
Detail drawing for the orders on the East Front
of the Library.

The letters relate the details to the small-scale drawing
of the whole front now at All Souls College.

40 Large-scale details of the orders on the east front of the Library: marked Figs. IX, X (Trinity College Library).

41 Plan and elevation of one of the recesses in the corners of the Library, not as built (All Souls, I, 102).

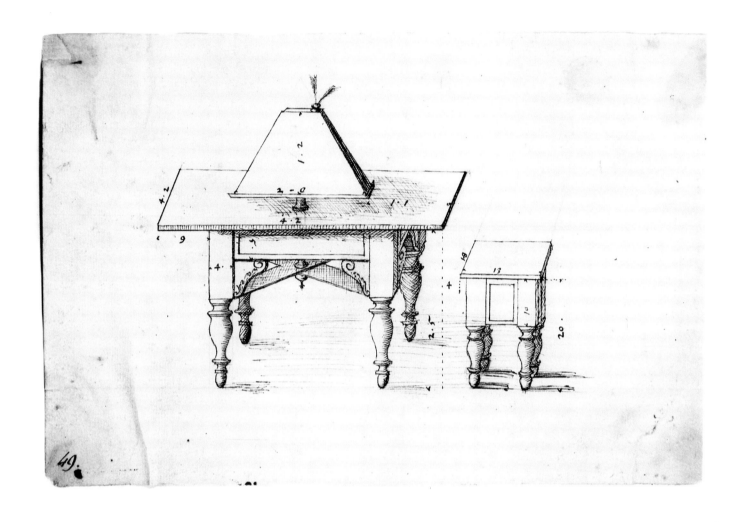

42 Sketch probably by Wren for a reading-desk and stand for the Library. See also fig. 7 (All Souls, I, 49).

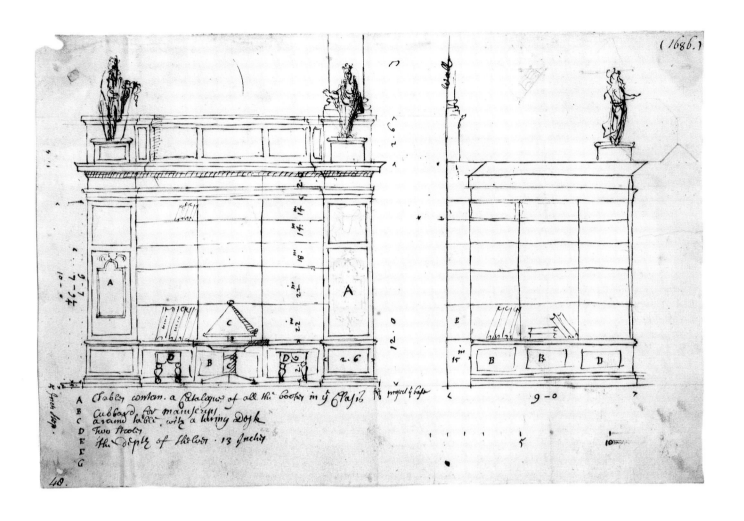

43 Sketch by Wren's assistant Nicholas Hawksmoor of a bookpress for the Library, dated 1686. Note the reading-desk as in fig. 42 (All Souls, I, 48).

CHAPTER THREE

BOOKS AND OTHER COLLECTIONS
David McKitterick

1 The age of Bentley

The College had built a great library. But it had given much less thought to how the books in it should be organised. The combination of a lack of an overall plan for the organisation of the books, and an emphasis on the importance of recognising and recording benefactions, led to an arrangement whereby for many years freshly added collections were shelved more according to their donors than to their subjects or their varying uses.[1] Uffenbach was one visitor who disapproved of such an arrangement, though he realised its value, like that of the coats of arms of benefactors carved by Grinling Gibbons and his workshop, in alluring further donors.[2] Apart from the major donations, subjects in the new library were shelved in much the same order as in the old. The new building did not bring new ideas in librarianship immediately. Nevertheless, some of the assumptions about the organisation of the Library and the presentation of the books in it to readers quickly proved to be out of date. The small boards at the ends of the cases (fig. 7), displaying lists of adjacent books and long familiar to readers not only in Oxford and Cambridge, were abandoned in the first years of the new century. As for the books themselves, they seem to have been turned front to back, so that the spines faced the readers in the new fashion, in 1706 – the same year as in the University Library.[3]

When Richard Bentley was admitted as Master of Trinity in 1700, he found much in need of reform and improvement, from the methods for electing new Fellows to the state of the Master's Lodge. The following four decades are celebrated as some of the most divisive in the College's history. Nowhere is the ambiguity of feelings at the time of his death more plainly seen than in the stone that marks his grave in the Chapel, its inscription making no mention of his place as Master. By contrast, the Wren now houses his bust in marble (fig. 93), carved posthumously and one of Roubiliac's

1 This was no innovation. It was common elsewhere, and had been followed at Trinity until 1640: see Gaskell, *Trinity College Library*, pp. 92–9.
2 *Cambridge under Queen Anne*, p. 126; Zacharias Conrad von Uffenbach, *Merkwürdige Reisen durch Niedersachsen, Holland und Engelland*, 3 vols. (Frankfurt, Leipzig, Ulm, 1753–4), 3, p. 4.
3 Junior Bursar's accounts, 1705–6, f.185r; Oates, *Cambridge University Library*, p. 479; McKenzie, *Cambridge University Press*, 1, pp. 290, 325; 2, pp. 286, 317.

finest achievements, in which his profile can be more plainly seen than in his portrait by Thornhill; much of his character may be thereby discovered. The bust was placed in the Library in 1756.[4] It is a vivid reminder of one who was a considerable benefactor (his Greek manuscripts formed by far the richest collection of such books ever given to the College), but also one who used the Library avidly (if not always responsibly), and who had been Royal Librarian since 1694. As Royal Librarian, he had been forward with proposals for improvement in London. In his first year as Master in Cambridge, the Conclusion Book records decisions that students were to be allowed to use the College Library, a privilege that in return required them to pay a part of the cost of purchasing books.[5] Two classes were to be set apart for their use, making practical use of a building that was at that time so far from full.[6] From the first, Bentley was determined that the Library should be adequately funded. Indeed, his anxiety to spend Hacket's money as it was intended, on books rather than on buildings, or allow it to be absorbed into the ordinary College revenues, led him into one of his earliest quarrels. No books were entered in the register of purchases with Hacket's fund between 1682 and 1698.[7] 'And when upon my coming in 1700', Bentley later remarked, 'I put a stop to this Corruption, *the Peace of the Colege was much disturb'd*, and the Seniors were very clamorous to have this Robbing allow'd again at every Audit for five or six years together.'[8]

In the sixteenth century, and for much of the seventeenth, the College Library had relied, like other parts of the University, on donations. It allocated no specific funds to the purchase of books. But with the gift by John Hacket of £1,200, allowing the College to rebuild Garret Hostel and thereby enabling it, with the rents from the new Bishop's Hostel, to provide an income specifically for the benefit of the Library, this haphazard arrangement was altered. Hacket himself died in 1670, and so did not live to see the manner whereby his benefaction was applied to the new library. With the Hacket fund, the College purchased books (mostly on mathematics) from Barrow's library in 1681; a copy of the *English atlas* in 1681–2; and ten volumes of the *Theatrum urbium celebriorum* in 1682.[9] To set beside this, it was able to add (in years when they were not occupied by members of the benefactors' families) the income from new rooms erected adjacent to the Wren, and the rent (set for many years at £12 per annum) for the old library in Great Court. In the first years of the eighteenth century, the rent of the old library, combined

4 Junior Bursar's accounts, 1756–7, recording expenditure of 19s. 6d. for carriage of Barrow's and Bentley's busts, and setting them up in the Library. But the bust may perhaps have been kept in the Library only temporarily: see the remarks by Malcolm Baker, p. 128 below.
5 See below, pp. 65–7.
6 Trinity College Conclusion Book, 19 August 1700; Monk, *Life of Bentley*, 1, p. 163.
7 MS R.17.6, f. 5r. After 1698 this register was no longer used.
8 Monk, *Life of Bentley*, 1, pp. 163–5; Richard Bentley, *The present state of Trinity College* (London, 1710), p. 14. The italics are Bentley's.
9 MS R.17.6, f. 4r-v.

with a balance of about £60 available once repairs and maintenance had been charged to the income from the new rooms in Nevile's Court and in Bishop's Hostel, produced a not untypical income from the Library.[10] To this was added the sum of £5 per annum bequeathed by Peter Samwaies in 1693 specifically for the purchase of books.[11] With this, the College met the cost of books, binding and minor repairs to the Library and its equipment. It was a modest income indeed; but in comparison with other, and larger, libraries elsewhere it was a generous one. In the Bodleian Library, expenditure rose from about £9 per annum in the first decade of the eighteenth century to just under £40 in the second. Although it remained healthy in the early 1720s, it dropped to about £7 per annum in the 1730s and 1740s.[12] In Oxford, as in Cambridge University Library, the 1710 Copyright Act brought some books by deposit; and all of these libraries gained much more by gift than they did by purchase. But the level of expenditure is none the less some guide to the ability and determination of the various bodies involved to build up their libraries. At Trinity, as elsewhere, expenditure inevitably varied very considerably from year to year. As any surplus or deficit in the Trinity library account was carried over to the following year, a quite substantial surplus eventually accumulated. By 1733, this amounted to £377, an amount so large that it was not carried over, but instead absorbed into the rest of the College revenues, to be resurrected only in 1744, so as to pay off the deficit that by 1743 had stood at £258.

The available funds were not always so unencumbered. In 1757, in the course of the restoration of Nevile's Court under the direction of James Essex (it was at this period that the court's facing of soft white clunch was replaced with Ketton stone, and the uppermost gable windows were altered for the new balustraded façade), the rent from the Library's rooms in the court had first to face bills for repairs and alterations amounting to over £500. The financial year 1757–8 began with a deficit of £689. Although attempts in the next few years to reduce this deficit met with some success, no serious inroads were made into it until the allocation in 1771–2 of thirty-two previous years' income from the Samwaies fund, amounting to £320. The Library's deficit was written off again in 1795, by a transfer of £590 from the plate fund: the same fund had met the cost of the *Encyclopédie* in 1779.

By these means, the College gradually increased its expenditure on the Library, and particularly on books. And yet, in some years it spent little or

10 The following is drawn from the Junior Bursar's accounts. All figures are quoted to the nearest pound, unless indicated otherwise.

11 Samwaies had been elected a Fellow in 1640, but he spent the later years of his life as an incumbent in Yorkshire. For a copy of his will (dated November 1690; codicil August 1692), see TC Mun., box 31, no. 8.

12 Ian Philip, *The Bodleian Library in the seventeenth and eighteenth centuries* (Oxford, 1983), pp. 74–5; Ian Philip, 'Libraries and the University Press', in Sutherland and Mitchell, *Oxford*, pp. 725–55 at pp. 728–31. The Bodleian possessed no regular book fund until the Crewe bequest provided £10 per annum in 1750: this remained the major contribution to the book fund for the next thirty years.

nothing. In 1702–3 the accounts record expenditure on stationery supplies, on binding, on bookplates for books bought with the Hacket bequest, and for minor repairs to the locks and windows, but nothing at all on books at a time when the accounts showed a credit standing to the Library of £457. By the following year, the credit had risen a further £100, but even so the College seems to have spent less than £10 on books and binding in 1703–4, and less than £16 in the next year. No books or binding at all graced the accounts for 1705–6. With Bishop's Hostel able to produce about £50 per annum, of which about £10 was available for books after the costs of maintenance, Bentley found such parsimony at the expense of the Library intolerable. Indeed, the College was reminded daily by the very words of Hacket's will, plain to see in the portrait (fig. 3) that had hung in the College for a quarter of a century: 'to furnish the Library of Trinity College with books'. So, under Bentley, these words stood in silent rebuke no more, and Hacket's money was put to its original purpose, and particularly to major works such as Baluze's *Concilia*, the *Acta conciliorum*, the Church fathers, Montfaucon on Greek palaeography, and Rymer's *Foedera*.

The Library always depended on one or two principal local booksellers. Cornelius Crownfield, the University Printer, acted as the principal supplier for the first part of the eighteenth century. Since bills were submitted months after the supply of books, it is impossible to correlate the figures in the audit books with the month when the cost was incurred, and the books arrived. It is therefore difficult to explain an exceptionally high account submitted by Crownfield in 1714–15, for £101, in a year where his previous figure had been £42 and the succeeding was to be £16: one possibility is that this represented expenditure from Hacket's bequest. No annual figure to an individual book-seller was to exceed, or even challenge, this until almost the end of the century. The total from Crownfield's equivalent as a bookseller and bookbinder in the 1780s, J. and J. Merrill, exceeded £100 for the first time in 1787–8, although by no means all of this was being spent on new books.

In the mid-century, periodicals began to figure regularly, including the *Acta eruditorum*, the *Histoire de l'Académie Royale des Sciences*, the *Histoire de l'Académie des Inscriptions et Belles Lettres*, and, from St Petersburg, the *Acta Academiae Scientiarum Imperialis Petropolitanae*. As with the others, the arrival of the *Philosophical Transactions* of the Royal Society was recorded somewhat haphazardly. For monographs, there was for many years less sense of urgency. Some books, in subjects otherwise well represented, were not acquired until surprisingly long after their publication. Thus, Morant's history of Colchester (1748) came only in 1757; Masters's history of Corpus Christi College came, a gift from the author, four years after publication in 1753; and Horsley's *Britannia romana* (1732) arrived in the 1740s.

Two of the Library's suppliers have already been mentioned: Cornelius Crownfield and J. and J. Merrill. As a critical part of Bentley's reform of the University Press, Crownfield had been brought from Holland and appointed to Cambridge as overseer of the newly restored University Press.[13] He established a bookselling business only subsequently. The College's first dealings with him were as a printer of bookplates; but in the same years, 1701–2, he also supplied the first volume of the Suidas Greek lexicon and a group of classical texts, both printed by himself. The publication of Ludolph Kuster's internationally acclaimed edition of the lexicon, and the arrival of a stock of books taken as exchange with the continental trade, seem to have helped to turn Crownfield into a bookseller. Within a few years, he was charging for the first volumes of Graevius' *Thesaurus antiquitatum et historiarum Italiae*. In 1709 his bill for (unspecified) books amounted to £18. 13s., and thereafter he became established as the Library's often sole supplier. From 1726, other names of local booksellers began to appear, beginning with William Thurlbourn. Merrill appeared in the mid 1740s, at first in a distinctly subservient role. John Deighton, whose surname was to figure so much in the Library's needs and in the publications of members of the College in the nineteenth century, seems to have supplied books for the first time in 1795–6, the same year as another local bookseller, William Lunn. Names of London booksellers occur only rarely in the accounts, including Samuel Harding in 1739–40, and John Nourse in 1753–4. Two other London booksellers, both dealing in foreign books, Baillière and Bossange, made a fleeting appearance in 1832–3, and Bossange appeared again in 1836–7. The simplicity of the accounts almost certainly conceals a more complicated chain of supply by the trade: in 1756–7, some of Merrill's account represented a choice of books made by the Master, Robert Smith, from a catalogue issued by the London bookseller Thomas Payne. Later on in the century, it is probable that Deighton also acted as local agent for London booksellers.

Apart from ordinary dealings with booksellers, the vogue for publication by subscription had its full effect on the Library, and helps to conceal patterns

13 Crownfield's early career as printer is fully discussed in McKenzie, *Cambridge University Press*. He became University Printer in 1705.

of supply. In the 1720s, the number of books published in this manner escalated.[14] Subscriptions had advantages for publishers and customers alike, since they required some prepayment but dispersed the cost sometimes over several years. But they also made it difficult to plan expenditure, since that depended on unpredictable and often unreliable timetables of publication. Not infrequently, plans for new books either had to be substantially altered, or they proved fruitless. In the late 1720s, the College's subscriptions included not only expensive works such as Martyn on botany, Pemberton's *View of Sir Isaac Newton's philosophy* and Buckley's edition of De Thou's *History of his own times* (exceptionally expensive, beginning at four guineas), but also cheaper works such as Bradley on the natural history of Cambridgeshire. Later on, Catesby on the natural history of the Carolinas and quantities of English local history and of descriptions of classical antiquities were bought in the same way. Although the College was recorded in many lists of subscribers, these printed lists are far from comprehensive as evidence. The lists of subscribers in such books, seemingly so clear in their identification of those who were most interested, are in practice unreliable guides to their first audiences. For Trinity, subscriptions were sometimes taken out via booksellers, and sometimes via members of the College. Sometimes, subscriptions simply arrived too late to be inserted in the printed list. On yet other occasions, books for which the College subscribed, such as an English edition of Julian's *Caesars* (in 1727–8) never appeared, while Robert Smith's work on optics, subscribed for in the same year, was finally published ten years later.

More particularly, the College seems to have had no policy with respect to copies on large or ordinary paper. Perhaps in anticipation of a gift, or perhaps in disappointment, since the author was a prominent Fellow, it subscribed only to a small-paper copy of Conyers Middleton's life of Cicero (1741), though King's, Corpus and Trinity Hall all subscribed for copies on large paper. Not surprisingly, the book was in immediate demand among the fellowship; a large-paper copy seems to have arrived in the Wren only with Robert Smith's bequest, in 1768. But for Francis Peck's history of Stamford, and for his *Desiderata curiosa*, large-paper copies were thought necessary. Clarendon's *History of the rebellion* was also bought on large paper. The practice of publication by subscription remained in the nineteenth century, but figured less in the accounts. Instead, books in parts became a more common

14 P.J. Wallis, 'Book subscription lists', *The Library*, 5th ser., 29 (1974), pp. 255–86.

feature of the book trade, and were reflected in the Library's accessions accordingly. The new edition of Estienne's Greek *Thesaurus*, published by Valpy in London, was divided into thirty-two parts plus index and glossary, at two guineas for each part, and its publication was spread over 1816–28: the Library embarked on a large-paper set, and so in 1822–3 found itself obliged to pay twelve guineas for six parts, in a total expenditure on books that year of only £57.

Since no proper donations register was kept for much of the eighteenth century, and the annual accounts are necessarily summary, the evidence for everyday accessions is far from comprehensive. It is, for example, unclear who was responsible in the mid-century for causing the College to invest in many of the standard works on English law published in the seventeenth and early eighteenth centuries. Nevertheless, the arrival of a series of major gifts, some of them of considerable number, must be viewed among these more mundane affairs. From the completion of the Wren Library, and even before 1695, these gifts dominated the Library; but in the end their treatment was ordained by the need to integrate the more miscellaneous collections.

By far the largest was the gift of Sir Henry Puckering, taking up most of four bays. Others followed: most substantially gifts or bequests from William Corker (d. 1702), who had been admitted as a Fellow forty-five years previously;[15] from John Laughton, Chaplain, Librarian and then University Librarian (d. 1712); and from Edward Rudd, Fellow of the College (d. 1727).

These donations, all of which had arrived by 1730, transformed the Library both in its appearance and in its subject matter. Indeed, they remain a formidable part of the Library's character today. The space so obviously available on the empty shelves of the new building served as a reminder not only of the College's hopes, and needs, but also of the fact that it could provide the means of preserving together what would otherwise have been dispersed. Roger Gale was to recognise this advantage for his manuscripts at the end of the 1730s: 'as good a way as any to preserve them from dispersion or the oven'.[16] A similar point had been made by Evelyn many years before.[17]

The Library was not finished before the arrival of the first, and (as it was to prove) largest collection of printed books to be received until the nineteenth century.

Sir Henry Puckering (fig. 4) died childless in 1701. He had begun to give his collection a decade previously, in time for the manuscripts to be listed by

15 For his will, dated 15 July 1700 and proved 12 May 1702, see TC Mun., box 31, no. 9. His books are listed in MS Add.a.150a.
16 Stukeley, *Family memoirs*, 1, p. 305.
17 See above, p. 21.

Laughton in Bernard's *Catalogi librorum manuscriptorum Angliae et Hiberniae*, published in 1697. The survey of Puckering's manuscripts, as published, is not quite complete. Many loose papers, particularly in Italian, were omitted, and it is probably to the confusion of papers faced by Laughton at this juncture that we may trace the separation of an important part of the Puckering gift from its fellows.[18] More intriguingly, the Bernard list makes no mention of the celebrated manuscript containing Milton's autograph versions of *Comus*, *Lycidas*, and minor poems (now MS R.3.4: fig. 44).

The collection dated back to the time of Sir John Puckering (1544–96), Lord Keeper of the great seal briefly under Queen Elizabeth. But its principal foundations lay in the books and papers of his son Sir Thomas Puckering, companion to Henry, Prince of Wales, and of Adam Newton, the Prince's tutor and then secretary. Newton's public career was principally remarkable for his holding the Deanery of Durham and yet not being ordained.[19] But the accumulations of the household of the Prince of Wales seem to have provided much that passed into his hands, from royal manuscript copy-books to an assortment of manuscripts intended to contribute to the instruction of his master, to books bearing all the marks of ownership by the royal household. Most notably, perhaps, there was an alphabetical catalogue of the library of Thomas, Lord Lumley, acquired for Prince Henry's own library.[20] Among the manuscripts that now returned to Cambridge was a copy of songs for lute and viol dedicated to Prince Henry by George Handford, perhaps of Emmanuel College, dated 1609. Further books came from other members of this circle, most numerously a group of manuscripts by Giacomo Castelvetro on subjects ranging from politics to conversation to cookery.[21] Yet other books, including a manuscript collection of Donne's poems (MS R.3.12) and probably the celebrated autograph collection of Milton's poems (MS R.3.4: fig. 44), had been added by members of the family in the course of the century.[22] By the end of the century, the collection was a substantial one, its printed books in particular rich in evidence of the royalist sympathies and friendships of Sir Henry Puckering and his wife Elizabeth.

Puckering's books seem to have arrived in stages. On 17 March 1690/1 the College approved a payment of £10 to John Laughton 'for his care & pains in cataloguing Sr Henry Puckering's Library at his house in Warwick'. Perhaps soon afterwards, but certainly by 1697, there had arrived the bulk of the collection, including the manuscripts: the College met the cost of transport.[23]

18 See further below, pp. 59–60. Many of the Puckering papers remained disorganised until after the arrival of Beaupré Bell's bequest in 1745 and the Bosanquet books in 1755: see, for example, the assortments bound up in MSS R.10.8,9.

19 Thomas Birch, *The life of Henry Prince of Wales* (1760), pp. 14, 66–7, 371–5; Roy Strong, *Henry, Prince of Wales, and England's lost renaissance* (1986).

20 Sears Jayne and Francis Johnson (ed.), *The Lumley library: the catalogue of 1609* (1956).

21 Giacomo Castelvetro, *The fruit, herbs & vegetables of Italy*, trans. and ed. Gillian Riley (1989). Most of the Castelvetro manuscripts are listed on pp. 166–7.

22 Adam Newton married the daughter of Sir John Puckering, and their son Henry took his mother's family name.

23 Accounts of Patrick Cock, Junior Bursar, 1695–8.

These were placed in the first bays to the left of any visitor to the Library, and were thus the most immediately obvious in the new building. Others, published in 1698–9, were added later, more or less as a group.[24] The family had assembled no outstanding collection of medieval manuscripts or of early printed books: indeed, very little among Puckering's gift had been published before 1550. Instead, here were the concerns of each generation, from the Elizabethan and Jacobean courts, through successive political upheavals and pamphlet wars, with an accompaniment of literature, books of instruction, and books with which to relax. Not surprisingly, the collection was especially strong in editions of French, Italian and Spanish literature of the late sixteenth and early seventeenth centuries. As a whole, it dominated the collections given in these first years, and it remains among the richest. On Puckering's death, the College commissioned for the Library a full-length portrait of its benefactor,[25] and so began to continue in the eighteenth century a practice already established of adorning the Library with portraits or representations of benefactors and those who might otherwise inspire readers.

Not everyone found the new arrangements at Trinity to his liking. Samuel Pepys, with his strong family connections in Cambridge, was also linked by marriage to Thomas Gale, who married his cousin Barbara Pepys, of Impington.[26] In the last weeks of Pepys's life, as his thoughts turned to the disposition of his library, he thought of the new library. His own college, Magdalene, was a preferable home; but failing that, Trinity would serve. As colleges, both were preferable to the University Library. But whether at Magdalene or Trinity, his books were to be kept in a separate room: 'and if in Trinity, That the said room be contiguous and to have communication with the new Library there'.[27] Though Wren's design had provided the main floor of the Library at the same level as the adjacent rooms, the deposit of Pepys's books at Magdalene meant that the question of extending the Library less than a decade after it had been completed did not arise.

The other three large donations in the Wren Library's early years came from Fellows. From the attestation given by John Laughton in 1700 that he had placed in the Library the books of William Corker, it would appear that Corker himself was unable to supervise his gift in person: he died two years later, in 1702. His books came to the Library, while the cash in his estate was divided between the improvement of the Chapel (one of Bentley's early projects) and the Library.[28] Though his collection was smaller than that of

24 Three hundred bookplates were printed in 1699 (Junior Bursar's accounts, 1698–9).
25 Conclusion Book, 4 August 1701; Junior Bursar's accounts, 1701–2.
26 Samuel Pepys's great uncle Talbot, and his cousin Roger, between them served as Recorders to Cambridge for a total of fifty-five years.
27 Codicil to Pepys's will, 13 May 1703, printed in E. Gordon Duff, *Bibliotheca Pepysiana: a descriptive catalogue of the library of Samuel Pepys*, part 2, *Early printed books to 1558* (1914), p. IX.
28 Conclusion Book, 12 June 1703.

Puckering, it still amounted to about seven hundred works. The list of his gift opened with the Eton Chrysostom (1613), but it is partly remarkable for containing the first issues of the *Philosophical Transactions* of the Royal Society to arrive in the Wren, albeit only a few odd numbers for the years 1665–73.[29]

In John Laughton, who took so large a part in organising the arrival of these collections, the College had a Fellow who enjoyed wide respect both in England and overseas. Knowledgeable, intellectually curious in both the humanities and natural philosophy, accessible and tactful, he had been born a few days before the execution of Charles I, and had entered Trinity in 1665. As was the custom, the librarianship at that period and for many years afterwards was usually placed in the hands of a young graduate. Laughton was appointed first Chaplain and then, in 1679, Librarian. In this position he served, officially at least, less than four years before returning to his post as Chaplain, and then, in 1686, being elected University Librarian. A close friend of Newton, he retained his interest in the College Library sufficiently to be responsible for the first catalogue of its manuscripts to be printed, in Bernard's *Catalogi* in 1697,[30] to be ready to show visitors appropriate attractions, and to be the acknowledged resident expert. Despite the fact that he was no longer College Librarian, but had been succeeded by Thomas Rotherham (to whom fell the task of supervising the removal of the books from Great Court into the new building), Laughton was still buying books for the Library even in 1695.[31] His erudition became celebrated; and besides his post as University Librarian he was also appointed *Academiae Architypographus*, charged with overseeing the running of the newly founded University Press – a duty which, however, was soon proved superfluous thanks to the competence of the University's Printer, Cornelius Crownfield.[32] His death in 1712 found even Thomas Hearne, in Oxford, ready to mourn: 'a learned Man, and understood Books well, and left behind him a good Collection not only of Books but old Coyns &c.'[33]

His books now in Trinity do not by any means constitute the whole of this 'good collection', a collection that Francis Burman had in 1702 found 'very curious'.[34] On Laughton's death, many of his papers, and in particular a sizeable portion of those that had once belonged to Puckering, passed into the hands of George Paul of Jesus College, whom Humfrey Wanley supported as a candidate as next University Librarian.[35] His remaining books were dispersed. Paul died soon after Laughton, but not before he had offered his

29 Corker's books are listed in a separate catalogue, MS Add.a.150a. For other early volumes of the *Philosophical Transactions* in the library, belonging to Thomas Kirke (d. 1706), see Gaskell, *Trinity College Library*, p. 131.

30 Edward Bernard, *Catalogi librorum manuscriptorum Angliae et Hiberniae* (Oxford, 1697), 2, p. 93, incorrectly naming Laughton as Henry rather than John.

31 Junior Bursar's accounts, July–December 1695.

32 McKenzie, *Cambridge University Press*, 1, pp. 97–8.

33 Hearne, *Remarks and collections*, 3, p. 458.

34 *Cambridge under Queen Anne*, p. 117.

35 Humfrey Wanley, *Letters*, ed. P. L. Heyworth (Oxford, 1989), p. 274.

new-found collection of Puckering and Newton papers to Robert Harley. The matter was further complicated because Thomas Baker, *socius ejectus* of St John's College, also had an interest in some of the papers in connection with his work on the history of the University. Within a few months, Baker, too (who was in correspondence with Strype over documents relating to Archbishop Whitgift, and who claimed to have contemplated passing part on to Ralph Thoresby, in Yorkshire) had sold his remaining papers from the same source to Harley. Baker's own part in the affair is not altogether clear, and Paul seems not to have been candid. The consequence was unfortunate. A letter from Paul to Harley provides a tantalising description of these stray Newton and Puckering papers, to set beside the more select series now surviving in the Harleian manuscripts:

> The last Possessor of these Papers had amassed an immense quantity of written Books and Treaties of all kinds, besides other papers of less Consequence. The Books consist cheifly of Pamphlets afterwards printed, Common Places Bookes, the Original Copys from Printing Houses of Bookes there printed, with a very few MSS on velum, of which there seems but one of Value.[36]

As much as the list provided by Wanley for Harley five months later, it suggests what was once in Trinity, but through misfortune, carelessness or deliberate act had now escaped. In this manner, Harley acquired papers from Adam Newton and the circle of Henry, Prince of Wales that would have remained more logically with the printed books and further papers already in the College Library.[37]

Thus the almost two thousand volumes that Laughton gave in his lifetime to the College represent but one part of his collection. Like the Puckering books, they included many in modern languages (but still principally French, Italian and Spanish). There was also a noticeable presence of books printed in northern and north-east Europe, from cities such as Uppsala, Warsaw and Danzig. Among half a dozen incunables, a copy of the *Legenda aurea* (Wynkyn de Worde, 1498) was the only example from an English press to enter the Library among the various collections of the early eighteenth century. It stands as a reminder that these were working collections, or the accumulations of generations, not collections inspired by the new fashions of bibliophily. The bookplate that now identifies Laughton's volumes is undated, but the gift is

36 George Paul to Harley, 9 July 1713 (British Library MS Harley 7007, at front). Baker found Paul difficult, and even dishonest: see his letters to Strype in Cambridge University MS Add. 10, especially 8 May, 28 May and 22 July [1714]; transcriptions in British Library MS Add. 5853.

37 Wanley included a list of Paul's papers in a letter to Harley, 30 December 1713: see Wanley, *Letters*, p. 289. The Newton, Puckering and Prince Henry papers are now scattered among the Harleian manuscripts.

likely to have been made in 1707, the date of the latest volume in the collection, the first volume of Sloane's *Natural history of Jamaica*.[38]

It was twenty years before a comparable collection was given to the College. Edward Rudd entered Trinity from Brasenose College, Oxford in 1695, and was elected a Fellow in 1701.[39] His elder brother Thomas, also of Trinity, had by then been appointed headmaster of the grammar school at Newcastle upon Tyne, where he was to remain before taking the livings successively of St Oswald's, Durham and of Northallerton. In Durham, Thomas Rudd marked his librarianship of the Cathedral Library by completing a catalogue of its manuscripts that was eventually printed only in 1825. In Cambridge, he was a benefactor to the College in his own right, his manuscripts, which were mostly of an antiquarian nature, including perhaps most appropriately a collection of transcripts made for Whitgift in 1595–6 (MS B.14.9), while his printed books included the gift in 1707 of a copy of Livy (Treviso, 1482) that had formerly belonged to Lincoln College, Oxford. These gifts arrived at various times between 1701 and 1714. But whereas Thomas made his career in northern England, Edward remained in East Anglia, first at Trinity and then, from 1719, as rector of North Runcton, a College living in Norfolk. When he moved to Norfolk, he calculated that he had spent at least £330 on buying books, very few of which could be described as antiquarian. About one-third were of theology. But something of the cast of his mind may be gathered from the heads under which he chose to list his collection, with emphases on mathematics, agriculture, history and travels, and poetry: under mathematics, he included Loggan's views of Oxford and Cambridge, for which he paid £4.[40] This early collection also contained several volumes of pamphlets concerned with Quakers. By the time he bequeathed his library to Trinity in 1727, it had grown considerably, now numbering over sixteen hundred volumes, and (with various pamphlet volumes) many more titles.[41]

However, apart perhaps from the Puckering collection, these printed books paled beside the manuscripts of Thomas and Roger Gale.[42] Thomas (fig. 11), the elder, had entered the College in 1655, and in 1672 had been appointed Regius Professor of Greek, a post he held only for a few months before moving to London to become High Master of St Paul's School.[43] He remained in London until his appointment as Dean of York in 1697. In York, he worked enthusiastically and effectively for the improvement and repair of the cathedral, but he died only a little later, in 1702. Cambridge had claimed

38 A list of Laughton's books is in MS Add.a.150, pp. 234–331.

39 In his diary (MS B.17.39), which was extensively quarried by Monk for his life of Bentley, Rudd provides many details of life in Trinity in the first years of the eighteenth century: see *The diary (1709–1720) of Edward Rud*, ed. H.R. Luard (Cambridge Antiquarian Society, 1860).

40 MS B.7.6.

41 A list is in MS Add.a.150, pp. 156–233.

42 For two sympathetic accounts of Thomas Gale's scholarly work, see David Douglas, *English scholars, 1660–1730*, 2nd edn (1951) and (inspired by his work on John Scotus Eriugena) Edouard Jeauneau, 'La Traduction Erigénienne des *Ambigua de Maxime le Confesseur*: Thomas Gale (1636–1702) et le *Codex Remensis*', in *Jean Scot Erigène et l'histoire de la philosophie* (*Colloques Internationaux du C.N.R.S.* 561). The most convenient account of the Gale family, on which subsequent authorities have largely relied, remains that in Nichols, *Literary anecdotes*, 4, pp. 536–55. For Roger and Samuel Gale, see also the correspondence assembled in *Bibliotheca topographica Britannica* 2 (1781).

43 A brief note of names of members of the College in the 1660s, and of books lent to them by Gale, is on the rear flyleaf of N.4.49 (Hesychius, Venice, 1514).

44 MS O.3.10.

45 Douglas, *English scholars*, pp.59–61, 171–5. Gale was prompted and urged to this pioneering collection by Fell, as a part of his programme of learned publications at Oxford.

46 Many of these had been listed by Thomas Hyde in 1679 (MS O.11.28 (3)); they are included (following Hyde's descriptions) in a separate section of the catalogue of Gale's manuscripts in Edward Bernard, *Catalogi librorum manuscriptorum Angliae et Hiberniae* (Oxford, 1697), 2, pp. 192–5. A somewhat skeletal catalogue of them was made by Sir William Jones in 1773 (now MS R.13.15). Many of them now stand together on shelf R.13 (which largely follows the order of the descriptions in the *Catalogi*), but Gale's are unfortunately not properly identified in E. H. Palmer, *A descriptive catalogue of the Arabic, Persian and Turkish manuscripts in the library of Trinity College, Cambridge* (Cambridge, 1880). This may be supplemented by Edward G. Browne, *A supplementary handlist of the Muhammadan manuscripts ... preserved in the libraries of the University and colleges of Cambridge* (Cambridge, 1922). Only some of the volumes given by Gale at this time bear a bookplate commemorating the fact. For Ansloo, most of whose books were bought by the University of Utrecht after his death, see *Nieuw Nederlandisch biographisch woordenboek* 9 (1933), pp. 26–7, and D. Grosheide *et al., Vier eeuwen Universiteits-bibliotheek Utrecht* 1 (Utrecht, 1986), especially pp. 71 and 74.

47 Publications of these years included Hickes's *Linguarum veterum septentrionalium thesaurus* (1703–5, including Wanley's catalogue of Anglo-Saxon manuscripts), Leland's *Itinerary*, ed. Thomas Hearne (1710–12), the first volumes of Rymer's *Foedera* (1704 etc.) and John Smith's edition of Bede (Cambridge, 1722).

48 Joan Evans, *A history of the Society of Antiquaries* (Oxford, 1956), p. 54. Some of his work on manuscripts in the Harleian Library may be followed in Humfrey Wanley, *Diary, 1715–1726*, ed. C. E. Wright and Ruth C. Wright, 2 vols. (Bibliographical Society, 1966).

49 A catalogue of part of his collection was transcribed by Thomas Hearne in 1716: Hearne, *Remarks and collections*, 5, pp. 250–4.

his first loyalties, and he had marked his election as a Fellow with the gift of a fine fifteenth-century manuscript Psalter from York (rather than the usual printed book) to the College library.44 In 1664 he had presented a copy of Robert Hooke's *Microcosmographia*, and as the Royal Society's order to print was only dated November that year, it may be that this was one of the first copies to reach Cambridge. In London he found himself further involved in the early activities of the Royal Society (he took his turn as Secretary in 1679–81, alongside Hooke, and again in 1685–93), as well as exceptionally well placed to develop his collection of manuscripts in particular. He was an ardent antiquary as well as a skilled Greek scholar, and his correspondence ranged across Europe. His interests in Greek, in Roman antiquities and in the early history of Britain are to be seen in a long series of publications, some (and most notably the great series of historians gathered in the two volumes of *Historiae Britannicae, Saxonicae, Anglo-Danicae, scriptores xv* (Oxford, 1687–91)) based partly on his own collections.45 On his departure to York, he presented his substantial accumulation of oriental manuscripts, some of it deriving from the library of the Dutch Hebraist and Arabist Gerbrandt Ansloo (d. 1643), to Trinity.46 At the same time he seems also to have presented his Greek *Heirmologion* (MS O.2.61), only to borrow it again soon afterwards. But the rest of his collection passed to his eldest son Roger (fig. 12). Like his father, he too was a member of the College, entering Trinity in 1691, in the last years of the construction of the Wren, and becoming a Fellow in 1697, the year his father gave his oriental manuscripts to the College Library.

Roger Gale's interests, more disparate than those of his father, were early reflected in the edition, prepared with the aid of his father's notes, of Antoninus' *Iter Britannicarum* (1709), thus contributing to a remarkable few years in which were laid the foundations of much English historical scholarship.47 As an antiquary, he has in this century been judged with some asperity: 'more pompous than his scholarship justified'.48 But in many respects he followed his father's reputation and footsteps fruitfully, adding to the collection of medieval manuscripts and taking an especial interest in numismatics.49 From 1728 to 1736 he served as Treasurer of the Royal Society. It was, however, the infant Society of Antiquaries that engaged most of his attention, from its first meeting in 1717 (when his brother Samuel was elected Treasurer), and which he served as its first Vice-President. He died in 1744; but by then he had already given to Trinity virtually the whole of the collection

50 Stukeley, *Family memoirs*, 2, p.36.

51 Roger Gale to Samuel Gale, 13 August 1738, Stukeley, *Family memoirs*, 1, p.305.

52 Gale's letter to the College, written on 21 July 1738 and now MS 0.11.29, f. 1r, is printed in James, *Western manuscripts*, 3, p. vi. The descriptions of Gale's manuscripts take up most of this volume of James's catalogue; for more recent work on some of them see also S.D. Keynes, *Anglo-Saxon manuscripts ... An exhibition organised in connection with the conference of the International Society of Anglo-Saxonists* (Cambridge, 1985). Three principal early lists survive of the Gale manuscripts other than that printed by Bernard: MSS Add.a.146, 147, 148.

53 Many of Young's manuscripts are now in Leiden University Library; see also the auction catalogue of the books of John Owen, of Christ Church, Oxford (1684).

54 MS 0.3.9; K. Tsantsanoglou, Το λεξικο του Φωτιου (Thessalonika, 1967), pp. 40–5: I am grateful to Colin Tite for drawing this to my attention. Porson's edition appeared in 1822.

55 MS 0.4.24, flyleaf.

56 MS 0.4.38. Sears Jayne and Francis R. Johnson (ed.), *The Lumley library: the catalogue of 1609* (1956). This was a class catalogue of the collection. Trinity had already acquired an alphabetical catalogue of it with the Puckering books (MS R.14.24).

57 MS 0.4.20. Edited in facsimile by Julian Roberts and Andrew G. Watson, *John Dee's library catalogue* (Bibliographical Society, 1990); Gale's manuscripts are listed on pp. 244–5.

58 MS 0.4.19. Though the volume was clearly described by M.R. James, the maps were none the less claimed as 'rediscovered' in William Ravenhill, *John Norden's manuscript maps of Cornwall and its nine hundreds* (Exeter, 1972). As Ravenhill explains, Thomas Gale originally possessed only the text, the maps of Cornwall migrating from the other copy of the text (formerly in the possession of James I and of the Cecil family) only after they had been engraved for the printed edition of 1728. See Thomas Hearne, *Remarks and collections*, 9, p.189 (8 September 1726).

of manuscripts gathered over a space of almost eighty years. It was the last of the great collections founded in the seventeenth century to come to Cambridge, following Samuel Pepys's bequest to Magdalene in 1703, and the purchase for the University by King George I of the entire library of John Moore, Bishop of Ely, in 1715. No collection of comparable size, quality and range has arrived since.

Gale announced to Bentley his intention of presenting the collection in 1735;[50] but it was a further three years before it was organised and dispatched to Cambridge. So, in 1738, and to supplement the Arabic and Persian manuscripts, received in 1697, the College now received well over twice the number that had been recorded in Bernard's *Catalogi* as being in Thomas Gale's possession in that year. 'I have made a present to Trin. Coll. Cant. of my manuscripts, which I thought was as good a way as any to preserve them from dispersion or the oven', he explained to his brother.[51] In presenting them, Roger Gale recognised that 'there must be some that may be lookt upon as trifles', while others were of more obvious importance, and some might be valued simply for the sake of their curiosity or rarity.[52] Perhaps most importantly, Gale also expressed his 'hope that they will not onely be more secure, but of greater service to the Public than in any private hand'.

It has proved to be a collection of diverse and formidable riches. Relatively little can be ascertained of the means whereby Thomas and his son Roger had gathered in their collection; but the group of notes, transcripts and other manuscripts either by or once in the possession of Patrick Young, Royal Librarian until 1649, may account for the presence in the collection of several others that have not since been associated with his name.[53] Of the Greek manuscripts, the eleventh-century manuscript of Photius' *Lexicon*, to be transcribed and edited by Porson many years later, attracted the especial attention of generations of classical scholars. It had been discovered in Florence in 1598, and by 1600 had passed to Sir Robert Cotton.[54] From Cotton it passed to Patrick Young, and Thomas Gale had possessed it since at least 1677, when Edward Bernard had borrowed it.[55] The manuscript catalogue of Lord Lumley's library may have come from the royal household – again, perhaps, through Young.[56] Among Gale's several manuscripts from the library of John Dee, mostly dispersed in the 1620s, was the catalogue of his library made in 1583.[57] John Norden's survey of Cornwall (fig. 45), Middlesex and Hertfordshire, dedicated to James I,[58] came, like a fifteenth-century manuscript of Eutropius,[59] from the library of the Earl of Ailesbury. The earlier manuscripts included two tenth-century copies of Juvenal (O.4.10, 11: the second from northern France) and a notably illustrated Boethius (O.3.7) – all three among an important group from Canterbury. A twelfth-century manuscript of Claudian, from Durham, and still in its early binding (MS O.3.22), had been acquired by Thomas Gale in 1697; and he had used his fifteenth-century copy of John Fordun and Walter Bower's *Scotichronicon* (O.9.9) for his edition of the text published in 1691. In two crucial twelfth-century manuscripts (O.2.1, O.2.41) were recorded the history and properties of Ely Abbey. His interest in the Northumbrian church is to be seen in a copy of Bede's life of St Cuthbert, *c.* 1200, written at Durham but later at Coventry, not least of interest today for the sake of its unfinished drawings (O.1.64), and in a copy of the *Historia ecclesiastica gentis Anglicarum* (1601), interleaved with his notes. Another Durham manuscript, containing the lives of Cuthbert, Oswald and Aidan, included music dating from the tenth century (O.3.55).[60] Among the thirteenth-century Anglo-French manuscripts were a copy of Roger of Salerno, with a series of uniquely detailed illustrations of medical and surgical subjects (O.1.20: fig. 46),[61] and a copy of Roger of Kent, *Roman de toute chevalerie*, a text much concerned with the legends of Alexander and accompanied by a prolific series of pictures of battles, sieges, and men in armour (O.9.34: fig. 47). Among the seventeenth-century books, one of several surviving manuscripts of Middleton's *Game at chess* (O.2.66) has provoked especial attention in the present century.[62] Of other books from overseas, and apart from the Greek collection, his copy of Hesiod (O.9.27) had belonged to Cardinal Grimani of Venice; a collection on geomancy by Guillaume de Meerbecke (O.9.35) to Charles V of France; and a volume of Livy (O.4.4) to King Matthias Corvinus of Hungary.[63] It is not necessary to speculate which parts Roger Gale had in mind when he spoke of 'trifles'; but by no means the least suggestive and evidential part is the mass of transcripts and notes accumulated by his father, in particular as he ranged across the libraries of England and of France. Amongst so much, it is only to be regretted that so little has survived of the Gales' incoming correspondence.[64]

As a class, readers in the Library tended to leave little obvious trace, save in their subsequent writings and in records of the books they borrowed. Many more read in the Library than borrowed from it; and, as always, members of the fellowship also possessed their own books – albeit in very varying quantities,

59 MS O.2.42, formerly the property of Petrus Aegidius and of Abraham Ortelius. It also bears the signatures of both Thomas and Roger Gale. James, *Western manuscripts*, mistranscribes the note about the Earl of Ailesbury, printing 1614 instead of 1684.

60 Iain Fenlon (ed.), *Cambridge music manuscripts, 900–1700* (Cambridge, 1982), no. 9 (notes by Susan Rankin).

61 The illustrations are all reproduced in A.B. Hunt, *The medieval surgery* (Woodbridge, 1992).

62 Edited by R.C. Bald (1929) and by Trevor Howard-Hill (Malone Society, 1990).

63 Casba Csapodi and Klára Csapodi-Gárdonyi, *Bibliotheca Corviniana: the library of King Matthias Corvinus of Hungary* (Shannon, 1969), p. 50 and pl. IX.

64 On 22 May 1722, Roger Gale presented to Lord Harley a few letters written to his father, now British Library MS Harley 7011, ff. 144–66. See Wanley, *Diary*, ed. Wright and Wright, pp. 84, 147. Further letters addressed to Thomas Gale survive, either in the original or in transcripts, among the Birch papers at the British Library: MSS Add. 4277, 4292, etc. Gale's printed books were auctioned by Thomas Osborne in 1757 and 1758. See also the notes by Edouard Jeauneau (n. 42 above).

just as they took similarly varying degrees of interest in the everyday affairs of the Library. In other words, by itself the known and recorded use of the Library is poor evidence for the interests and activities of members of the College. But among the authors who were borrowed, the name of Newton dominated, his works represented in the Library by multiple copies. Of the borrowers, Richard Bentley was distinctive. Others borrowed more books; but none kept them consistently for such long periods, while he also took full advantage of his position also to borrow manuscripts – usually for himself but on occasion for others. In 1716, for example, his work on the text of the Bible led him to borrow two of the College's most valued manuscripts, the eighth-century copy of the Epistles written in northern England, and the early eleventh-century Winchester Gospels.[65] Among the books he borrowed on behalf of others was a twelfth-century copy of Livy, from Canterbury, for the use of his friend John Brookbank of Trinity Hall in 1714.[66] It was to be many years before the manuscripts were returned, like many of the other books borrowed not only by Bentley but also by many in the fellowship at large.

For several years in the first quarter of the century, the otherwise unused space in the Wren offered special provision for undergraduate reading. The origin and proposed management of this imaginative arrangement is most concisely summed up in the College's Conclusion Book, a few months after Bentley had taken office as Master:

> Agreed & orderd by the Master & Seniors that Two Classes in ye College Library (or more as hereafter may be thought convenient) be appropriated for such Books as shall be purchas'd or given to the Use of the Scholars of this College, viz, of all under ye Degree of Masters of Arts.
>
> That henceforth at the time of every one's admission there shall be paid by their respective Tutors into the hands of the Senior Bursar for a Nobleman or Fellow Commoner one pound sterling, for a pensionar Ten Shillings, for a Sizer five shillings; wch money is to be laid out from time to time in proper Books for the said Scholar's Library by order of the Master or in his absence of the Vicemaster: and an account is to be taken of the said payments & disbursments at every Audit.
>
> That all the present scolars of this College under the degree of Batchelors of Arts shall pay as above; in consideration of the Years wherein they will have the use of the said Books.

65 MSS B.10.5. (olim C.3.5), B.10.4 (olim R.15.26). See MS Add.a.117, p. 2.
66 MS R.4.4. (olim B.10.36). See MS Add.a.117, p. 2.

That the Master, or such as he shall appoint, are hereby impowerd to select such Books out of the Fellow's Library, as in their judgment they shall think may be spared from thence & are proper for the Scholars: wch Books are to be prised & purchasd for the Scholars Library; and the money acccruing from thence to be laid out in other Books that are wanting to the Fellows Library.

That the said Scholar's Library be under all the statutes & regulations that the Fellow's Library is under, & the Library keeper to be chargeable with the custody of the said Books. Provided, that the scholars are to make use of these Books, not in the Library, but in their chambers: and the Library-keeper is hereby impowerd to deliver any of the said Books to any of the Scholars of this College, entering the name of every Book, and of the person borrowing it, & the Year, month & day of Delivery in a Book appointed for that Purpose.[67]

Between then and at least 1726, there existed alongside the ordinary collections a further collection of books intended for undergraduates – of literature, some of the common reading for the undergraduate syllabus, and of what may be broadly termed works of reference.[68] There was less sign of the sciences or mathematics; and among the last books to be added were copies of *Don Quixote* (1725) and *Gulliver's travels* (1726). Despite the presence of these and a few other modern books, including Pope's *Iliad* (1720) and the first volume of Burnet's *History of his own time* (1724), the collection was composed overwhelmingly of seventeenth-century books.[69] If there were ever any hopes of modern books, rather than simply of unwanted books from the Fellows, they must quickly have been disappointed. The collection is as a consequence poor evidence of the details of the early eighteenth-century Cambridge curriculum. It was dispersed, and partly amalgamated with the rest of the Library, in the mid eighteenth century, but a few books, bearing the inscription *Liber publicus*, may be relics of this enlightened acknowledgement that undergraduates might benefit from freer access to books than was customary in the University: these *libri publici* include Ray's *Historia plantarum*, Estienne's Latin dictionary and, magnificently, Cowper on human muscles, *Myotomia reformata* (1724), as well as some smaller volumes.

The idea of an undergraduate library seems to have been Bentley's; and it came to an end during the term of office of his nephew Thomas Bentley, Librarian from 1721 to 1729. In the latter year Thomas was obliged to resign

67 TC Mun., Conclusion Book B, p. 206, 19 August 1700.

68 Similar ideas in Oxford are described in I. G. Philip, 'Libraries and the University Press', in Sutherland and Mitchell, *Oxford*, pp. 725–55, at pp. 749–51. Balliol, Exeter, Magdalen, Merton, Queen's, Trinity, University and Wadham all had undergraduate libraries in some form for shorter or longer periods. See also Paul Morgan, *Oxford libraries outside the Bodleian*, 2nd edn (Oxford, 1980).

69 This is based on the books listed in the first part of MS Add.a.110, which is no more than an alphabetical catalogue, and does not appear to reflect the order in which they were shelved (cf. Gaskell and Robson, p. 25).

after his absences from Cambridge, pursuing research on behalf of his uncle, had become notorious: for once, Bentley's adversaries in the fellowship found an easy target.[70] After a brief interval, in which another Yorkshireman, William Gossip, found himself appointed to this singularly hapless position between College factions,[71] he was succeeded by Sandys Hutchinson, recently graduated and the nominee of the Archbishop of Canterbury. As a pawn in the contest between Master and Fellows, Hutchinson, like his predecessors, was not in a comfortable situation. But his first years were further marred by a series of thefts. Henry Justice, a member of the College, admitted in 1716, returned in 1733 as a Fellow-Commoner. With the privileges of that position, he was able to gain easy access to the Library and to steal books on a considerable scale. He took advantage of the disorganisation of the University Library to steal from there as well.[72] His eventual exposure was stimulus to further investigations of the organisation of the College Library. In 1738–9, a systematic check of books missing and on loan was carried out. Much of it was carried out by Charles Mason, a man who now enjoys a rather ambiguous reputation as the first Woodwardian Professor of Geology,[73] but also a keen antiquary and a man devoted to the College and its library. Mason's analysis unearthed a depressing list of books not simply long in the hands of Fellows, but also borrowed by those who were no longer Fellows, or who were even dead. Of several books returned in the course of the exercise, no record of borrowing could be found. New regulations were drawn up, and agreed; and a fresh series of borrowers' registers was begun, though no provision was made for regular checks to be made. But the seriousness with which the matter was viewed may be seen more clearly in a rule that henceforth books lost or damaged were to be replaced by copies of the same edition, or their value paid for.[74]

Events and necessities such as these do not suggest great care – by either the fellowship or the Librarians. The long-running battle between Master and Fellows was undoubtedly a drain on energies and thought that might have been applied to better effect. Much of the stimulus for the well-being of the Library in the first part of the century had been Bentley's, whether in finances, provision for undergraduates, or even day-to-day supervision. As he withdrew from everyday contact with the fellowship, so too his influence on the College Library waned. Mason, who led the attempt to regulate borrowing, and avoid losses, was no friend of Bentley. In 1740, Hutchinson was succeeded by Timothy Lee, who had graduated but three years previously.

70 Monk, *Life of Bentley*, 2, pp. 275–9; H. R. Luard, *Biographical notes on the Librarians of Trinity College* (Cambridge Antiquarian Society, 1897), pp. 43–52; John Byrom, *Private journal and literary remains*, ed. R. Parkinson, 2 vols. in 4 (Chetham Society, 1854–7), 1.1, pp. 317–18.

71 A copy of a letter in Gossip's letter-book, addressed to an unnamed correspondent, summarises the situation from his point of view: Leeds District Archives, Thorp Arch papers, T. A. 3/2.

72 Philip Gaskell, 'Henry Justice, a Cambridge book thief' *TCBS* 1 (1952), pp. 348–57; McKitterick, *Cambridge University Library*, pp. 198–200.

73 See below, p. 99. An account of Mason's unprepossessing appearance, his work in the Library at Trinity, his unsuccessful love for Bentley's daughter, and his work on Cambridgeshire cartography is given in Willis and Clark, 2, pp. 674–7.

74 MSS Add.a.115 (list of books outstanding); Add.a.126 (new regulations, inside the front cover of the borrowing register).

For half a century after the first books were moved into the Wren, no consistent attempt was made to classify them by subject. Instead, as we have seen, they were shelved by donor. The same system was followed until after the death of Bentley in 1742. By that time, the printed books given or bequeathed by James Duport (1606–79), Sir Henry Puckering (d. 1701), William Corker (d. 1702), John Laughton (d. 1712), Thomas Smith (d. 1714), Edward Rudd (d. 1727) and Bentley himself were all shelved as discrete collections, sometimes coherent to the extent that groups of books in modern languages tended to be grouped together, but otherwise with little regard for subject matter.[75] The stock of books had grown from about seven thousand volumes at the beginning of the century to 16,355 by 1735–6, and it could not be said that the organisation of the Library had kept pace with its expansion. It is tempting to see in Bentley's passing the stimulus for changes that were by then long overdue, though the direct responsibility lay with yet another new Librarian, appointed in the year of Bentley's death.

2 From Robert Smith to William Whewell

For a century after his death, the memory of Bentley dominated the College. His struggles with the fellowship fed gossip and scandal; his scholarship and European fame lived on in his publications; his books and papers were, so far as possible, gathered into the Library; his letters were published in two editions, one by Charles Burney in 1807 and another, more fully, by Christopher and John Wordsworth in 1842. The College devoted considerable money to preserving his genius, for in some of this there was substantial expenditure. The slab in the floor of the Chapel recording his last resting place made no mention of his position as Master; but in the Library subsequent generations found it easier to reconcile his reputation with the records of his learning. His busts, the gift of his daughter, and that of Isaac Barrow, were both placed in the Library in 1756.[76] They were the first to be added after the initial four of Bacon, Newton, Ray and Willoughby had been set in place earlier in the 1750s.

Apart from the Gale collection, the largest group of manuscripts to enter the Library in the eighteenth century came from Bentley, by bequest.[77] In his lifetime, he had been an active, and generous, user of the Library, though he had been seriously mistaken in supposing that the fellowship would countenance

75 MS Add.a.150. On this evidence, it would appear that once the decision had been made to build a new library, it was not thought advisable to catalogue bequests such as that of Duport, which would have to be reorganised in the new building. Although this manuscript has considerable value as a donations register, in the absence of anything more organised, it does not list all donations received during the period it covers: the Beaupré Bell and Benjamin Bosanquet books are especially remarkable for their absence.

76 See below, p. 134.

77 An early list survives in MS Add.a.111. At first, Bentley's manuscripts were kept apart, as a special class.

his nephew Thomas as an absentee Librarian.[78] Among his gifts during his lifetime were not only copies of his own publications, but also, and rather unexpectedly, a group of medical books from the sixteenth and seventeenth centuries.[79] On his death, he divided his library. The College received a collection of Greek manuscripts almost all of which had come from Mount Athos, many of them bearing the notes of ownership of the monastery of Pantokrator. The rest of his library, including his printed books and adversaria, he left to his nephew Richard Bentley, who immediately sold off the less important parts of his portion.

With the Greek manuscripts thus acquired, to set beside the Gale and earlier collections, the College found itself in possession for the first time of a substantial group emanating not from the West, but from the East. On the whole, the collection was theological: several volumes of the works of John Chrysostom and of Gregory Nazianzenus, and lives of the saints. Most dated from the eleventh to the thirteenth centuries, though two volumes of Chrysostom (MSS B.7.1; B.8.8), one of them in an especially fine hand, dated from the tenth. A copy of the New Testament, written in 1316 (MS B.10.16), came originally from Mount Sinai and then passed to Pantokrator. In a fifteenth-century *Sticharion* (MS B.11.17), the Library had an example of Greek musical notation to set beside a fourteenth-century *Heirmologion* given by Thomas Gale in 1697 (MS O.2.61), of which Gale had been particularly proud.[80] The route by which Bentley had obtained his manuscripts from Mount Athos is no longer clear. In the 1720s and 1730s monks from Pantokrator and other monasteries on Mount Athos made several attempts to sell manuscripts in England.[81] But only in the nineteenth century was it discovered that the binding of one of Bentley's manuscripts from this source concealed fragments of a ninth-century uncial copy of St Mark's Gospel.[82]

The eventual disposition of the rest of Bentley's library, in the hands of his nephew, was complicated. His nephew Richard died in 1786, having given a small group of Greek manuscripts to the College in 1757. These had included a fourteenth-century copy of Tzetzes on Homer (MS R.16.33) and a late copy of the *Iliad* (MS R.16.35) that had at one time belonged to John Moore, Bishop of Ely, whose library had meanwhile passed to the University Library in 1715.[83] Other books, especially those containing adversaria, and quantities of notes, passed to Richard Cumberland, and so for the present remained in the family. But in 1786 the younger Bentley bequeathed an

78 See above, p. 67.

79 Listed in MS Add.a.150, pp. 470–5.

80 Humfrey Wanley, *Letters*, ed. P. L. Heyworth (Oxford, 1989), pp. 120–1.

81 W. D. Macray, *Annals of the Bodleian Library*, 2nd edn (Oxford, 1890), p. 205; F. H. Stubbings, 'Anthony Askew's *Liber amicorum*', *TCBS* 6 (1976), pp. 306–21, especially p. 316. For the cool reception accorded by Conyers Middleton, *Protobibliothecarius* at Cambridge, see McKitterick, *Cambridge University Library*, pp. 177–8.

82 Now kept in a special mount in class B. See James, *Western manuscripts* 1, p. 549.

83 For related manuscripts, see E. Gamillscheg *et al.*, *Repertorium der Griechischen Kopisten, 800–1600.* (Vienna, 1981), A, no. 14.

important group of books to Trinity. On his death there arrived a further two manuscripts, and fifteen volumes bearing Bentley's adversaria. Of all the elder Bentley's early Greek manuscripts there had been only one, and that from the West, of whose acqusition he had made a note: a tenth-century Greek and Latin parallel text of the Epistles (MS B.17.1: fig. 48), bought in 1718 and originating in Reichenau. This had formed no part of the Mount Athos bequest, but now came from his nephew. Among the printed books, many of them reminders of uncompleted projects for publication, were a series of heavily annotated copies of the Greek and Latin New Testament, and annotated copies of Homer, Hesychius' *Lexicon*, and Hephaestion.[84] Following this substantial group, it then remained for Cumberland (who did not die until 1811) to pass his portion of the papers to the College. Among these last was a family copy of his grandfather Richard Cumberland's *De legibus naturae* (Lübeck, 1694), partly in proof, and bearing corrections by Bentley against a second edition: the hope that, once this was at Trinity, it might be published by the University Press, came to nothing.[85] Cumberland allowed (so it was alleged) the rest of what was by 1811 perceived as a residue of unusual importance to pass into the hands of the London bookseller James Lackington. From this portion of the collection, the British Museum acquired a substantial holding in Bentley's work, to be supplemented with the library of the classical scholar and book collector Charles Burney bought as part of his entire library by the British Museum after his death in 1817.[86]

The effect of all this was to drive up the price of what had escaped. In a period that set exceptional store by Greek and Latin classics, in which collectors strove against each other and thus increased prices still further, the results might have been foreseen. On the one hand, and despite some grumbling, the country gained a bargain in the price it paid for Burney's library in 1818; but on the other, individual prices for some books could seem extraordinary. It was in these circumstances that the College was driven to pay Bentley Warren, of Uppingham, no less than fifty guineas for but three of Bentley's annotated books.[87] They included his copies of Collins's *Discourse of free-thinking* (1728), Boyle's *Dr Bentley's Dissertation on the Epistles of Phalaris examin'd* (1698), and Parker's *Double ephemeris*, Bentley's pocket diary for 1701.[88] The price was, no doubt, enhanced by the personal interest of each of these three volumes. The College's commitment to Bentley was to be further demonstrated in its purchase of a group of papers bought from

84 A list survives inside the front cover of Adv.bb.2.1 (Jerome, Paris, 1693). The Junior Bursar's accounts include a charge of sixpence for porterage.

85 Richard Cumberland, *Memoirs*, 2 vols. (1807), 1, p. 7.

86 *Museum Criticum* 1 (1814), p. 370; Edward Edwards, *Lives of the founders of the British Museum* (1870), pp. 435–42. Many of Bentley's books can be discovered through the index to Robin Alston, *Books with manuscript* (1994).

87 Junior Bursar's accounts, 1819–20.

88 Some of Bentley's adversaria are discussed in R.C. Jebb, *Bentley* (1882). In an act of co-operation that has since become celebrated in the annals of scholarship, the College lent his copy of Estienne's *Poetae graeci* to Heyne, in Göttingen.

Walker's descendants in 1829 – a year before J. H. Monk published his authoritative biography.[89] With so much thus in place, it could only be a matter of time before a full edition of Bentley's own correspondence was published; and in 1838 the College gave its blessing for a new edition.[90] It was published in 1842, the centenary of his death.

Later in the year that Bentley died, the Librarian Timothy Lee resigned, to return to his native Yorkshire and take the living of Pontefract. In Thomas White, who was elected Librarian in the same year that he graduated, the College found a man well suited to reordering what in the previous few years threatened to become an embarrassment.[91] He was to remain in office for twenty-one years, longer than any of his predecessors since the mid seventeenth century, and he died in office, still in middle age, in 1763. For the whole of his career, the Master of the College was Robert Smith (fig. 80), to whom the Library owes much of its modern appearance.

Under White's guidance, the Library was reorganised and recatalogued. One of his first acts was to arrange for a new bookplate to be engraved.[92] He acknowledged, and removed, an inconvenience that must long have been obvious, and one pointed out, with regard to the University Library, by Conyers Middleton, Fellow of the College, as long ago as 1723:[93] that the retention of the convention, dating from medieval times, of attaching letters to each stack, and seeking to accommodate Wren's wall-cases to this system, meant that the manuscript classes in particular (housed in their walled-off compartments) were poorly defined. Instead, when the Library was recatalogued in the 1740s, the projecting stacks no longer remained the defining elements, and the letters were now allocated to each bay, as they remain today.[94] But although the printed books were rearranged, the manuscripts, shelved in classes B, O and R, still reflected much of their origins. Those from Roger Gale, given in 1738, were placed in class O, save for his father's oriental manuscripts given in the 1690s, and placed in class R. Most of classes B and R were taken up with earlier acquisitions, not only the great collections of Whitgift and Nevile, but also the miscellaneous volumes received before and since: subsequent eighteenth- and nineteenth-century additions were also placed in these classes. These same classes also served to receive the printed books deemed to be the most valuable, including a group of Caxtons, a copy of Galen, *De affectorum locorum notitia* on vellum (Paris, 1513, the gift

89 Senior Bursar's accounts, 1828–9.

90 Conclusion Book, 27 March 1838.

91 Sinker, *Biographical notes*, p. 63, does little justice to White's achievements.

92 By Stevens (Junior Bursar's accounts, 1742–3). Further impressions taken off in 1752 and 1756 attest to the increases in the Library during these years (Junior Bursar's accounts, 1751–2, 1755–6).

93 Conyers Middleton, *Bibliothecae Cantabrigiensis ordinandae methodus* (Cambridge, 1723).

94 MS Add.a.111, f. 143.

of Sir Edward Stanhope (d. 1608)), a particularly splendid illuminated copy, again on vellum, of Seneca in French (Paris: Vérard, not before 1500), Henri Estienne's copiously annotated copy of Xenophon ([Geneva] 1561) and a small group of Chinese printed books.

The first collections of printed books to be shelved not as entities, but by subject, were the bequests of Beaupré Bell, numismatist and antiquarian, who died in 1745, and of John Colbatch, Knightbridge Professor of Moral Philosophy until 1744, and Rector of the College living of Orwell, who died in 1748. Some of Colbatch's books went to the University Library.[95] But more came to Trinity, including many of those he had acquired when chaplain to the English community in Lisbon in the seventeenth century.[96]

In Beaupré Bell, who lived close enough to the western boundary of Norfolk to take an interest both in his own county and in the fens more generally, the College had a benefactor with sympathetic interests. He was a close friend of the Vice-Master, Richard Walker, but Bell's principal acquaintance was with his antiquarian contemporaries, both in London and in fenland circles in Spalding and Wisbech. He had graduated from Trinity in 1725, and led a life very different from that of his dissolute father, who was principally remembered by some for the remarkable numbers of unbroken horses that he owned. Instead, Bell devoted his energies to the study of antiquities, helping Francis Blomefield on the history of Norfolk and Cambridgeshire;[97] to the study of Chaucer (whom he had thought to edit);[98] and in particular to numismatics. Although he issued proposals for a work on Roman coinage, *Tabulae Augustae*, and gathered in subscribers, the book was never published. It was to have been drawn very largely from his own collection, which he bequeathed to the College[99] with many of his books and papers. Among the 450 or so volumes that came with his coins were not only a good working collection on numismatics, but also papers on the history of the fens, and books on building, fishing, spas and the pictorial arts.[100] His own annotated copy of Dugdale's *History of imbanking and drayning* (1662) caused immediate interest in colleges quite apart from Trinity. With his further bequest of money, the College seized the opportunity to spend £100 in London on further standard works on numismatics of all periods, at an average price of a little over £1 each: in view of the fact that this included many usually expensive illustrated works, it was money acutely as well as knowledgeably spent.[101]

95 McKitterick, *Cambridge University Library*, pp. 244–5.
96 Listed, sometimes rather inaccurately, in MS Add.a.150.
97 David A. Stoker (ed.), *The correspondence of the Reverend Francis Blomefield (1705–52)* (Norfolk Record Society and Bibliographical Society, 1992).
98 Bell to Roger Gale, 14 January 1733/4, in *Bibliotheca topographica Britannica* 2 (1781), p. 169. See also below, p. 78.
99 See below, p. 100.
100 Bell's books are listed in MS Add.a.110, pp. 145–59. Some of his papers have since disappeared.
101 The purchases are listed in MS Add.a.108.

The Bell and Colbatch bequests, received in quick succession, made urgent the beginning of a new and wholesale reclassification and recataloguing of the Library. In this, Trinity was not alone. In the previous decade, the University Library had also undergone recataloguing, as the *Protobibliothecarius* John Taylor faced the organisation of the library of John Moore, received as long ago as 1715 but still lying in disorder a generation later. By his own account, Taylor's method of classifying books was haphazard.[102] At Trinity, there is evidence of some anxiety lest books and subjects should be wrongly placed. In one of the catalogues written at the time, various questions and notes covered most of a page:

> Qu: Where the Mytholog: Writers are to be placed.
> NB: I have put Romances under Consulendi and such as Barclays Argenis under Modern History because they are pretended to be Secret History ...
> Heraldry I have enter'd under Modern History, but shall separate them.
> Fortification under Mathem; de re Militari under Politicks ...
> Rei Musicae Authors under Math:
> Botany is under Physick & the history of Animals. Quaere whether these two wd not make one head.

Other questions related to individuals. Was Sir Walter Raleigh's *History of the world* to be treated as ancient or modern history? Were Dionysius Cassius and Herodian to be accounted Latin or Greek historians? Should criticism of authors be placed in a general heading *Critici*, or should they be shelved next to their subjects?[103] That this was a part of a debate on how the Library was to be classified is borne out in a series of notes written inside the front board of the same manuscript. Here, beginning with liturgies and Bibles, distinctions were made that introduced various innovations for the organisation of knowledge as it had been developed over the previous eighty or so years.[104] Medicine, philosophy, mathematics (treated as a subdivision of philosophy) were each divided, like history, orators and poets, between ancient and modern. Numismatics was divided from architecture, sculpture and painting. A special heading was invented for the literature of travel; and another distinguished English writings dating between 1640 and 1700 – a separation that has been widely preserved in bibliographical circles to this day.

By the mid eighteenth century, the Library required more than classification according to modern standards. No less seriously, thanks to

102 McKitterick, *Cambridge University Library*, p. 191.
103 MS Add.a.114.
104 Some of the principal library classifications in France, from Naudé (1627) and Clément (1635) to Gabriel Martin (1705) and G.-F. de Bure (1763), are conveniently summarised in Claude Jolly, 'Naissance de la "science" des bibliothèques', in Jolly, *Histoire*, pp. 380–5.

73

the succession of major collections that had been received over the past half-century, there were quantities of duplicates of which the College had no need. On the death in 1755 of Benjamin Bosanquet, who had been elected a Fellow in 1733, there arrived about two hundred medical books that were all the more valuable in that recent books on the subject were not well represented in the Library.[105] As for more general collections, by the time of the bequest of Richard Walker (Vice-Master; d. 1764) there is evidence that some selection was taking place. From this occasion since, few personal libraries have been accepted in their entirety.[106] Thus of Walker's books a few, such as Bentley's Horace, works by Newton, and Conyers Middleton's Cicero, were clearly retained as extra copies. But here also were Corelli, a copy of the Baskerville Virgil of 1757 to set beside the College's subscription copy, and a copy of the last four books of *Paradise lost* interleaved with a manuscript translation into Latin verse.[107] Walker had succeeded Colbatch as Knightbridge Professor in 1744; and in 1762 had shown himself to be imaginatively generous in making over to the University a plot of land for a new botanic garden, to the south of the old house of the Augustinian canons and on what is now the new museums site.[108] His botanical, and specifically horticultural, interests were well represented in his books, which included copies not only of Miller's *Gardeners dictionary*, but also of Evelyn, of London and Wise (1701), Richard Bradley (1718), *The vineyard* (anonymous, 1727), and Nicholas Gauger on building chimneys (1715). Although there is no direct evidence for it, Walker's interest in promoting botany may perhaps have influenced the choice of John Ray and his friend Francis Willoughby for two of the original four busts by Roubiliac in the Wren Library (figs. 69, 70).

Walker's copy of Corelli, indicative as it was of mid-eighteenth-century musical taste in the College, was one of the few books of music to enter the Library.[109] Amateur music-making was popular in the College, as in the University. In 1768 the Vice-Chancellor of the day, Sir James Marriott of Trinity Hall, sought to apply a bequest of £500 from Walter Titley (a member of Trinity, and for many years envoy extraordinary to the court of Denmark) to a University building suitable for concerts and lectures. Some thought the money would be better applied to the Botanic Garden, which Walker had so actively promoted.[110] But the performance of music was not much reflected in the books in the Wren Library. At the beginning of the century, the bequest of Thomas Smith, Vice-Master (d. 1714), had provided an encouraging beginning.

105 Listed in MS R.20.8, ff. 140r–143v.
106 In the nineteenth century, even the large bequests of Julius Charles Hare (d. 1855), William Grylls (d. 1863) and William Whewell (d. 1866) were in practice selections.
107 MS Add.a.150, pp. 529–32.
108 [Richard Walker] *A short account of the late donation of a botanic garden to the University of Cambridge* (Cambridge, 1763); Willis and Clark, 3, pp. 145–7; Clark, *Endowments*, pp. 468–74. Walker's will is printed in *Trusts, statutes and directions affecting (1) the professorships of the University, (2) the scholarships and prizes, (3) other gifts and endowments* (Cambridge, 1876), pp. 251–4.
109 Sir John Hawkins (*General history of the science and practice of music* (1776)) attests to the especial popularity of Corelli in England. The College had bought his forty-eight sonatas in 1744 (now L.6.14–15), and his organ works in 1747–8 (Junior Bursar's accounts 1747–8: £2.7s.). See also William Weber, *The rise of musical classics in eighteenth-century England* (Oxford, 1991), especially pp. 75–89.
110 *Cambridge Chronicle*, 5 November 1768. Titley also left £100 to Trinity. He was, presumably, instrumental in arranging the visit of the King of Denmark to Cambridge in August 1768.

Smith had first entered the College as a chorister, in 1672, and he had retained his interests. His estate included copies of Henry Lawes's *Treasury of musick* (1669), Purcell's *Orpheus Britannicus* (1698–1702) and Thomas Mace's *Musick's monument* (1676), the last almost *de rigueur* as the work of a member of the College community. John Paris bequeathed a volume of songs from Francesco Mancini's opera *Hydaspes*. But otherwise the principal music to enter the College's possession was evidently (to judge by the multiple copies) for the Chapel: not only Corelli in 1744, but also five sets each of John Garth's adaptation of Marcello's *First fifty psalms*, in eight volumes (1757); of Nares; of Boyce's collections in 1778–9 and for years afterwards; of William Hayes's *Cathedral music* (1795); and of James Kent's anthems in 1796–7 – the last the work of one who had been College organist in the 1720s.[111] The first music by Handel to enter the Library seems to have been the arrangement of some of his vocal works for organ or pianoforte by John Clarke, organist at the College in 1799–1820, and acquired in 1810.[112] Of the personal enthusiasms for amateur music-making by members of the College there was little sign.[113]

Robert Smith died in 1768. His reserved manner does not seem to have endeared him to the fellowship, but by his death he had a reputation for having greatly improved the finances of the College since the days of his predecessor.[114] His influence alike on the appearance of the College, and on teaching in the University, had been profound. Under him, the College had seen Great Court repaired and refaced with stucco, Nevile's Court restored, and a new bridge built over the river. He died unmarried, and was generous in his bequests to the College. With a part of his considerable estate, the new stained glass was inserted in the south window of the Library. To his term of office, and probably to his personal inspiration, the Library also owes the beginning of the series of busts by Roubiliac and others that now grace the interior: they were but one aspect of an iconographic programme devised to make plain the College's historic claims to pre-eminence. For Smith, these claims lay mainly in the sciences, based principally on Bacon and, yet more importantly, on Newton, their two busts by Roubiliac flanking the window created to commemorate them after his death. As Plumian Professor of Astronomy in succession to his cousin Roger Cotes, as supervisor of the completion of the observatory over the Great Gate, as founder of the University

111 Details of these purchases are from the Senior and Junior Bursars' accounts. But William Glover, a member of the College choir in the 1830s, recalled that since engraved music was very costly, 'even at Trinity Chapel nearly all Handel's and Haydn's compositions were played and sung from manuscript copies' (William Glover, *Memoirs of a Cambridge chorister*, 2 vols. (1885), 2, p. 30).

112 Now L.0.18–; see MS 0.4.49, under 1810.

113 Frida Knight, *Cambridge music from the Middle Ages to modern times* (Cambridge, 1980), ch. 4, gives some details of musical life in eighteenth-century Trinity. Although Robert Smith was an accomplished cellist, no scores were retained by the Library among his books in 1768.

114 *Cambridge Chronicle*, 6 February 1768. See also British Library MS Add. 5811, f.54v.

prizes for mathematics that bear his name, and as author of two major influential treatises, on optics (1738) and harmonics (1749), Smith strove to ensure that Newton's mathematical legacy was not lost to Cambridge.[115] Not surprisingly, the books from his private collection that were retained for the Library bear witness to these preoccupations. Besides Galileo, Tycho Brahe, Bernouilh, Copernicus, Kepler and Descartes, there was a useful selection of recent work in English mathematics. Literature was less well represented, though the presence of Boccaccio, *Gulliver's travels* and other works by Swift, *Le Diable boîteux,* Molière and *La Princesse de Clèves* attested to more leisurely interests.[116] Other parts of Smith's estate came to the College on the death of his relative Edward Howkins in 1780, including papers relating to Newton and Cotes, and the original copper plates for the illustrations to Smith's own books.[117]

His successor, John Hinchliffe, had little of Smith's strong sense of place, or of his innate sympathy with the College's past members. Whereas both Bentley and Smith died in office, leaving the most important parts of their libraries to the College, Hinchliffe had by the time of his death left Cambridge. At first, however, prospects were encouraging. In his gift of much of the work of Piranesi, he not only marked the beginning of his term but also acknowledged, magnificently, one aspect of the College's interest in illustrations of classical antiquity.[118] It was to prove a poor guide; for although his connections with the circle of the Duke of Grafton, to whom he owed much of his success in his career, may (as will be seen) have encouraged one of the most remarkable gifts ever received by the College, events were to show him in many respects out of sympathy with both the Library and the fellowship.

Meanwhile, Thomas White, the Librarian, turned the College's attention to the duplicates, although it was still to be many years before agreement was reached on what might be discarded. Thanks to a longstanding policy of accepting duplicates or even triplicates, the Library had become crowded with multiple copies of both older standard works and more modern ones. Thus, to set beside its own subscription copy of the Baskerville Virgil of 1757, there were by 1768 also the copies of Richard Walker and of Robert Smith, both of whom had also subscribed to this most fashionable of books. Now, lists were drawn up as a preliminary to a prolonged debate. But only in 1784, the year in which it received the bequest of Richard Jackson, founder of the Jacksonian chair in Natural and Experimental Philosophy,[119] did the College at last agree to dispose of many of the extra copies of several hundred titles,

115 Clark, *Endowments,* pp. 93–5.

116 MS Add.a.150, pp. 533–54.

117 MS Add.a.150. Howkins, who had been elected a Fellow in 1752, spent his last years as Rector of North Runcton, in Norfolk.

118 MS Add.a.150, p. 555. *Le antichità romane* was presented in 1769; the rest of Hinchliffe's gift is not dated.

119 A list of Jackson's bequest is in MS Add.aa.3: not all the books were retained. For the Jacksonian chair, see Clark, *Endowments,* pp. 206–16.

and to sell them to Robert Faulder, bookseller in New Bond Street. The criteria applied in identifying duplicates did not include strict regard for dates, so the list of candidates included, for example, six copies of Herbert's *The temple* dated between 1633 and 1679. As a result, some books that would not now be accounted duplicates were no doubt lost to the College. But even so, the quantities were alarming. By 1784, the Library could offer three copies of Estienne's *Thesaurus* (1572), five of Castell's *Lexicon heptaglotton* (1669), five of Clarendon's *History of the rebellion*, six sets of the Walton polyglot Bible (1657), and five or six copies each of the quarto editions of the Latin poets printed by the Cambridge University Press for Tonson in the first few years of its new foundation in 1698.

All was not gain. The disposal of duplicates produced gaps on the shelves at irregular intervals, which it was proposed to fill by moving up books from the cupboards beneath, so that the shelves would still appear full. To the Librarian, Thomas Green, who was by now the Professor of Geology but who as a young graduate of three years' standing had inherited the reformation wrought by White twenty years previously, and added his own mark of organisation, this proposal was thoroughly irresponsible. It would have destroyed years of labour that had been devoted to bringing the Library into a reasonable subject order. It may be that Hinchliffe had by this stage seen enough of arguments over the duplicates; or perhaps he really did have no idea of why libraries tend to be organised so that books on the same subject are grouped together for the convenience of readers. But his opinion, and tone, were unambiguous:

> There is a General Catalogue, by consulting which, any Book may be found, and consequently the separate arrangement of every Science is of no importance.[120]

The opinion was as inescapable as the consequences were, for the present, inevitable. But fortunately, this arrogant and misguided assumption did not bind future generations. Green himself died only four years later.

Much of what had been done in the Library under Robert Smith had been motivated by *pietas*. By the end of the century, the College was investing heavily in the bibliographical evidence of its history, motivated by a mixture of interests in classical scholarship and in the human passions and complexities of Bentley's relations with his contemporaries within and outside Cambridge.

120 This and other details of duplicates are taken from MSS Add.a.143 and 144.

But the eighteenth century also witnessed a shift towards new attitudes to the literature of the English Renaissance, and with it a fresh bibliographical awareness of books that had hitherto been little regarded as possible rarities. On the one hand, William Ames and like-minded historians of printing investigated the course of printing in England in the fifteenth and sixteenth centuries (but less, so far, in the seventeenth); and on the other, collectors and editors such as Richard Farmer, Thomas Percy and George Stevens applied themselves to unearth and preserve a wide range of literary activity. For Trinity, the Milton manuscript attracted the attention of Thomas Newton, who incorporated his observations in his edition of 1749–53. In earlier literature, Beaupré Bell had quarried the manuscript of Chaucer, R.3.15, given by Thomas Nevile, and entered its readings in his copy of Urry's edition of 1721.[121] Neither, however, had so great and long-lasting effect as the Shakespearian library assembled by Edward Capell, one of the first substantial collections centred bibliographically and historically on a single writer ever to have been made in England.[122]

Indeed, of all the collections, small and great, that entered the Library in the eighteenth century, none has had a greater importance. From Capell's collection of Shakespeariana, presented in 1779, has flowed a tradition of scholarship and of editing Shakespeare that has expanded, generation by generation, across the world. Capell's own reputation among his contemporaries, both as a scholar and as a person, was a mixed one; but he provided amply and authoritatively for subsequent generations, both in his edition of Shakespeare and in his collection of books. In the work of W. G. Clark, John Glover and William Aldis Wright (all members of Trinity) on the nine-volume edition published in 1863–6 may be perceived the beginning of a clear line of influence on the text of Shakespeare; and for W. W. Greg (Librarian from 1907 to 1913), the collection was to prove a vital stimulus in developing modern bibliographical methods more generally.

Capell's edition of Shakespeare was derided by his contemporaries; indeed, it remains *sui generis* in its idiosyncratic typography, and irritating in its division of text and notes into separate volumes of greatly different size that were never designed to sit together comfortably on the shelf. That Capell was difficult in his personal relations, and eccentric in his private life, was indisputable. But his principles in editing Shakespeare, and especially his insistence on returning to a consideration of the early quartos as well as the

121 Now H.18.38.

122 The standard catalogue is W. W. Greg, *Catalogue of the books presented by Edward Capell to the Library of Trinity College, Cambridge* (Cambridge, 1903). Thirty copies of a catalogue of the gift were printed in 1779, apparently at the behest of George Stevens, who had been plagued with requests for information (note by Richard Farmer in a British Library copy, 82.e.21).

1623 folio, have proved to be more firmly based and convincing than the speculations of many eighteenth-century editors from Pope onwards. He set out his founding principles clearly:

> Let it then be granted that these quarto's are the Poet's own copies, however they were come by; hastily written at first, and issuing from presses most of them as corrupt and licentious as can any where be produc'd, and not overseen by himself nor by any of his friends. And there can be no stronger reason for subscribing to any opinion than may be drawn in favour of this from the condition of all the other plays that were first printed in the folio; for in method of publication they have the greatest likeness possible to those which preceeded them, and carry all the same marks of haste and negligence.[123]

His conclusions, the result of careful collation of quartos against each other and against the first folio of 1623, were drawn from his working library. The collector and the textual scholar were one.[124]

Capell had formed his collection at much the same time as his friend David Garrick had also been at work amassing his own much more general collection of early English drama, now in the British Library.[125] Garrick and Capell had met through the latter's employment as Deputy Inspector of Plays, and the two struck up a friendship that usually withstood Capell's somewhat varied reputation amongst contemporary Shakespearians – of whom he was quite willing to be openly critical. It seems even to have weathered Capell's difficult behaviour as he became increasingly reclusive. There is evidence to suggest that Capell not only helped Garrick in his collecting, but even stood aside in order to allow him to acquire some particularly choice items. Though in the end the two men came to regard each other with some reservations, Capell was in many ways responsible for the creation and organisation of Garrick's collection. His manuscript catalogue of Garrick's plays survives in the British Library. When, on his death in 1779, Garrick bequeathed his collection to the British Museum, Capell was quickly moved to give his own to Trinity (fig. 49). He had formed it with two views in mind: first, a new edition of Shakespeare based on the earliest printed texts; and second, an accompanying compilation of sources, drawing together extended quotations from the literature available to Shakespeare's contemporaries in order to illustrate the contexts of sixteenth- and early seventeenth-century

123 Edward Capell, introduction to Shakespeare, *Comedies, histories and tragedies*, pp. 10–11.

124 For Capell's life, see Samuel Pegge's account in Nichols, *Illustrations*, 1, pp. 465–76; for recent assessments, see especially Alice Walker, 'Edward Capell and his edition of Shakespeare', *Proc. British Academy* 46 (1960), pp. 131–45, and Brian Vickers (ed.), *Shakespeare: the critical heritage. 5. 1765–1774* (1979), pp. 32–7 etc.

125 George M. Kahrl and Dorothy Anderson, *The Garrick collection of old English plays: a catalogue with an historical introduction* (1982). The introduction to this catalogue provides an illuminating account of some of Capell's activities.

79

England. His edition of Shakespeare was published in ten volumes in 1767–8, with further volumes of notes and variant readings beginning in 1774 (the first volume met with such hostility that Capell began again). The long-planned volume of accompanying extracts, *The school of Shakespeare*, appeared only after Capell's death in 1781. With characteristic exactitude, Capell provided a summary description of the collection of early editions on which this work was based:

> All the several Editions of the Works of Shakespeare, old & new; divers rare old Editions of Writers, prose-men & verse-men; with a Variety of other Articles, chiefly such as tend to illustrate him.[126]

The collection ranged from Chaucer and Gower to Cervantes and Montaigne. Particular attention had been paid to Elizabethan and Jacobean poetry; among various books, Capell had lent his rare 1557 copy of Surrey's *Songs and sonnets* to Bishop Percy.[127] Capell's interests had not stopped with the death of Shakespeare, and thus there were also copies of Crashaw, of *Paradise lost* and of a late edition of *Scogin's jests*. Beaumont and Fletcher were the only major dramatists apart from Shakespeare of whom it could be said that Capell had paid serious attention to them as a collector. Shakespeare, and literature that might serve to support work on his plays, overshadowed everything, on a scale much more noticeable even than in Garrick's collection. Capell's efforts to be as comprehensive as possible in his assembling of early editions are all the more remarkable in that his collection was formed over quite a short space of time in the mid eighteenth century, and that in the end it had strengths that even Garrick could not match. Among the quartos, he possessed first editions of *Richard II* (acquired thanks to the help of Bishop Percy), *Romeo and Juliet, Love's labour's lost, Henry IV part 2, Henry V, King Lear, A midsummer night's dream* (previously in the possession of the Shakespeare editor Lewis Theobald[128]), *The merry wives of Windsor, Much ado about nothing, Pericles, Othello* and *The taming of the shrew*. His copy of the 1599 edition of *The passionate pilgrim* is one of only two complete copies now extant. There also arrived with this collection of printed books a copy of the Chandos portrait, and a cast from the face of the bust in Stratford-upon-Avon parish church, as well as a fair copy transcript of Shakespeare's works and Capell's accompanying commentaries, and his unpublished edition of *Paradise lost*.

By November 1779, Capell could write of 'my work's conclusion'. His edition of Shakespeare had appeared, and the volumes of commentary and

126 Manuscript catalogue of the collection (fig. 49): see Greg, *Catalogue*, p. 163.

127 *The correspondence of Thomas Percy and Richard Farmer*, ed. Cleanth Brooks (Baton Rouge, 1946), pp. 31, 64, 101.

128 Theobald's Shakespeare collection is discussed in Peter Seary, *Lewis Theobald and the editing of Shakespeare* (Oxford, 1990), pp. 231–6. A little of Capell's relations as a collector with another Shakespeare scholar, Edmund Malone, may be seen in W. W. Greg, 'Editors at work and play: a glimpse of the eighteenth century', *Review of English Studies* 2 (1926), pp. 173–6. In April 1779, having just had some success, Malone wrote, 'There is hardly an old play of any rarity now to be got under four or five shillings – and some they even ask half a guinea for. I paid, a few days ago, two guineas for the old "Taming of the Shrew", (not Shakespeare's) and Mr. Capel was so miserable about it, that he wrote three letters to the bookseller that sold it, requesting to let him have a sight of it, a circumstance which, you know, adds a great value to these sorts of things.'

accompaniment were all but complete. As if to draw a line under this work, he had a few months previously sent his library to his binder, to be dressed up in a style so that in the future the books should boast their common ancestry on the shelf:

> What leisure I had in the course of last spring, was employ'd in digesting a book-collection, and conveying it to my binder in parcels, which I *had* bequeath'd to the publick, but thought it right (upon further considering) to see lodg'd myself, and expect your Lordship's approof for it ... [I] could wish you had seen the Collection's self, its neatness & its entire uniformity would have pleas'd and surpriz'd you; especially the latter, when you had consider'd the difficulty of bringing that about in a business so miscellaneous: the deposit is large, has been many years in collecting, and at much expence, and (perhaps) the public owes me some thanks for it; but the pay I expect, is – abuse in great plenty, and the loss of some hundreds by what I am now publishing.[129]

He had rearranged his volumes of pamphlets and plays according to their size; and where necessary he had broken up existing volumes so as to avoid unnecessary bulk. For at least one group of plays, bibliophily overcame bibliography, in that his desire for neatness and convenience led to his separating into two a volume of Shakespeare's plays in quarto, evidence of an attempt by the stationer Thomas Pavier to publish a collection of Shakespeare's works in 1619 – four years before William Jaggard's first folio of 1623.[130] All the books now in Capell's collection in the College Library have been either rebound or rebacked, and decorated in gilt with his entwined initials, E.C. (fig. 50). So, with Garrick's death, the long process of exchange and sharing had come to an end, and the books were found a permanent home.

The choice of Trinity as a resting place at first sight seems odd. Capell himself had been at St Catharine's, and his father at Queens' and Corpus. His eye lit not on his own college, or on the University Library, but the college of his younger brother Robert, who had like him come up from school at Bury St Edmunds. While Edward had gone to London, Robert had been admitted as a Fellow in 1739. There were other ties to the College, and in a series of circumstantial details we may guess at the course taken by Capell's deliberations. As Deputy Inspector of Plays from 1737, he had made the friendship of Garrick. In the same post, he would have come across Richard Cumberland,

129 Capell to Lord Dacre, 26 November 1779, Osborn Files 6.347, Beinecke Library, Yale University. Part of the letter is printed in Kahrl and Anderson, *Garrick collection*, p. 29. (I am grateful to the Beinecke Library for permission to quote from this letter.)

130 Now Capell Q.11, Q.12. See A.W. Pollard, *Shakespeare folios and quartos: a study in the bibliography of Shakespeare's plays, 1594–1685* (1909), pp. 81–3.

grandson of Richard Bentley, educated like the Capell brothers at Bury St Edmunds, who was elected a Fellow of Trinity in 1752, and who in the 1760s embarked on a prolific career as a dramatist. A further link is to be found in Arthur Kynnesman, headmaster of the school at Bury for thirty years, and friend alike of Cumberland and of Capell, to whom he bequeathed his copy of the Oxford Shakespeare of 1743–4.[131] But perhaps the strongest personal link lay with John Hinchliffe, Master of Trinity from 1768 – the year in which Capell's edition of Shakespeare was published. Capell had owed his appointments both as Deputy Inspector of Plays and as Groom of the Privy Chamber to the Duke of Grafton, to whom he dedicated his Shakespeare, crown (and for him in many ways justification) of his life's work. Hinchliffe, too, was in the Grafton circle, having been presented by him to the living of Greenwich only two years previously and also owing to him his place as royal chaplain.[132] In addition to all this, Capell was well aware that in Trinity lay the manuscript of Milton's so-called minor poems, used extensively by Thomas Newton for his edition. Apart from Shakespeare, Capell had given much energy to editing *Paradise lost*, though his edition was never published. It cannot have been difficult to make an irresistible case. Thus time and connections conspired, and the decision to present this remarkable collection to Trinity became in effect inescapable. Perhaps, too, the hand of the Master is to be seen in the College's readiness to accede to Capell's unusual conditions: not only to keep the collection together, but also to treat it as it had no group of printed books hitherto, and to forbid its being borrowed from the Library.[133]

Despite all these riches, to some the College Library seemed less than it might be. William Cole, of King's, was not one to be shy of criticising his contemporaries, and he was most readily critical of those outside his own coterie. Quite justifiably, he considered Beaupré Bell's notes on local history inferior to his own; but he also found that they were not easily consulted. Instead, he explained, to his fellow antiquary Richard Gough, Trinity held them 'in Durance: as are many other curious Things that are inaccessible to'.[134] In itself, Cole's irritation signifies little. But when it is placed alongside the erratic and often small numbers of new books bought in the latter part of the eighteenth century, and beside a destructive and prolonged argument over the very arrangement of the Library, there seems room for doubt. In the context of what was happening to the book collection, the exhibits from Captain Cook's voyage[135] were glorious distractions.

131 Now Capell D.1–6. A note by Capell in the first volume records the circumstances of his acquiring them.

132 Hinchliffe's career is described in the *DNB*.

133 Seniority minutes, 26 June 1779; the decision is also recorded in the manuscript catalogue of the collection.

134 Cole to Richard Gough, St Thomas's Day 1780: British Library MS Add.5834, f. 236r.

135 See below, pp. 104–6.

For all of the eighteenth century, the College depended much more on donations than on buying books. There was nothing very unusual in this. But such a policy left the overall well-being of the Library as a comprehensive repository for the subjects of interest to the College too much at the mercy of those who bequeathed their books. It also tended to build in a sometimes considerable delay between the publication of a book and its reception. The long series of bequests through the century, especially but not exclusively by Masters and Fellows, left the College with a library in some parts stronger than the University Library itself. In the absence of a systematic policy in parallel for buying new books, it also encouraged conservatism.

But in the 1770s there was a notable change in the Library's fortunes, as for a few years accessions increased in number and more attention was paid to the most recent publications. The College was pursuing a deliberate policy of purchase in modern books over a chosen range of subjects, and especially in classical and later antiquities, in lexicography, in English local history, in foreign travel, and in law. These subjects had been established in the Library many years before, and curiosity in foreign countries had also been expressed in purchases of many of the standard works on natural history in parts of the world of especial colonial interest: Sloane and Patrick Browne on Jamaica, Catesby on Carolina, Adanson on Senegal, and Griffith Hughes on Barbados. In 1775–6, no doubt with an eye to current political events, the Library acquired Thomas Jefferys's *American atlas*, published that year, and William Douglass's older *Summary ... of the first planting, progressive improvements, and present state of the British settlements in North America* (1760). Priestley on air (1775) and Smith on the wealth of nations (1776) were bought promptly, as were Gibbon's *Decline and fall of the Roman Empire* (the first volume bought in 1776, the year of publication) and both Burney and Hawkins on the history of music. The Rowley poems (1782) were also bought in the year of publication: this last was one of the very few books of English poetry to enter the Library at this time, to join Mason's edition of Gray (York, 1775, bought in the same year) and Tyrwhitt's gift of his edition of Chaucer (1775–8). In 1772, the College received the first volume of the *Transactions* of the new American Philosophical Society: such series had, by virtue of their dates and method of publication, the advantage of insisting on their immediacy.

Acquisitions such as these were sure signs of change in the air, reflected to some extent in the records of books borrowed from the Library by Fellows either for their own reading or on behalf of undergraduates or others. In term-time there were occasionally as many as a dozen or more loans in a single day, many of them clearly for undergraduate use. Other than the predictable classical texts, the most persistent appearances among these records are Smith on optics, Simpson and Maclaurin on fluxions, and Cotes on hydrostatics; Burnet on the Thirty-nine Articles; and dictionaries not only of Greek and Latin (of which the Library possessed multiple copies) but also of Spanish and Italian. Occasionally books were borrowed to be lent out of the College: the Master of Christ's, for example, kept Dugdale on drainage from November 1770 until February 1772, and Edward Gregory, Fellow of Trinity Hall, kept Flamsteed's *Atlas coelestis* from January 1771 until March of the following year. Since books could be as well read in the Library as when they were borrowed, and were quite probably passed round amongst members of the College once out of the Library, these records are not an entirely satisfactory means of discovering how much particular books were read: Gibbon, for example, had been borrowed four times by the end of 1777, the year following publication, but it is reasonable to surmise that the copy had been seen by many more people. Even so, few readers were of so devotedly imaginative a frame of mind as T. J. Mathias (author of *The pursuits of literature* (1794 and many later editions)), whose reading after he became a Fellow in 1776 included Molière, Boileau d'Espréaux, Milton, La Fontaine, Chaucer, Cowley, Swift, Shakespeare, Cervantes and Ariosto.[136]

It is not clear to what extent this new sense of urgency in buying books was due to the Librarian appointed in 1763, Thomas Green, who became Professor of Geology in 1778. But it was in stark contrast to the inactivity distressingly obvious under his successors, John Clark and Charles Hoyle. Green died in 1788, the year in which Clark took his MA. In 1787–8, for the first time since 1714–15, the annual bill from a local bookseller exceeded £100. But this was not all expenditure on books. In 1789–90, for example, one of the few years for which detailed accounts survive, the Merrills, local booksellers, were supplying paper, quills and sand, as well as books. Most of all, expenditure was due to a programme of repair and rebinding, and to the great cost of the kind of expensive illustrated book that the fellowship found much to its taste: it certainly did not herald a change in buying policy with an eye to increasing the quantities of the more ordinary modern books. Out of a total of just under £40, only about a quarter was for new books. Most tellingly,

136 MS Add.a.132, pp. 209–12.

in that it represents the true state of the Library's health as measured by accessions of modern books, only five of these new books were not continuations of previous publications.[137]

In all this, opportunity for change was offered with a change of Master. In 1789, two years after the College had been shown to have failed to have followed its statutes in electing new Fellows, Hinchliffe resigned, to take up appointment as Dean of Durham.[138] The affair of the fellowship election was widely seen as a turning point in the fortunes of the College, in that it set a firm terminus to the sometimes scandalous ways of the *ancien régime*.[139] The Library eventually – but not for some years – reflected this change of mood. Hinchliffe was succeeded by a senior Fellow, Thomas Postlethwaite, a man who well knew, and clearly cherished, the need for a period of rest after the scandals and recriminations of recent memory.

By the 1790s, the energy that had characterised the 1770s had evaporated. In 1796, only six works published that year were bought, other than periodicals or continuations of existing sets: the year was more positively remarkable for the purchase of issues of the *Allgemeine Literatur-Zeitung*, and for two gifts of early printed books, one a 1594 Bible and the other a copy of Copernicus, *De revolutionibus orbium coelestium* (1543), heavy with contemporary annotations and formerly in the library of Trinity College, Oxford.[140] But the opening years of the nineteenth century found the Library employing booksellers even less. In 1803, the College bought a single book that was published that year, out of eight purchases in all: by comparison, it also received fifteen donations. In 1804, the only new publication to be bought was the *Philosophical Transactions* of the Royal Society: no books published that year were bought at all.[141] These two years coincide with the brief tenure of the librarianship by Charles Hoyle, a man whose slight acquirements as a poet exceeded his achievements as a librarian.[142] After just over a year in office, he was quickly replaced by Aldous Henshaw, who was to remain until his death in 1837.[143]

While it may be unfair to charge individual Librarians with the faults and negligences of the fellowship as a whole, it remains that the years of deepest inactivity in acquiring books coincide with those of Henshaw's two predecessors. The extent of the change in the mood of the College by the 1820s is to be seen in its regularly spending over £200 on new books, though even then the year 1822–3 found it in no mood for extravagance, as it faced the start

137 TC Mun., box 30, no. 10b.
138 D. A. Winstanley, *Unreformed Cambridge* (Cambridge, 1935), pp. 241–55. The fellowship election was of 1786, and the protest against its conduct, instigated by ten Fellows, was heard by Lord Thurlow in November 1787.
139 Henry Gunning, *Reminiscences of the University, town and county of Cambridge from the year 1780*, 2 vols. (Cambridge, 1854), 2, p. 109.
140 S.4.11. It had formed part of the library of Edward Hindmarsh (1545–1618), whose books passed to Trinity College, Oxford on his death; the volume was bought from the London booksellers R. and J. White in 1794, for 15s. Since it bears a bookplate clearly from Oxford, it seems improbable that it was presented to the Library under the misapprehension that it had been in Cambridge originally.
141 Details of acquisitions in these years are taken from the accessions register, 1770–1815, MS O.4.49.
142 Manuscripts of Hoyle's poems are gathered in R.17.14–32.
143 Sinker, *Biographical notes*, pp. 63–5.

of building in what became New Court – the first extension to the College since the building of the Wren Library.

Whatever the need, there is scant evidence to suppose that serious reform was in mind when in February 1790 the Master and Seniors agreed that suggestions for new books should be formally considered twice a year, and a quarto notebook was provided to receive such suggestions. That there were gaps in the Library was all too clear: one of the earliest suggestions was for a copy of Thomas Rutherforth's *System of natural philosophy*, published at Cambridge in 1748.[144] But over the first few years of the existence of this recommendations book (whose modest extent was not filled up until 1849), few Fellows chose to use it regularly. A subscription to Cowper's translation of Homer was suggested by Richard Ramsden, and the new edition of the works of Algernon Sidney by Thomas Cautley; suggestions for standard editions of classical texts came from William Lax, better known as a mathematician and astronomer. But many of the books suggested were expensive, such as Jean Houel's *Voyage pittoresque des Isles de Sicile* (Paris, 1782–7; £24, unbound), Linnaeus in the 'best edition', or John Latham's *General synopsis of birds*, illustrated with coloured plates (1781–5). A bequest from Mark Hildesley, Bishop of Sodor and Man (d. 1772), enabled the purchase of Linnaeus in 1793–4.[145] Latham's *Synopsis* was suggested by John Hailstone, Green's successor as Woodwardian Professor of Geology, who took a lively interest in keeping up the Library. It was on his recommendation that in 1796 the College bought the *Allgemeine Literatur-Zeitung* as (in his words) 'a periodical work of established reputation containing the best account of German Literature'. Unfortunately this progressive effort was nipped in the bud, as only the issues for that year were bought and the series was allowed to lapse.[146] The recommendation of the Vice-Master, Thomas Gilbank, for Young's *Annals of agriculture* found better favour. On the whole the list remained firmly committed to books of travel, to illustrated books, to mathematics, and to classical literature and antiquities.

A principal difficulty was that no clear idea was held as to the Library's purpose: whether it was to buy books unaffordable by most people, or whether the existence of a copy in the University Library made a purchase by the College unnecessary. In the first years of the nineteenth century, several suggestions were deferred on the latter grounds. When, therefore, the *Transactions* of the infant Geological Society were recommended, it was pointed out that this

144 MS Add.a.123. The new recommendations book cost 2s. 6d. (Merrill invoice, 1789–90, TC Mun., box 30, no. 10b).

145 Junior Bursar's accounts, 1793–4. For Hildesley, a former Fellow of the College, see *DNB*. In 1763–4 the College had subscribed twenty guineas towards his pioneering translation of the Bible into Manx (Senior Bursar's accounts, 1763–4).

146 Evidence of emergent interest in German in the 1790s is inconsistent. W. Render, translator of Kotzebue, Schiller and Goethe, 'Teacher of the German language in the University of Cambridge' (see *DNB*), gave his *Concise practical grammar of the German tongue* (1799), but it remains even today in pristine condition.

was 'the only work extant from which any scientific knowledge of the Geology of this Country is attainable – They *are* in the Publick Library but are in so great request that it is scarcely possible to obtain a sight of them.' The recommenders were young in the fellowship; but the senior of them, the geologist Adam Sedgwick, had brought in as allies William Gilby, W. H. Mill (later a distinguished Arabist and Sanskrit scholar) and the youthful George Peacock, mathematician and in 1819 one of the founders of the Cambridge Philosophical Society. William Whewell was elected a Fellow only a little later, in 1817. He, too, brought new ideas, though they were not always easily digested by the more senior members of the College. His suggestion, made with Sedgwick, that a set of the new one-inch Ordnance Survey maps should be bought at £2 12s. 6d. a sheet, was deferred indefinitely. And when he recommended a subscription to Cuvier's *Recherches sur les ossemens fossiles des quadripèdes*, it was thought better to wait until the series was complete. The impatience of a fresh generation at what seemed wretched incompetence was further reflected in Peacock's observation that several series from foreign academies had been allowed to fall behind, that for St Petersburg terminating at 1784, and in Julius Hare's noting that even *Archaeologia* had been allowed to lapse. In response, the Master and Seniors charged Peacock with procuring copies to complete runs that he found imperfect.

In general, the recommendations book had been used only very sparingly in the early years of the nineteenth century. This changed with the arrival of men such as Peacock, Sedgwick and Whewell, elected Fellows in 1810–17, and J. W. Blakesley and Robert Pashley, elected in 1830–1. Subject always to the will of the Master (and Christopher Wordsworth, Master from 1820, seems in this to have preferred hesitation to action), the Library was gradually, albeit painfully slowly, buying a higher proportion of its intake.

By the later part of the eighteenth century, there seems to have been a change in policy in that undergraduates had less restricted access to the Library, and a greater supply of books relevant to their instruction. In 1778, undergraduates were permitted to borrow two books each. Christopher Wordsworth, later Master, used the Library as an undergraduate in 1793–4 both for study and for casual reading, or 'lounging', and borrowed books for both purposes.[147] J. M. F. Wright, who matriculated in 1814, and who was proud to be a reading man, has left a vivid image of the scene at the beginning of the Easter term, as undergraduates sought to prepare themselves:

147 MS O.11.8.

87

At the hour of ten, on the first day of the opening of Trinity Library, I found the entrance in the Cloisters beset by an ocean of pale countenances undulating to and fro with each succeeding effort to get foremost. Immediately the doors flew open in rushed the torrent, fifty perhaps wanting the same identical book. Such was the eagerness displayed by all, that some tripped up in ascending the lofty stairs, others stumbled over them, caps and gowns flying in most irreverent academical confusion. 'But necessity has no law', and 'cares not a fig for fine feathers.' Books many wanted I, but being short-legged and weak-muscled, brought up just in time to meet them on their way out of the Library.[148]

The borrowing register shows Wright to have been assiduous. But perhaps his memory exaggerated. In 1818, four years after Wright had matriculated, the young Macaulay entered the College. As an undergraduate, he carried off a series of prizes and scholarships, including the Latin declamation prize, the University's Craven scholarship and the Chancellor's medal for English verse. In January 1822, he took his BA without honours, having been defeated by mathematics. For much of the following three years, he remained in Cambridge, eventually winning a fellowship in 1824. But, if his correspondence with his mother is to be believed, he began to use libraries seriously only after his graduation, having relied until then on purchases from local booksellers. In a process of financial retrenchment, he explained on 16 February 1822, he had 'found that books may with a little management be got out of the College libraries, and that my Bookseller's bill may be materially reduced without denying myself any work that is necessary for study'.[149] Unlike Wright, Macaulay had not borrowed many books: but he had equally not neglected his reading. A few years later, the young W. M. Thackeray's reading included not only Hallam and Strutt on the Middle Ages, but also the plays of Ben Jonson and of Beaumont and Fletcher, as well as works on medicine.[150] 'I went to our library to day, & got out five stout quartos', he told his mother in 1829. 'But just as I was bearing them off, the library Keeper told me they must be all returned by this day week! Which will give me rather hard work if I intend reading them. They allow you to keep 6 books out a whole quarter of a year, but they must be returned by quarter day wh. is next Wednesday. It is a most splendid room.'[151]

Like many others, no doubt, he found the Wren Library an agreeable place in which to sit, but less satisfactory when he was obliged to work. It certainly

148 [J. M. F. Wright] *Alma mater; or, seven years at the University of Cambridge*, 2 vols. (1827), 1, p. 183. Wright's authorship of this book is not certain.

149 T. B. Macaulay, *Letters*, ed. T. Pinney, 5 vols. (Cambridge, 1974), 1, p. 170.

150 Borrowing registers, 30 March and 19 May 1829.

151 W. M. Thackeray, *Letters and private papers*, ed. Gordon Ray, 4 vols. (Oxford, 1945–6), 1, pp. 42–3.

did not include many multiple copies of the books most recommended; and to Thackeray at least its riches of early books were ambiguous compensation when he needed more recent work. So, the next month he wrote again to his mother,

> You mistake about the Library, it is not for my use. I may have five books out of it, by applying to a fellow of the College, & as Whewell is the only one I know, it is a bore both for him & me to receive & to give many tickets of admission – Besides the books are so outrageously old that there is hardly a book wh. wd. be of use to me in the library – Mitford's Greece I must have, I know where there is a copy quite new & very handsomely bound for five guineas.[152]

In practice, the College was only one – if, for Trinity men, the principal – source of books other than their own shelves. The library of the Union Society, founded in 1815, was another source; and in King's Parade, the popular book-seller 'Maps' Nicholson, whose full-length portrait now hangs in the University Library, ran a circulating library including a substantial supply of textbooks. Even the University Library was available to an undergraduate who could (and it was readily done) persuade an MA to allow him to use his name.[153]

Certainly more books were being borrowed from the College Library by undergraduates, even if the needs imposed on them by their studies were not all being met. But while new preoccupations are to be traced in the books recommended for the Library, the long-term strengths came, as had almost always been the case, by gift and by bequest. The series of bequests of classical books in the first decades of the nineteenth century ensured that the tradition already discernible at the end of the eighteenth was fortified and enlarged. This change of emphasis in the Library's accessions in some measure reflected different emphases in the undergraduate curriculum; but it was far more powerful in the extent to which it preserved the interests and influence of a generation, in the last years of the eighteenth century and the beginning of the nineteenth, that laid the foundations for the extraordinary increase in the power of the classics as a central field of study. In examinations, the mathematical tripos had existed since 1748. The subject had been encour-aged, as we have seen, by Robert Smith's provision for prizes. The introduc-tion of a classical tripos in 1824, initially requiring that those seeking hon-ours should first have gained them in mathematics, was a milestone on a road that had already been paved towards reform. As was anticipated, in

152 *Ibid.*, 1, p. 57.
153 *Alma mater*, 1, p. 120.

most years Trinity dominated the class-lists for the new tripos, in a manner that it did not, during the 1820s and 1830s, in mathematics.[154]

For many, both in Cambridge and in other parts of the country, the dominating figure at the end of the eighteenth and beginning of the nineteenth centuries was Richard Porson. He was only one among a group of gifted classicists of his generation that made Cambridge a centre of study in the subject as never before; but his personality, his wit, his brilliance as a scholar, his sheer devotion to classical studies, his illness and finally his premature death ensured him a reputation of a kind that has never been surpassed. He had come up to Trinity in 1778. As a Fellow of the College, he was able to use the Library much more fully than as an undergraduate, and he took advantage of it. In the space of three days in July 1783, he borrowed Apian, Sophocles, Estienne's *Thesaurus*, a Greek New Testament, Arrian, Diodorus Siculus, Plutarch, Petavius, Salmasius, Philostratus, Pausanias, Pollux, Suidas, Gruter and Bossuet.[155] Had he stayed in Cambridge, this might have continued. But he found himself obliged to resign his fellowship on his decision not to take holy orders, and so, to his friends' distress, he moved to London. None the less, fourteen years after he had matriculated he was elected Regius Professor of Greek. It was an election that did little to tie him to Cambridge. Most of his life thereafter was spent in London, in circumstances that, if anything, conspired to ensure that he was held in ever greater esteem among his friends still at Cambridge. He died in 1808.

In his lifetime, and in order to enable him to survive after his quitting his fellowship, a group of friends had subscribed to provide him with an annuity. But when his estate came to be examined, not only was this fund intact; he was also discovered to be in possession of an unusually good library, valued by the London booksellers Paine and Nichols at £1,186. This was quite apart from his work on Photius and other notes thought to be ready for the press. The booksellers' figures proved to be a considerable underestimate; for when in June 1809 Leigh and Sotheby sold the more straightforward part, that alone reached a hammer price of £1,254. The rest of the collection, amounting to something over two hundred volumes, posed a much more difficult question. It consisted not only of work either virtually ready (as was believed) for the press, but also of Porson's annotated copies of classical texts. These seemed all the more valuable in that Porson had himself published relatively little of this work in his lifetime. Matthew Raine, one of his

154 D. A. Winstanley, *Early Victorian Cambridge* (Cambridge, 1940), p. 67. Tripos results may be followed in the *Historical register*.
155 MS Add.a.132, p. 227.

closest friends, who had entered his fellowship at Trinity only a year after Porson and had taken a lead in promoting his annuity, was determined that they should be preserved as a collection, an opinion shared by members of Porson's family, and notably by his brother-in-law James Perry. By a simple process of arithmetic, based on the assumption that as the books which had been auctioned had reached about twice their valuation figure, a price of a thousand guineas was set on the rest. Lest Trinity should prove unable or unwilling to find so great a sum, Raine also approached the British Museum, and was thus able to rattle the Museum's Trustees at the Senior Bursar of Trinity.[156] He need not have worried; for the College agreed to pay half at Lady Day 1810 and the rest on the safe delivery of what had always been regarded as the prize amongst Porson's work: his transcript of the College's manuscript of Photius' *Lexicon*, given by Gale and then still thought to be unique.[157]

As an acknowledgement of the central importance of the work of a member of the College, there was no precedent – even in Bentley. In the financial years 1809–10 and 1810–11, the bills of Deighton, the local bookseller, and the Library's principal supplier of ordinary books, amounted to just under £50 and just under £45 respectively; the only other book bought during these years was a copy of J. E. Bode's ambitious series of engravings of the heavens, *Uranographia*, price £9 10s. The figure of a thousand guineas may be compared with the dividend of £920 received by the Master, and with £2,660 received by the Junior Bursar from the College treasury, as it was then called, for running most of the domestic affairs of the entire College in the same financial year. But to some degree it could be looked on as a straightforward investment, in that the following April the College agreed further to publish Porson's manuscripts and adversaria for its own benefit. Over the next few years, this policy led to a series of volumes edited by J. H. Monk (Porson's successor as Regius Professor), C. J. Blomfield, James Scholefield and Peter Paul Dobree, the College paying for printing and then selling any remaining stock into the trade after meeting its immediate requirements. As each volume was published, provision was also made for a small stock of copies on large paper; especial care was taken with the printing to ensure that the series should be a monument worthy of Porson himself. But as the well-informed and sympathetic reviewer of his *Adversaria* in the *Museum Criticum* realised, the exercise had proved somewhat more difficult than had been anticipated, in that Porson's notes had been left in a far from coherent order.[158]

156 Then J. H. Hailstone, who had entered his fellowship in the same year as Raine.
157 The papers respecting these transactions are in MS Add.c.152; for Raine and the British Museum, see his letter to Hailstone, 2 December 1809, in c.13.26. The College agreed to accept the offer twelve days later (Conclusion Book, 14 December 1809). A summary of Porson's estate is printed in J. S. Watson, *The life of Richard Porson* (1861), pp. 337–8. The circumstances of the loss in a fire of Porson's first transcript of the Photius, and of his settling to recopy it, are related in Watson, pp. 129–31. Inevitably (and indeed deliberately) some of Porson's books bearing manuscript notes escaped; many of them have found their way back to the Library by various routes since. A second early manuscript of Photius, derived from the Trinity manuscript, was discovered only in 1959; see N. G. Wilson, *Scholars of Byzantium* (1983), p. 92.
158 *Museum Criticum* 1 (1814), pp. 115–22.

The Porson industry (it can have seemed little less) continued for over fifty years, culminating in H. R. Luard's edition of his correspondence, published by the Cambridge Antiquarian Society in 1867.[159] For the College, it was financially of no little interest. But for the history of the College, as well as for classical studies, the publication first of Bentley's letters, edited by Charles Burney in 1807, then of the first edition of Monk's authoritative biography in 1830, and finally a fuller edition of Bentley's correspondence, edited by Christopher and John Wordsworth in 1842, all combined to emphasise the degree to which two generations were prepared to celebrate what had been preserved in the Wren Library. Perhaps not surprisingly, the gifts in these years reflected some of these preoccupations, in the bequests of Dobree and of Robert Hole, Fellow of the College, both in 1826, and of Jonathan Raine in 1831.

Porson's books had not been especially remarkable for their binding. He was also notoriously careless of his everyday clothes. But his handwriting, and in particular his Greek, was celebrated for its neatness and beauty. In the care that Trinity took with printing his posthumously published works, ensuring good type and arranging for copies on large paper, the bibliophile influence of Matthew Raine may be visible yet again. It was also an acknowledgement of the detailed interest that Porson himself had taken in type design.[160] Raine's own books, bequeathed by his brother Jonathan, were those of one who had allowed his tastes to be formed in the more fashionable circles of London book collecting.[161] After his fellowship at Trinity, his post as headmaster of Charterhouse School had given him ample opportunity. The bindings, by Hering, Rodwell and others, stand out in smart contrast with the books that had hitherto entered the Library from most earlier benefactors, who had given less thought to the outward appearance of the volumes in their possession. Raine's scholarly inclinations at Cambridge had combined with the interests of stylish book collecting in London to produce a library that introduced a distinctly metropolitan air. Where others in previous generations had sought out standard texts in the best edited versions, Raine and others of his like-minded contemporaries sought out *editiones principes*, and therefore paid especial attention to the Aldine press, whose Greek books in particular offered an authority unparalleled in the history of classical scholarship. Subsequently, this collection of Aldines was to form a centrepiece in the Library's buying policy, as further examples were added and the whole was shelved together.

159 Luard's own working copy, with various insertions, stands at c.13.9. His abortive attempt in 1843 to have published a collection of Porson's opuscula survives only as a working volume, c.13.17.

160 James Mosley, 'Porson's Greek types', *Penrose Annual* 54 (1960), pp. 36–40. Porson Greek was cut for Cambridge University Press by Richard Austin in 1806–8.

161 Raine's collection is listed with Porson's in MS Add.aa.6. For a dispute over the word-ing of Jonathan Raine's will, see TC Mun., box 31, no. 9.

Raine was the more associated with Porson in that he died only a few months afterwards, in 1811. But in Cambridge it was Peter Paul Dobree who seemed to offer most in common, and whose career as Regius Professor of Greek (in which he succeeded Porson at one remove) was cut short by his premature death. Partly as a result of his work on Porson's Aristophanes and his Photius, partly even in his physical appearance, he seemed to inherit much of his predecessor's mantle. Nowhere is this more vivid than in the monuments to the two men in the College Chapel, alike in their design yet fifteen years apart. Dobree left his own adversaria to the University Library rather than to his college;[162] but Trinity received a valuable addition to its store of books of Greek literature in particular.

Dobree's bequest arrived in 1825; that of Robert Hole in 1826; of Raine in 1831; of Daniel Pettiward in 1833; and in 1835 Robert Evans added to the series, this time not by bequest, but by gift.[163] Of these, Hole and Pettiward had both entered the College in the same year, 1785. Evans was to be accounted one of the next generation, having taken up his fellowship in 1813, three years after Sedgwick and a year before Peacock, with whom he shared duties as a tutor from 1823 to 1835. Pettiward, on the other hand, friend and supporter of Sedgwick,[164] never held a fellowship, and lived for thirty-five years, a little over half his life, as Rector of livings near Stowmarket in Suffolk.[165] Here, supported by the family estate, he found sufficient ease to enjoy a life befitting a country gentleman, as well as to accumulate a collection of pictures and other works of art that he bequeathed with almost three thousand volumes to the College.[166] Thanks to its systematic collection of English literature in particular it did much to bring the Library's holdings up to date.

Between them, these men shaped much of the Library's future, not only in the attention increasingly placed on early printed texts of the classics, but also in the appearance of the Library shelves, as the plain calf and vellum of earlier acquisitions was interrupted by the fashionable leathers such as russia or variously coloured morocco.

These collections dominated by their numbers, and by their subjects. They were accompanied by smaller donations, usually of recent works, whose regular arrival marks a change in the perception of the Library as a centre of College activity. One was outstanding, and was a rare example of a manuscript in these years. The well-known Trinity carol roll (MS O.3.58: fig. 51), dating from the first half of the fifteenth century, was the gift of H. O. Roe, of Weston, near Baldock,

162 Listed in H. R. Luard, *A catalogue of adversaria and printed books containing ms. notes preserved in the library of the University of Cambridge* (Cambridge, 1864), especially p. 66; see also McKitterick, *Cambridge University Library*, pp. 462–3. Two volumes of Dobree's adversaria, edited by his successor James Scholefield, were published in 1831–3, and a third in 1835. A summary of the relevant portion of his will is in TC Mun., box 31, no. 11.

163 The Dobree, Hole, Evans and Pettiward collections are all listed in MS Add.a.151, that from Dobree additionally in MS Add.aa.2. That from Pettiward (including his works of art) is in MS Add.aa.5. His entire bequest was valued at £1,290 (Senior Bursar's accounts, 1834–5).

164 J. W. Clark and T. McK. Hughes, *The life and letters of Adam Sedgwick*, 2 vols. (Cambridge, 1890), 1, pp. 124–7, 162–3.

165 Pettiward is associated variously with Great Finborough and with Onehouse, both near Stowmarket: the family owned the livings of both.

166 Among his bequest were three tables with tops made of specimens of different stones: of marbles from Italy, of lava from Vesuvius, and of marbles from Devonshire. For many years two of them ornamented the Wren Library, as scientific exhibits as well as furniture; they are now in the Fitzwilliam Museum. For a description of the table made of Italian marbles, made in Rome, see Q.17.32.

in 1837. It has been attributed to Norfolk or perhaps elsewhere in East Anglia, and it concludes with the popular 'Ther is no rose of swych vertu'; but its unique importance lies in preserving the so-called Agincourt song, commemorating Henry V's victory in 1415.[167]

Not surprisingly, by the 1830s the Library was beginning to show signs of strain. In a college where the ascendancy of classics had been so vividly demonstrated by an exceptional series of purchases, gifts and bequests, mathematics and the sciences now commanded increasing attention. Further concerns were signalled in the Library's subscriptions to the Oriental Translations Fund and to the Instituto di Corrispondenza Archeologica in Rome. Reform was in the air. In three years, from 1833 to 1835, Sedgwick's *Discourse on the studies of the University*, originally a commemoration sermon preached in the College Chapel, went through four editions. Whewell got into his stride as a polemicist eager to use the resources of the printing press. The University showed its hand in new journals, including the *Philological Museum* (edited by Julius Charles Hare) in 1832, and the *Cambridge Quarterly Review* in 1833. The *Cambridge Mathematical Journal* was founded in 1837.

In 1836, in order to meet increased demands of funds for purchasing, it was agreed that fines (half a crown for each offence) levied on undergraduates for walking on the grass should be applied to buying books for the Library.[168] A new Librarian, Charles Warren, was appointed in 1837, and he quickly found occasion to report on the faults of his predecessors, including missing manuscripts and 'utter confusion' in the catalogues.[169] But the horse had already bolted. Just as Henry Justice had found in the disorganised state of Cambridge libraries during the 1730s opportunities for theft, so Trinity now suffered again, this time at the hands of an undergraduate. James Orchard Halliwell had come up in 1836, aged but sixteen. In the Wren, he proved to be unable to separate his budding interest in medieval manuscripts from the urge to steal, and he systematically pilfered Gale's scientific and mathematical medieval manuscripts. From Cambridge, he took them to London, where in due course some were sold to the British Museum. But thanks partly to the fact that the College was unable to demonstrate conclusively from its inadequate and disordered records that the manuscripts had recently belonged to it, no case could be brought against Halliwell, and the Museum kept what it had bought in good faith.[170]

167   Roe to Christopher Wordsworth, 30 December 1837, MS Add.a.157a, no. 5; Iain Fenlon (ed.), *Cambridge music manuscripts, 900–1700* (Cambridge, 1982), no. 27 (notes by Richard Beadle); reproduced in facsimile, ed. J. A. Fuller-Maitland and W. S. Rockstro (1891).

168   Conclusion Book, 16 February and 10 December 1836.

169   MSS Add.a.167(1), Add.a.166, f. 2r. The catalogue of Gale's manuscripts against which Warren checked the collection is MS 0.15.62.

170   D. A. Winstanley (and R. W. Hunt), 'Halliwell Phillipps and Trinity College Library', *The Library*, 5th ser., 2 (1947–8), pp. 250–82. Further contemporary detail may be sought in *Statement in answer to reports which have been spread abroad against Mr. James Orchard Halliwell* [1845], which prints much of the correspondence from Halliwell's point of view. Further papers and correspondence from the College records are in MS Add.a.120. Halliwell migrated to Jesus College in 1838. Among his many literary publications, in 1841 there appeared *Shakesperiana: a catalogue of the early editions of Shakespeare's plays*, including notes of those in the Capell collection.

Within the Wren, in 1832–4 Joseph Wentworth had been paid for fitting up bookcases, and substantial repairs were carried out.[171] Then, in 1840, the Library was transformed. Into the generous spaces left by Wren for tables and stools between each of his cases, a total of twenty-four new cases were introduced to the designs of C. R. Cockerell, their execution again the work of Wentworth.[172] The spaces intended by Wren for study were invaded, in a sequence of alterations that was to lead a little over twenty years later to further destruction of his concept when dwarf bookcases were set in two long lines down the centre, principally to receive the books of Julius Charles Hare in 1855, and of William Grylls (d. 1863) in 1864. The collections, each uniquely important of its kind, added magnificently to the Library. The visual consequences of these years were disastrous. In these decades, also, the Library became a focus of attention for more than books or (as is shown below[173]) antiquities and curiosities. As Malcolm Baker demonstrates, it was probably in this generation that the several busts by Roubiliac and Scheemakers, hitherto scattered round the College, were gathered in the Wren to join the four of Bacon, Newton, Ray and Willoughby. Thorvaldsen's statue of Byron, refused for Poets' Corner in Westminster Abbey, and rejected for the College Chapel, came to rest in the Library in 1845.[174] The interior of the Wren Library took on the appearance it was to keep for over a century.

More important for the College and the University as a whole, in 1841 William Whewell moved into the Master's Lodge. He was to remain there until his death in 1866.

171 Junior Bursar's accounts, 1832, 1833, 1834.

172 TC Mun., box 30, no. 13.

173 See pp. 108–9.

174 Mrs Stair Douglas, *The life of William Whewell* (1881), pp. 292–3. Some of the correspondence concerning the commissioning and eventual location of the statue is printed in Robert Sinker, *The library of Trinity College, Cambridge* (Cambridge, 1891), pp. 125–32.

3   The library as a Museum

Like many libraries in the seventeenth century, that in the College housed more than books. During the eighteenth and nineteenth centuries, the various curiosities, specimens, antiquities and scientific instruments both grew in number and, in varying degrees at different periods, acquired an importance in their own right. By the years before the First World War, the Wren housed what the Librarian of the day, A. G. W. Murray, was to describe as a raree show: a collection of scientific and ethnographical specimens, archaeological remains, tourist souvenirs and the whims of several generations of undisciplined antiquarianism. By then, what had once been a serious collection had degenerated into a neglected group of curiosities. Indeed, the transition from a collection with some basis in the sciences to the assumption that the College Library was the proper place for relics had begun in the eighteenth century: in this, the gift in 1770 of a lock of Sir Isaac Newton's hair set a precedent that subsequent generations were to follow with alacrity.[175] Although the College still possesses specimens of Newton's hair, these collections are now, for the most part, either deposited in collections more suitable for their understanding, or (as in the case of a zebra's head, which was found to be vermin-ridden) have been necessarily destroyed.[176]

The origins of such collections, and the spirit which prompted them, are to be found in the cabinets of antiquities and natural curiosities in the sixteenth and seventeenth centuries: for Trinity, perhaps in particular in that originally envisaged for the Royal Society, though neither at Trinity nor in the Royal Society did the collection develop as once may have been hoped.[177] There is no evidence that, until the second half of the seventeenth century, the College kept anything other than books in the old library in Great Court.[178] But even as the Wren Library was being built, the foundations for new forms of collecting were being put in place. During these twenty or so years, the Library's book collections expanded as never before, growing to about 3,570 volumes by 1695, an increase of 24 per cent since 1667.[179] This expansion took place against changes in the organisation and administration of knowledge that are most obviously perceived, in England, in the foundation and gradual development of the Royal Society. The foundation (or, in some estimates, the refoundation) of the Society of Antiquaries in 1707 was a further manifestation of changes in the academic organisation of knowledge, complementary to the established centres of the universities.[180] Both societies, whose membership overlapped to a marked degree, encouraged previous tendencies, giving them fresh direction, in collecting exhibits as accompaniments to book learning. Elsewhere in the country, and nowhere more successfully than at Spalding in Lincolnshire, more or less formal groups pursued similar aims, sharing their membership partly with the two principals in London and partly with university circles.[181] Gradually, if by no means easily, the cabinet of curiosities familiar since the sixteenth century was modified into collections more familiar in the nineteenth- and twentieth-century museum, whether of anatomy, ethnography or antiquities.

175   This, the first of its kind, was given by Edward Howkins, as part of a collection of papers relating to Newton, Cotes and Smith. Another was bequeathed by Charles Burr in 1823 (MS Add.a.157a, no. 4).

176   Murray's list of 1914, and related lists, are in MS Add.a.167. The exhibits are now principally in the Museum of Archaeology and Anthropology and (in the case of coins and classical sculpture) the Fitzwilliam Museum.

177   For the Royal Society, see Nehemiah Grew, *Musaeum Regalis Societatis. Or, a catalogue & description of the ... rarities belonging to the Royal Society and preserved at Gresham College* (1681), and Michael Hunter, 'The cabinet institutionalized: the Royal Society's "Repository" and its background', in O. Impey and A. MacGregor (eds.), *The origins of museums: the cabinet of curiosities in sixteenth- and seventeenth-century Europe* (Oxford, 1985), pp. 159–68.

178   Gaskell, *Trinity College Library*, pp. 120–2.

179   *Ibid.*, p. 128.

180   Joan Evans, *A history of the Society of Antiquaries* (Oxford, 1956), ch. 3.

181   For Spalding, see *An account of the Gentlemen's Society at Spalding, Bibliotheca topographica Britannica* 3 (1790) and *The minute-books of the Spalding Gentlemen's Society, 1712–1755*, selected and ed. by Dorothy M. Owen and S. W. Woodward (Lincoln Records Society, 1981).

The association of books, and libraries, with such collections was well established. In the most celebrated picture of all cabinets of curiosities, belonging to Ferrante Imperato in Naples,[182] books and specimens are shown housed in different parts of the same room. In Paris, at the very time that the Wren Library was being built, Claude du Molinet was assembling the great library at the Abbey of Sainte-Geneviève, and the equally celebrated collection of numismatic, historical, artistic and natural history specimens associated with it: 'un cabinet de piéces rates & curieuses, qui regardassent l'étude, & qui pûssent servir aux belles lettres'. There, the building was begun in 1675, and du Molinet died in 1687 – the two events coinciding almost exactly with the development and construction of the Wren Library, and thus offering an unusually vivid contemporary parallel.[183] In Cambridge, a dramatic turn in the Library's collections during these years was nowhere more vividly illustrated than in the list of objects presented by Sir William Mainstone, an East India merchant retired to Gamlingay, even as the Wren Library was being built. His gifts in 1682 represented natural history (a rhinoceros horn, 'an excrescency upon the head of a Deer'), ethnography (poisoned Indian arrows), exotic civilisations (an unspecified Chinese printed book, Chinese paper made of feathers and of silk, Chinese ink and chopsticks and a sheet of Malay papyrus) and medicine (antidotes derived from pig, ape and porcupine).[184] Two oriental documents given shortly afterwards by John Laughton had much the same curiosity value: one was entered in the accessions register merely as 'Grand Seigners Love letter'. More substantially, Laughton also provided a part of what was described as an Egyptian mummy, and an 'Egyptian Scarabeus',[185] while others found a petrified fig and a pair of bracelets engraved in Persian.

These piecemeal accumulations might have been precursors of a greater collection, had that made by the architect William Talman (1650–1719) and his son John (1677–1726) come to the College, as the younger Talman at one stage intended. Although nothing is recorded in the College of the course that led John Talman, a founder-member of the Society of Antiquaries, to Trinity, it is likely to have been through his friendships in the Society, and with the Gale brothers in particular. Such a gift would have brought an accumulation of sculpture, copies after the antique, vases, bronzes and furniture, much of it gathered in Italy, as well as an enormous collection of drawings of architecture, ecclesiastical ornaments, jewellery, antiquities and costumes, either by or

182 Ferrante Imperato, *Dell'historia naturale di Ferrante Imperato Napolitano libri xxviii* (Naples, 1599). See also Impey and MacGregor, *The origins of museums*, pl. 4.
183 Claude du Molinet, *Le Cabinet de la Bibliothèque de Sainte-Geneviève* (Paris, 1692); *Le Cabinet de curiosités de la Bibliothèque Sainte-Geneviève, des origines à nos jours* (exhibition catalogue, Bibliothèque Sainte-Geneviève, Paris, 1989).
184 MS Add.a.106, f. 26r. Mainstone died in 1683: see *Victoria county history: Cambridgeshire*, 5 (1973), pp. 73, 85.
185 MS Add.a.106, f. 53v.

commissioned by John Talman, much of it, again, in Italy. But Talman was clearly in several minds. While naming the College as beneficiary in his will, he also busied himself in repeatedly offering most of his drawings to Lord Harley.[186] In the event, although he passed some of his collection to the Antiquaries in his lifetime, the bulk was dispersed at a series of sales for the benefit of the family.[187]

But even without Talman's collection, the list by the 1720s was sufficiently varied, including loadstones, a Lapland drum and drumstick, 'a Romish Pix set in Gold', an ivory comb reputed to have belonged to Henry VIII, Sir Samuel Morland's speaking trumpet, wood from a Spanish shipwreck and various fragments of Roman urns. The natural history collection now also included the dried skin of a lizard and 'a large Sea-Weed'. There had been two skeletons in the Library since the early years of the century,[188] but one had disappeared by the time this extraordinary list was drawn up. The catalogue gave prominence to one of the skeletons, and to a plaster of Paris model of Isaac Barrow's head.[189] In the mid eighteenth century, the anatomical portion of the collection was given rather more weight with gifts from Dr Layard, as a result of which, for the first time, it was possible to examine in the Library preserved human and animal hearts, a cranium, several foetuses, various human abnormalities and, inexplicably, a tarantula.[190] For many years afterwards, the College accounts included a regular charge for spirits for their preservation in various bottles.

It was not an organised collection; and it was certainly not a very great one. Trinity had produced no figure such as Du Molinet at Ste Geneviève or Athanasius Kircher in Rome, or August Francke at Halle, men determined to assemble collections of major importance for their various institutions.[191] Though by the mid-century the College possessed an assemblage in which natural curiosities, medical preparations and scientific instruments could be accounted part of a single collection, it was hardly a cabinet in the sense understood, for example, in Paris.[192] Other than in the systematic equipping of the College's observatory (in which, not surprisingly, the Library played only a very modest role), there was evidence of disciplined collecting and cataloguing in but two fields: in the coin collection and in the collection presented by Lord Sandwich following the first voyage of Captain Cook to the Pacific, to which we shall return.[193] In these two, the collections were outstanding. Elsewhere in Cambridge, there were more organised and better-defined collections. The minerals, fossils and archaeological miscellanea collected

186 Humfrey Wanley, *Diary, 1715–1726*, ed. C. E. Wright and Ruth C. Wright, 2 vols. (Bibliographical Society, 1966) 1, pp. 16, 18, 22, 25, 123.

187 Details of the Talmans are drawn from H. M. Colvin, *A biographical dictionary of English architects, 1600–1840* (1978), pp. 800–7. Further drawings in the collection were offered in the Sammlung Rudolf von Gutmann (Sotheby's, 2 April 1993), Lot 96. For some of his time in Italy, the younger Talman was the travelling companion of William Kent: see Hugh Honour, 'John Talman and William Kent in Italy', *Connoisseur* 134 (1954), pp. 3–7, and John Dixon Hunt, *William Kent, landscape garden designer: an assessment and catalogue of his designs* (1987).

188 Junior Bursar's accounts, 1712–13, payment for a case for the 'lesser skeleton'.

189 Now missing.

190 A list of Layard's gifts is pasted into MS Add.a.106, f. 214v.

191 William Schupbach, 'Some cabinets of curiosities in European academic institutions', in Impey and MacGregor, *The origins of museums*, pp. 169–78.

192 Cf. C. R. Hill, 'The cabinet of Bonnier de la Mosson (1702–1744)', *Annals of Science* 43 (1986), pp. 147–74.

193 See p. 104–6.

194 Clark, *Endowments*, pp. 196–202;
V. A. Eyles, 'John Woodward, F.R.S.,
F.R.C.P., M.D. (1665–1728): a bio-
bibliographical account of his life and
work', *Journal of the Society for the Bibliography
of Natural History* 5 (1971), pp. 399–427; David
Price, 'John Woodward and a surviving
British geological collection from the early
eighteenth century', *Journal of the History of
Collections* 1 (1989), pp. 79–95.

195 E. Saville Peck, 'John Francis Vigani,
first Professor of Chemistry in the University of Cambridge (1703–12), and his materia
medica cabinet in the library of Queens'
College', *Proc. Cambridge Antiquarian Soc.*
34 (1934), pp. 34–49; L. J. M. Coleby, 'John
Francis Vigani', *Annals of Science* 38 (1982),
pp. 46–60.

196 McKitterick, *Cambridge University
Library*, pp. 231–41.

197 MS Add.a.106, f. 88v. The University
Library (in 1681) and Pembroke College
also acquired Castlemaine globes, with
a celestial planisphere set beneath the
terrestrial globe, in the same year: Oates,
Cambridge University Library, pp. 441–2.

198 Celia Fiennes, *Journeys*, ed. Christopher
Morris (1949), p. 65.

199 MS Add.a.106, f. 25v.

200 MS Add.a.109, p. 311; Derek J. Price,
'The early observatory instruments of
Trinity College, Cambridge', *Annals of
Science* 8 (1952), pp. 1–12. The College
agreed to the erection of the observatory on
5 February 1705/6 (Conclusion Book). Such
as remain of these instruments are now in
the Whipple Museum.

201 Junior Bursar's accounts, 1703–4. It
had to be repaired several times in the
following years.

202 Junior Bursar's accounts, 1707–8, 'by
order of the Master'.

203 For coin cabinets in Oxford, including
the Bodleian and several colleges, see S.
Piggott, 'Antiquarian studies', in Sutherland and Mitchell, *Oxford*, pp. 757–77, at
pp. 759–60.

and arranged by John Woodward, founder of the chair in geology, were bequeathed by him in 1728 to the University – only to be set in disorder by the first incumbent of the chair, Charles Mason.[194] The cabinet of *materia medica* assembled by Giovanni Francesco Vigani, the University's first Professor of Chemistry, at the beginning of the century passed to Queens';[195] and even the cabinet of oriental curiosities left to the University by George Lewis in 1727 had more organisation.[196] Very sensibly, Whewell arranged for the anatomical preparations to be passed to the Anatomy School in the nineteenth century.

More conventionally, the Library served also to house a collection of globes, including a Castlemaine globe bought in 1681,[197] and two pairs of celestial and terrestrial globes, by Jansson and by Moxon. It was these that Celia Fiennes saw at each end of the Library in 1697.[198] The College acquired a microscope in about 1680. A small group of mathematical instruments, presented by Thomas Scattergood, remained apparently the only such things of their kind until the eighteenth century, apart from a 'Brazen quadrant', given by Sir Thomas Turner of Essex.[199] But when in 1706 plans were set in hand under Bentley for the erection of an observatory over the Great Gate, the emphasis was firmly changed. In August–September 1703, the Library had already received the equipment for an observatory, including a sixteenfoot and an eight-foot telescope, as well as dials, a barometer, a micrometer, compasses and quadrants.[200] A 'Dyall & Brass figure' cost £3 4s. 6d. from Carter in 1704.[201] In 1707–8, a new, and expensive, sextant was supplied by John Rowley, the London instrument maker, for £100.[202] It may be presumed that with the completion of the observatory, much delayed for lack of funds, these instruments passed to the other side of Great Court.

The numismatic collection, a natural adjunct to the books and manuscripts, was to become much more important.[203] Little is known of it before the eighteenth century, when it was greatly increased by the addition of the collection of Beaupré Bell; and it is now impossible to compare the significance of the College's collection at that time with the much older collection of the University Library. In the mid seventeenth century, Anne Sadleir, donor of the glorious thirteenth-century *Apocalypse*, had also presented a collection of early coins, though no details of what it was composed of can now be extrapolated. At the end of the seventeenth century, donors included Henry Firebrace, Fellow (who gave a small group of English commemorative medals of the 1680s), Dudley North, Daniel Skynner, also a Fellow, and Robert Montagu, younger son of the Earl of Manchester. A medal case was commissioned to house the collection in 1728.[204] In the eighteenth century, some may have regretted that Roger Gale chose to present his collection not to the College, and thus keep it together with his manuscripts, but to the University Library, where it quickly became muddled with earlier accumulations.[205]

These earlier collections were transformed by the bequest of Beaupré Bell, who died in 1745 – shortly after Gale had given his manuscripts to the College. For many years, Bell had assembled materials for a volume, *Tabulae Augustae*, to be printed by Cambridge University Press, only to find his plans thwarted by difficulties in obtaining satisfactory illustrative engravings and by his own illness. He died of consumption, unmarried.[206] The close ties that he kept with Cambridge may be gathered from his keeping a room there, in which he stored most of his antiquities, and in the memorable hospitality to which Richard Walker, the Vice-Master, paid tribute when he came to write his own will in 1764, almost twenty years after his friend's death: Walker's bequest was specifically to help make good what the elder Bell had allowed to decay at the family house at Narford in Norfolk.[207] The arrival of Bell's coins and medals in the Library, to join those of Anne Sadleir and other more recent benefactors, led directly to the recataloguing of the entire collection. This was undertaken by the indefatigable antiquarian, arranger and Professor of Geology who has already been mentioned, Charles Mason.[208] Bell's primary interests were in Roman Britain: but something of their scale may be glimpsed in that in 1741 he was reported to have lately purchased about five hundred Greek and Roman coins brought from overseas by the late Mr Hanson, lecturer at Wisbech.[209] Apart from his Greek and (in particular) his Roman coins, he also possessed a handful of Anglo-Saxon coins, while among his later English types the series of Civil War and Inter-Regnum examples were of notable interest. His modern English series continued, rather haphazardly and incompletely, down to 1740. Very few modern foreign coins came with his bequest. In many respects, it was an admirable complement to the already strong collections in many of these areas at Trinity.

While the collection of coins and medals prospered, supported by a carefully nurtured and eventually extensive section of books on numismatics, other parts of the more miscellaneous collections languished as inadequate or inappropriate. Additions continued to arrive, more or less relevant, throughout the

204 Junior Bursar's accounts, 1727–8: £9 8s. 1d. The gifts are also summarised in Gaskell, *Trinity College Library*, pp. 121–2.
205 Nichols, *Literary anecdotes*, 4, p. 548. The Trinity College collection of coins and medals, by then estimated at three thousand pieces, was deposited in the Fitzwilliam Museum in 1937.
206 John Nichols, *Literary anecdotes*, 5, pp. 278–82; Stukeley, *Family memoirs*, 2, pp. 22, 281–2. Although Bell did not live to see his *Tabulae Augustae* in print, he had gathered together a list of subscribers: see MS R.10.13, ff. 94–107.
207 For Walker's will, see *Trusts, statutes and directions affecting (1) the professorships of the University, (2) the scholarships and prizes, (3) other gifts and endowments* (Cambridge, 1876), pp. 251–4.
208 Mason's catalogue (MS R.17.12) has been transferred with the coin collection to the Fitzwilliam Museum. Bell's own catalogue of his collection is now MS R.13.116. Some information may also be gleaned from Bell's annotations; see, for example, his copy of John Evelyn, *Numismata* (Y.17.29).
209 Maurice Johnson to Roger Gale, 3 April 1741, in *Bibliotheca topographica Britannica*, 2 (1781), p. 345.

nineteenth century. In many respects, the Library had few defences against much that in the end proved trivial. In other respects, it began to fulfil some of the duties of a local museum, in taking under its wing the group of vases and other Roman objects unearthed in a gravel pit near Trumpington and presented by a former Fellow-Commoner, Porter Thompson.[210] However, in three particular areas of collecting the Library gained some national significance: in sculpture from ancient Greece and from Roman Britain, and, most importantly, in south Pacific ethnography.

The foundation of these parts of the collection, which stood for many years at the top of the stairs, was the so-called Sandwich marble, named after its discoverer, Lord Sandwich, and given to the College in 1766 by the Countess of Bute. This large slab was said to have been found by Sandwich in the lumber yard of the English consul at Athens. Shortly after it had been brought back to England in 1739, it caught the interest of John Taylor, Fellow of St John's College, whose account of the inscription was published at Cambridge in 1743. There, Taylor demonstrated its importance as a survival of Athenian public accounts, though in his excitement he convinced himself that it was somewhat earlier than the now accepted date of the fourth century BC.[211]

But before arriving at the history of ancient Athens, visitors to the Wren Library in the latter part of the eighteenth century had first to pass the collection of inscriptions and sculpture from Roman Britain, presented by Sir John Cotton in 1750 and arranged in the vestibule at the foot of the staircase.[212] The collection had been formed by his ancestor the antiquary Sir Robert Cotton, who had set the stones into the walls of a building in his garden at his house at Conington, just north of Huntingdon. Most of it came from sites on or near Hadrian's Wall, fruit of an expedition in 1599 with his friend and mentor William Camden – a survey made, in the words of Philemon Holland, Camden's translator, 'not without the sweet food and contentment of our mindes'.[213] Camden had included Cotton's transcriptions, and illustrations of several of the sculptures, in the much-revised folio edition of his *Britannia* in 1607, and he paid repeated compliments to his companion in research, 'who over and beside other vertues, being a singular love and sercher of antiquities, having gathered with great charges from all places the monuments of venerable antiquitie, hath heere [at Conington] begunne a famous Cabinet, whence of his singular courtesie, he hath often times given me great light in these darksome obscurities'.[214] Half a dozen of

210 Stukeley, *Family memoirs*, 2, p. 37. Thompson (Fellow-Commoner 1725; d.1741) also presented about five hundred books, mostly standard classics and modern history, listed in MS Add.a.150, preceding p. 321.
211 John Taylor, *Marmor Sandvicense* (Cambridge, 1743). Something of Taylor's enthusiasm can be caught in his letter of 2 November 1742 to an unnamed correspondent (probably Anthony Askew), printed in Nichols, *Literary anecdotes*, 9, pp. 325–8. The copper plates from which the two large reproductions of the inscriptions were printed are preserved in the Library.
212 For more details on the following, see D. McKitterick 'From Camden to Cambridge: Sir Robert Cotton's Roman inscriptions and their subsequent treatment', in C. Wright (ed.), *Sir Robert Cotton as collector* (1995).
213 William Camden, *Britain* (1610), p. 769.
214 *Ibid.*, p. 500.

Cotton's sculptures came from Risingham, north-west of Corbridge, including a large dedication slab erected by a cohort from Gaul and measuring almost five feet in length by over two in height. An altar from the same site, dedicated *Deo invicto Herculi*, was almost four feet tall and two feet thick.[215] These were heavy stones to move along the roads and rivers of Elizabethan England, to a house in Huntingdonshire on the edge of the fens, and Camden's remarks concerning the expenses entailed by Cotton in their collection were made from personal knowledge. Following Camden, Speed too turned to Cotton's cabinet, or *armarium*, using his coins as models for illustrations, and incorporating drawings of some of his more remarkable inscriptions into the margin of the map of Northumberland in *The theatre of the empire of Great Britaine* (1611).[216] Cotton's initial visit to the North in 1599 proved but the beginning of his task, for even fifteen and more years later he was still seeking to get his discoveries and acquisitions back to Conington.[217] Eventually he had amassed stones from half a dozen sites connected with the Wall.[218] But his interests ranged beyond Cumberland and Northumberland. A tombstone in his collection, from Silchester, had been discovered in or before 1587; and in 1600 Camden referred to altars from Greetland (just south of Halifax) and Bowes in Yorkshire.[219] A milestone, almost four feet high, was found near Cotton's home, probably on Ermine Street.[220]

In an early example of antiquarian display in England, Cotton had set up the inscriptions around the inside wall of his summer house in Huntingdonshire. It was here that they were first seen by John Horsley when he was compiling his *Britannia Romana* (1732). Horsley came from Morpeth, so the fact that Northumberland was so well represented in the collection offered, initially, an especial appeal.

> When I looked round me in that summer-house, and observed particularly the inscriptions which had been removed from our own country and neighbourhood, it gave me for some time a great deal of pleasure; tho' it was afterward much abated, by reflecting on the ruinous state both of the house and inscriptions.[221]

Horsley was not the only person to remark with disappointment on the state of the collection. In 1731, with the eyes of the learned world on the damaged Cotton manuscripts after the fire at Ashburnham House, James West reported to Hearne that the main house at Conington was desolate, and the Roman

215 *RIB* 1227, 1215; both are illustrated in William Camden, *Britannia* (1607), pp.663–4.
216 John Speed, *Theatre* (1611), map at p.89.
217 British Library MS Cotton Julius C.III, ff. 210, 314.
218 Old Carlisle (*RIB* 897), Risingham (*RIB* 1215, 1225, 1227, 1237, 1241, 1254), High Rochester (*RIB* 1270), Halton Chesters (*RIB* 1433), Housesteads (*RIB* 1589) and Carvoran (*RIB* 1792).
219 *RIB* 68, 627, 730.
220 *RIB* 2239.
221 John Horsley, *Britannia Romana* (1732), p.182.

inscriptions were broken and trodden under foot.[222] The roof of Cotton's summer house had fallen in, and the stones set into the wall were in evident danger. Horsley included the collection in his series of facsimile engravings, and very usefully rearranged both this and other collections according to the counties in which they had been found. But it was not until eighteen years after his book had appeared that the stones were established in a secure home. Sir Robert Cotton's books had been settled on the nation by Act of Parliament in 1700; but at Conington both the summer house and the main house were in poor condition; and in 1731, the year before Horsley's account was published, Sir John Cotton died. He was succeeded by his uncle, who had been educated at Trinity and who himself died in 1749 at an advanced age. His son survived him for only three years; but he was sufficiently in touch with antiquarian opinions and advice to make provision for what he had inherited. In the eighteenth century it was still believed that Sir Robert Cotton had been an undergraduate at Trinity – a long-lived misapprehension that was only to be corrected just in time for his entry in the *Dictionary of national biography*.[223] And so the College became, with the University of Glasgow, one of the earliest substantial university owners of Roman inscriptions in Britain.[224]

Of the importance of the Cotton collections, antiquaries had no doubt. Apart from Camden and Horsley, a further account of parts of the collection was included in John Warburton's *Vallum romanum* in 1753, and the College itself was to pay for the production of an engraving of the collection a little later. No part of the Library had ever been given such attention. Indeed, the pictorial representation of antiquities such as these, either as woodcuts or engravings, had for generations been much more common that that of manuscripts. No manuscript from the Library was to be reproduced until the Society of Antiquaries published the plan of Canterbury Cathedral priory and the portrait of Eadwine, both from the Eadwine Psalter (MS R.17.1), in 1755.[225]

The influence of the printing press in the publication and interpretation of such collections, and particularly the existence of a group of highly skilled reproductive engravers of copper-plates, became critical in the mid eighteenth century. Pictorially, the work of Horsley and Warburton provided a stimulus as well as offering in their engraved illustrations a means of reproducing antique artefacts. While the medieval manuscripts did not at first attract such attention, and Vertue's engravings of the Eadwine Psalter for the

222 Hearne, *Remarks and collections*, II, pp. 10–11.

223 In fact, he was at Jesus College.

224 For Glasgow, see John Anderson, *Monumenta Romani imperii, in Scotia ... iconibus expressa* (Glasgow, 1771) and David Murray, *Museums: their history and their use*, 3 vols. (Glasgow, 1904), 1, p. 160 and 2, p. 256. In 1759, Trinity paid the local artist P. S. Lamborn for drawing, engraving and printing two hundred copies of pictures of the Roman altars in the Library (Junior Bursar's accounts, 1758–9): a copy is preserved in MS Add.aa.7. This work may be added to J. M. Morris, 'A check-list of prints made at Cambridge by Peter Spendelowe Lamborn (1722–1774)', *TCBS* 3 (1962), pp. 259–312. The house at Conington was much altered after Sir John Cotton's death.

225 David McKitterick, 'The Eadwine Psalter rediscovered', in M. Gibson, T. A. Heslop and R. W. Pfaff (eds.), *The Eadwine Psalter: text, image and monastic culture in twelfth-century Canterbury* (1992), pp. 195–208, at pp. 202–3.

Society of Antiquaries offered a means to scholarship whose importance could not have been predicted, by the end of the eighteenth century, thanks to the work of Joseph Strutt and others, the manuscripts had been made known to a wider public than ever hitherto.[226] A similar course can be perceived in the history of guidebooks to the city, of which the first modern one to deal with Cambridge alone, *Cantabrigia depicta,* was published in 1763: it marked the beginning of a tradition that was to bloom by the end of the century and become ever more competitive with the advent of popular tourism – particularly in the wake of the new railways in the nineteenth century.

The course of illustrative traditions, and public scientific instruction, is nowhere more evident than in the illustrated volumes of travels and natural history that proliferated in the last decades of the eighteenth century. A combination of expert engraving and printing, with new attention to the recording of natural and ethnographic curiosities by often specially commissioned draughtsmen, and a new emphasis on the importance of bringing back plants and artefacts to Europe in recognisable condition, stimulated and maintained levels of public interest that found their most widespread expression in the print trade and in public or private museums.

For Trinity, artefact and image had combined in the publication of Cotton's Roman inscriptions and in the large plates accompanying John Taylor's account of the Sandwich marble. Vertue's engraving of the plan of the waterworks at Canterbury Cathedral, taken from the Eadwine Psalter, was similarly archaeological in purpose. But none of these was to have the extraordinary appeal of the voyages and discoveries of Captain Cook, which seized the popular imagination in pictures, poetry, fiction and the stage. The collections from the voyage of the *Endeavour,* which proved to be the other major curiosity in the Library, apart from books, were never the subject of such detailed pictorial publication as some of the archaeological remains in the Library. But many of the same considerations arose as the public, either in London or Cambridge, contemplated the fruits of this and Cook's subsequent voyages. The achievements of the first voyage were made vivid by the engravings included in Hawkesworth's account of voyages to the South Seas, published in 1773, and even more so in John Webber's evocative drawings published as an elephant folio of engravings to accompany Cook and King's account of their voyages in 1776–80.

In 1771, Captain Cook sailed home to fame, promotion, and presentation at court. His voyage in the *Endeavour* had taken him to Tahiti, the Society

226 A. N. L. Munby, *Connoisseurs and medieval miniatures, 1750–1850* (Oxford, 1972), pp. 26–30; for pictorial developments in other disciplines, see Francis Haskell, *The painful birth of the art book* (1987) and *History and its images: art and the interpretation of the past* (1993).

227 *The journals of Captain James Cook on his voyages of discovery: The voyage of the Endeavour, 1768–1771*, ed. J.C. Beaglehole (Hakluyt Society, 1955, repr. with corrections and addenda 1968).

228 Bernard Smith, *European vision and the south Pacific, 1768–1850: a study in the history of art and ideas* (Oxford, 1960; 2nd edn, New Haven, 1985); see also, in a large literature, A. M. Lysaght, 'Banks's artists and his *Endeavour* collections', *British Museum Yearbook* 3 (1979), pp. 9–80, Rüdiger Jopien, 'Philippe Jacques de Loutherbourg's pantomine "Omai, or a trip round the world" and the artists of Captain Cook's voyages', *ibid.*, pp. 81–136, and D. J. Carr (ed.), *Sydney Parkinson: artist of Cook's* Endeavour *voyage* (1983).

229 *Journals of Captain Cook ...1768–1771*, ed. Beaglehole, p. 638. These and the collections acquired on subsequent voyages have proved difficult, and often impossible, to disentangle. See, in particular, Adrienne Kaeppler, *'Artificial curiosities': an exposition of native manufactures collected on the three Pacific voyages of Captain James Cook, R.N.*, Bishop Museum Special Pubns 65 (Honolulu, 1978), which includes photographs of several items from the Trinity collection; Adrienne Kaeppler, 'Tracing the history of Hawaiian Cook voyage artefacts in the Museum of Mankind', *British Museum Yearbook* 3 (1979), pp. 167–97; Wilfred Shawcross, 'The Cambridge University collection of Maori artefacts, made on Captain Cook's first voyage', *Journal of the Polynesian Soc.* 79 (1970), pp. 305–48; Peter Gathercole, 'The Maori collection at the Cambridge University Museum of Archaeology and Anthropology', in *Taonga Maori conference, November 1990* (Dept of Internal Affairs, New Zealand, n.d.), pp. 80–5.

230 Green's list (evidently derived from a larger one, retained in the Admiralty or by Sandwich) is now MS Add.a.106, ff. 108r–109v. An early exhibition label, attributing a gift of quiver and arrows to Cook himself, survives in MS o.11a.4(8).

Islands, the circumnavigation of New Zealand, and the east coast of Australia from New South Wales northwards.[227] Within three years, western Europe was to be intoxicated by illustrated accounts of his voyage, by Hawkesworth, Parkinson and others. Thanks to newspapers, magazines and the book trade, the voyage was celebrated on an unprecedented scale. It provided a heady patriotic mixture of scientific observation, traveller's tales, accounts of remote civilisations, and discovery of lands that sounded all too inviting. But Cook, Banks and Solander had also brought back material evidence, in their botanical, zoological and ethnographic collections assembled during the course of the voyage. On the conclusion of the voyage, this passed to the Admiralty, and so into the control of the Earl of Sandwich, as First Lord. The British Museum was an early beneficiary, and Sandwich also seems to have retained some examples for himself. The illustrations in the various accounts of this and subsequent voyages, and the eventual special public display in the Museum, fuelled popular and artistic excitement, as well as literary inspiration.[228] Cambridge now found itself in the van. Sandwich, who had entered Trinity in 1735, presented an important part of Cook's material to the College Library in October 1771 – only two months after Cook had transmitted what he termed 'the bulk of the Curiosity's' to the Admiralty.[229] Though it was but the latest of Sandwich's gifts to his college, for many it was easily the most spectacular. It retained its popular interest long into the nineteenth century. In scale, it may even have been comparable with the selection that went to the British Museum itself. In importance, it has proved to be unique, since (unlike the collections from Cook's several voyages which passed to the British Museum) it never became confused with trophies and specimens collected on the subsequent voyages. Those who had taken part in Cook's voyage had been struck by the discovery of civilisations wholly unacquainted with metals, and this remained a feature of especial curiosity to those who viewed the artefacts on their return. With the help apparently of an accompanying inventory, the ninety items that now arrived at Trinity were duly recorded by the Librarian, Thomas Green, with details of their geographical origins. They included tools, bark cloth, personal ornaments and musical instruments (including a nose flute) from Tahiti and paddles, household equipment, clothes, ornaments and weapons from New Zealand, as well as a smaller group from Tierra del Fuego and a pike and a fish gig, or spear, from New South Wales.[230] In all this, there was a deliberate attempt to provide the

College with a specimen collection, one deliberately selected for the sake of its representative qualities.

The effect of these accessions was inescapable. For the College, the Wren was its library. For the public who came to visit, it was as much, if not more, a museum. The foundation of the British Museum in 1753, and its conjunction of books, manuscripts, antiquities, artefacts and natural history, created the most obvious place in the country where the search for knowledge ignored the bounds otherwise set to disciplines. There, the exhibits from the South Seas proved to be an especial attraction, albeit one marred for many years by the difficulties in visiting the Museum thanks to strict limits on the numbers of visitors and to the unwelcoming and unhelpful attitude of those responsible for showing round the unavoidable guided parties.[231] In Cambridge, as in most places until the mid nineteenth century, there was no museum. Until the arrival of Edward Daniel Clarke's marbles from the Mediterranean in 1803, and their display in the vestibule of the University Library, there was no public display of classical sculpture in the town.[232] Only in 1821, with the bequest to St John's by the antiquary Thomas Dunham Whitaker of a group of pieces from Ribchester, in Lancashire, were there any other inscriptions to be found from Roman Britain. In the fine arts, the Fitzwilliam Museum was founded by private benefaction in 1816, and had no suitable building until 1848: it quickly attracted the collection of classical sculpture assembled by Thomas Hollis and his friend Thomas Brand Hollis in the mid eighteenth century and presented to the Museum by John Disney.[233] The University Museum of Zoology was founded in 1864, and the Museum of Archaeology and Ethnology in 1882. With its exhibits from Roman Britain, from the eastern Mediterranean and from the South Seas, as well as its coins, its portraits and its sculpture, the Wren Library served as a museum of some significance until the early twentieth century.[234] In the eighteenth century, the importance of its collections in a national context was emphasised by publication; by Sir John Cotton's decision to present his ancestor's collection of inscriptions and sculpture only a few months before the Cotton manuscripts became part of the new British Museum; and by the repeated generosity of the Earl of Sandwich.

By the second half of the nineteenth century, such acquisitions had become a principal part of visitors' experiences of the Library, to be viewed with the manuscripts and printed books. Laid out in a series of small display cases, hanging from the bookcases, protected under glass domes, or simply

231 Edward Edwards, *Lives of the founders of the British Museum, 1570–1870*, 2 vols. (1870), 1, pp. 323–4, 336–41.

232 E. D. Clarke, *Greek marbles brought from the shores of the Euxine, Archipelago, and Mediterranean* (Cambridge, 1809); McKitterick, *Cambridge University Library*, pp. 362–70.

233 Adolf Michaelis, *Ancient marbles in Great Britain* (Cambridge, 1882), pp. 69, 241–68; L. Budde and R. Nicholls, *A catalogue of the Greek and Roman sculpture in the Fitzwilliam Museum, Cambridge* (Cambridge, 1964); W. H. Bond, *Thomas Hollis of Lincoln's Inn: a Whig and his books* (Cambridge, 1990). The Cotton collection was deposited on indefinite loan in the Museum of Archaeology and Anthropology in 1969.

234 The items from the Cook collection transferred to the Museum of Archaeology in 1914 are listed in *Cambridge University Reporter* (1914–15), pp. 1177, 1190.

set out on top of the dwarf bookcases introduced to accommodate the ever-increasing numbers of books, they formed one of the most remarkable tourist sights in the University. What had been accepted for its scientific or historical importance in the eighteenth century, and had often been put to serious use, was soon to be dismissed as out-dated. Yet many of these curiosities, specimens and instruments had been exhibited for at least a century. In 1790, a local guidebook, having remarked the artefacts brought back from the South Seas, went on to list other memorabilia:

> There is also a dried human body of one of the original inhabitants of the Madeiras; a curious Chinese pagod, a lock of sir Isaac Newton's hair, head of Newton in wax, an universal ring dial, quadrant and compass of sir Isaac Newton's; a large lizard, the greatest in the kingdom; a quiver of arrows fought with by king Richard the III. against Henry VII. at the memorable battle of Bosworth; a curious skeleton of a man in miniature, cut out by a shepherd's boy; a stone taken from the wife of a locksmith at St. Edmund's Bury after her death; it weighs 33 oz. 3 gr. troy. There appears to be at least half an ounce taken off, which was done before king Charles II at Newmarket, to shew him it was formed in the manner animal stones usually are; a copy of king John's great charter; a copy of a letter of indulgence from pope Clement XII ...[235]

As most of these guides to Cambridge, like their counterparts elsewhere, drew heavily and often verbatim from each other, they are not altogether reliable reflections of the position at any one time. None the less, the series of local guidebooks produced from 1748 onwards claimed to offer a view of the Library, like the rest of the University and town, such as the tourist might expect to see.[236] So, with the eyes of each generation of tourists, we may follow the arrival and subsequent display of the mummy and the ibis presented by the Earl of Sandwich (mentioned in a guidebook of 1748), Sir John Cotton's inscriptions and Roman sculpture (described in 1763), Sandwich's further gifts, following Cook's explorations, and the marble inscription from Athens, given by the Countess of Bute in 1766 (described in 1776), the mummified body from Madeira (described in 1784), and the antique effigy, said to be of Aesculapius, found near Rome and presented by the distinguished army doctor Sir Clifton Winteringham (described in 1796). Inevitably, tourism brought changes. The longstanding convention that visitors usually depended

235 *A concise and accurate description of the University, town and county of Cambridge* (Cambridge [1790]), p. 90.
236 The earliest such guide is Thomas Salmon, *The foreigner's companion through the Universities of Cambridge and Oxford* (1748).

on the courtesy of the Librarian or a Fellow to inspect the Library could not cope with large numbers, and in 1829 *The Cambridge guide* remarked that someone was in attendance every day except Sundays to show the collections to visitors.[237]

Since no provision had originally been made in the Library for the exhibition of such miscellaneous collections, they had to be fitted into whatever available space could be found. The Cotton and other marbles were straightforward, and formed a coherent group on the ground floor in the vestibule, where the plain walls provided an agreeable background. Other exhibits began to litter the bays that had been designed for readers. But the ethnographic specimens were for many years stored in one of the lock-up studies that Wren had designed for manuscripts.

In one crucial respect, however, these guidebooks are most remarkable for what they do not describe. If they are to be believed, by the second half of the eighteenth century manuscripts and early printed books seem to have been of less account than sculpture, portraits and other curiosities. It had not always been thus. Before the century turned away from manuscripts, John Chamberlayne's much-reprinted *Magnae Britanniae notitia; or, the present state of Great Britain* had remarked three manuscripts in particular: Origen in Greek, the eighth-century copy of the Epistles from Durham (supposed, erroneously, to be in Bede's own handwriting), and the twelfth-century Eadwine Psalter ('the most valuable Latin Psalter in England'), the last two given by Thomas Nevile.[238] In 1803, more than half a century of uninterest was broken, with a brief account of the manuscript of Milton's poems.[239] For years it was to remain the only manuscript of which any particulars were given; it may be surmised that it was, indeed, the only book usually produced for display. When in 1840 a new glass-topped showcase was made for it, there is every reason to assume that this was its first.[240] By the end of the nineteenth century it had been so much handled that parts had been worn or broken away.[241] In comparison, the medieval manuscripts seem to have escaped lightly – further evidence that they did not form a regular part of exhibitions to merely casual visitors.

All this made for an untidy arrangement; but it had about it an air almost of domesticity that some clearly viewed with affection. In 1858, the College decided to dispose of some of the anatomical exhibits, as Joseph Romilly, Fellow and University Registrary, recorded in his diary;

237 Further details of opening times are provided for this period in *A new guide to the University and town of Cambridge* (Cambridge, 1831), p. 129: from 10 a.m. to 3 p.m. in the summer quarters, and from 11 a.m. to 3 p.m. in the winter. With the opening of the railway from London to Cambridge in July 1845, Cambridge was brought within easy reach of large numbers of day trippers: the first special excursion train ran on 1 September that year. See Joseph Romilly, *Romilly's Cambridge diary, 1842–1847*, ed. M. Bury and J. Pickles Cambridgeshire Records Society, (1994), pp. 139–40, 142.
238 John Chamberlayne, *Magnae Britanniae notitia: or, the present state of Great Britain*, 27th edn (1726), p. 290.
239 *A guide through the University of Cambridge*, new edn (Cambridge [1803], p. 98.
240 The case was made by Joseph Wentworth, who also made the new bookcases designed by Cockerell. TC Mun., box 30, no. 13.
241 W. Aldis Wright, *Facsimile of Milton's minor poems preserved in the library of Trinity College, Cambridge* (Cambridge, 1899).

We voted that the skeleton man and monkey & certain snakes in bottles &c &c should be given to the Anatomical Museum: (– Clark wd have liked our Mummies also, but we would not part with them) – So now we shall lose one of our sights for visitors to the Library. – Still there will remain Newton's reflectg Telescope, with the standg joke to any Lady that in it she will se Venus, – & the ossified heart of a woman who jilted a fellow of a College. – The closet of 'the Man & Monkey' is wanted for a hand-washing place.[242]

242 13 February 1858. Cambridge University Library MS Add.6838.

45 Map of Cornwall, by John Norden, *c.*1604. MS 0.4.19. See p. 63.

ne tente od oignement uert. si deuez faire en ceste cure
si cū deuant dit ē teske ala fin. E metez la puldre q deuant
dit ē al genciues quant cancre ni est. ~~A dolur de den~~

A la dulur dedenz. E des genciues faites une qchun en
la funteinrele de rere en la char q est dereire lozaille.
E en ce metez un petit mu. E puis si pnez la semence jĥ
be que ē casSilago E de la pozere. E metez uelemēt sur les
charbons. El li maledī receue la fumee p un chanal qē
apele embottun ceo la zeume q la dulur merueilluse
ment deslie. E nient hors q sasuagist. ~~A bozbeletes ke aue~~

A s burblettes q auienent en la face ~~nunt en la face.~~

oster. pnez unces trois de miel u de latt. defiez unces
dous del uis de mal tre unce une. E ses choses metlez en
semble. El metez en la poin. E de tre croīsi e metez sur
lent fu boillir emetez ces puldzes ouec q rechoīt. tar
tan blanc. de seneue unce une de peiure. u de alum
zucre uelemēt unce demie. bozacis unces dous. del gros
encens. E del os de la seche uelemt unces dous. E ces mis
en puldze metez en tele liquoz. E longemt mouez en
semble emetez en un equant mestier serra eschaufez
le linsil oinguez. E quant les burblettes creuerunt

46 Roger of Salerno,
Chirurgia. c.1230–40.
MS 0.1.20. See p. 64.

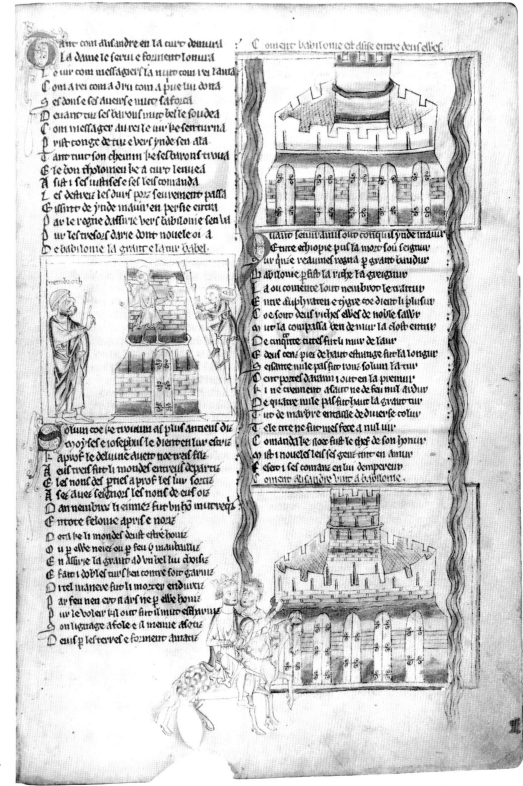

ЄΛΛΙΟC · ΚΑΙ ЄΠΙ ΤΟΝ ΙΗΛ ΤΟΥ ΚΥ ·
ΤΟΥ ΛΟΙΠΟΙ ΚΟΠΟΥC ΜΟΙ ΜΗΔΕΙC
ΠΑΡΕΧΕΤΩ · ЄΓΩ ΓΑΡ ΤΑCΤΙΓΜΑ
ΤΑ ΤΟΥ ΚΥ ΗΜΩΝ ΙΥ ΧΥ ЄΝ ΤΩ
CΩΜΑΤΙ ΜΟΥ ΒΑCΤΑ ΖΩ · Η ΧΑΡΙC
ΤΟΥ ΧΥ ΗΜΩΝ ΙΥ ΧΥ ΜΕΤΑ ΤΟΥ
ΠΝC ΥΜΩΝ ΑΔΕΛΦΟΙ · ΑΜΗΝ

ЄΤΕΛЄCΘΗ ЄΠΙCΤΟΛΗ
ΠΡΟC ΓΑΛΑΤΑC

ΑΡΧΕΙΑΙ ΠΡΟC
ЄΦЄCΙΟΥC

ΠΑΥΛΟC ΑΠΟCΤΟΛΟC
ΙΗΥ ΧΥ ·
ΔΙΑ ΘЄΛΗΜΑΤΟC ΘΥ ΤΟΙC ΑΓΙΟΙC
ΤΟΙC ΟΥCΙΝ ЄΝ ЄΦЄCΩ · ΚΑΙ ΠΙC
ΤΟΙC ЄΝ ΧΡΩ ΙΥ · ΧΑΡΙC ΥΜΙΝ ·
ΚΑΙ ΙΡΗΝΗ ΑΠΟ ΘΥ ΠΑΤΡΟC ΗΜΩΝ
ΚΑΙ ΚΥ ΙΥ ΧΥ · ЄΥΛΟΓΗΤΟC
Ο ΘC · ΚΑΙ ΠΑΤΗΡ ΤΟΥ ΚΥ ΗΜΩΝ
ΙΥ ΧΥ · Ο ЄΥΛΟΓΗCΑC · ΗΜΑC
ЄΝ ΠΑCΙ ЄΥΛΟΓΙΑ ΠΝЄΥΜΑΤΙΚΗ ·
ЄΝ ΤΟΙC ЄΠΟΥΡΑΝΙΟΙC · ЄΝ
ΧΩ · ΚΑΘΩC ЄΞЄΛЄΞΑΤΟ ΗΜΑC ·
ЄΑΥΤΩ ΠΡΟC ΚΑΤΑ ΒΟΛΗC · ΚΟC
ΜΟΥ ЄΙΝΑΙ ΗΜΑC ΑΓΙΟΥC · ΚΑΙ

misericordia · et super istrahel di
De cetero nemo mihi mo
lestus sit · Ego enim stigmata
ihu in
corpore meo posto · Gratia
dni nri ihu xpi cum
spiritu uro fratres · Amen ·

EXPLICIT EPISTOLA
AD GALATAS ·

INCIPIT AD
EFESIOS ·

PAULUS APOSTS
IHU XPI
per uoluntatem di scis
omnib; qui sephesi · & fideli
bus inxpo ihu · Gratia uobis
& pax a dø patre nostro
& dno ihu xpo · Benedictus
ds et pater dni nri
ihu xpi Qui benedixit nos
in omni benedictione spitali
in caelestib · in
xpo sicut elegit nos in
ipso ante mundi constitutio
nem ut essemus sci &

48 The Pauline Epistles in Greek and Latin, written at the monastery of Reichenau. Tenth century. MS B.17.1. See p. 70.

CATALOGUE

of a COLLECTION of SHAKESPERIANA;

comprehending

All the several Editions of the Works of Shakspeare,
old & new; divers rare old Editions of Writers, prior-
over & post-over; with a Number of other Articles,
chiefly such as tend to illustrate him;

made by his last Editor, E. C.;

and by him deposited in the Library of Trinity College
in Cambridge, this eleventh Day of June in the Year
1779.

A.

1.	Adam Bell, a Poem. n.d. 4° b.l.	Q.	14.
2.	Albion's England, D° 1602. 4°	R.	9.
3.	L'Alcionista, comedia di Loanbruolo. 1602. 12°	*.	14.
4.	Amendment of Orthography, Bullokar. 1580. 4° b.l.	Q.	10.
5.	Answer to Pr. Pope's Preface. 1729. 8°	S.	28.
6.	Apology for Actors, Heywood. 1612. 4°	S.	32.
7.	D° & d. d. D°	R.	18.
8.	Apology for Poetry.	S.	18
9.	Apuleius's golden Ass, by Adlington. 1596. 4° b.l.	I.	3.
10.	Arbor of amorous Devises, Poems. c. t. 4°	S.	8.

49   The opening of Edward Capell's catalogue of his collection of Shakespeariana. See p. 81.

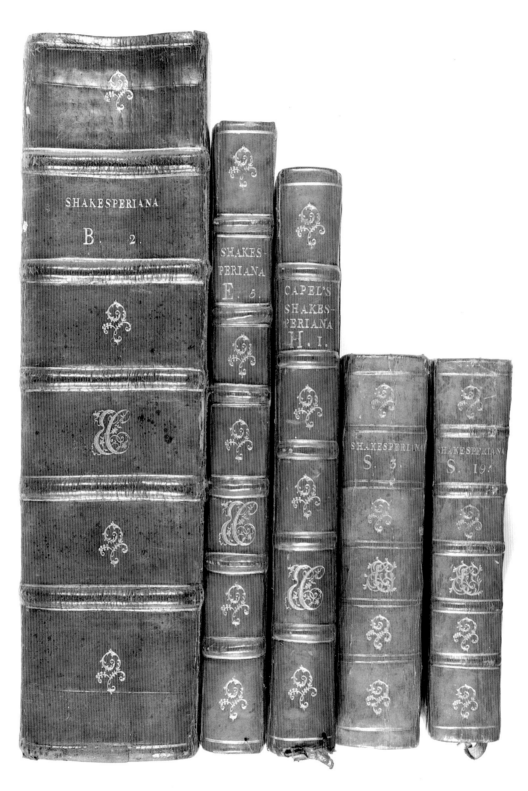

50 A group of books bound or repaired for Edward Capell. See p. 81.

51 The Trinity College carol roll, showing the Agincourt song 'Deo gracias Anglia'. East Anglia, first half of the fifteenth century. MS 0.3.58. See pp. 93–4.

CHAPTER FOUR

THE PORTRAIT SCULPTURE

Malcolm Baker

This chapter, which is based on research for a larger study of Roubiliac and sculptural portraiture in eighteenth-century England, draws considerably on earlier work by Dr Robert Robson and Professor David Bindman, who has generously allowed me to make use of his unpublished paper given at the Mellon Centre for Studies in British Art in 1981. I am also grateful to David McKitterick for his advice and encouragement and for the comments of Kathleen Adler, Craig Clunas, Aileen Dawson, John Larson, Alan Morton, David Pearson, Margaret Rose, Charles Saumarez Smith, John Styles, Marjorie Trusted and Rowan Watson. I am indebted to the Trustees of the British Museum for permission to consult their Minute Books and to the archivists there for arranging for me to do this.

1 A. Cunningham, *The lives of the most eminent British painters, sculptors and architects*, 3 (1830), p. 57.
2 The Wren Library portraits are cited as the 'most spectacular surviving example' of library sculpture, for example, in D. Piper, *The image of the poet* (Oxford, 1982), pp. 52–3, and individual busts are discussed at length in the standard account of post-medieval English sculpture, M. Whinney (rev. J. Physick), *Sculpture in Britain 1530–1830* (Harmondsworth, 1988), pp. 221–4. The most detailed account is K. A. Esdaile, *Roubiliac's work at Trinity College Cambridge* (Cambridge, 1924); corrections and additions to this were made in K. A. Esdaile, *Louis François Roubiliac* (1928), pp. 98–103.

When Allan Cunningham commented in 1830 on the admiration shown by the sculptor Sir Francis Chantrey for the portrait busts of Louis François Roubiliac, the leading sculptor of mid-eighteenth-century England, he singled out for praise the 'far-famed specimens at Trinity College, Cambridge'.[1] By describing them as 'of surpassing beauty' and quoting Chantrey's comment that he knew 'of no works of that kind which may be safely compared to them', he was acknowledging the central place which that remarkable series of marbles lining the Library must have in any account of portrait sculpture in eighteenth-century England.[2]

While portrait busts had long been recognised as appropriate to the decoration of a library, the Wren Library and its sculpture would appear to be the classic English example of this conjunction. The formation of this apparently coherent ensemble was, however, more complex and ambiguous than might at first seem to have been the case. The history presented here of the portrait sculpture therefore involves not only the Library as a location where the College's institutional history was constructed visually but also the use throughout the College of various forms of portraiture, painted as well as sculptural, to define and articulate Trinity's intellectual affiliations and identity as these were being worked out in the eighteenth century. Neither the process of commissioning the busts nor their place was straightforward or stable, but involved the whims of individual patrons, the availability of appropriate models and a later reconfiguration of the College's iconography and history.

In its present state the Library's sculptural portraiture consists of both plaster and marble busts and the two statues of the Duke of Somerset and Byron. The plaster busts placed on the ends of the cases consist of thirteen ancient and thirteen modern authors, along with later portraits of Hooper and Porson, the latter added in the early nineteenth century. The marble busts comprise busts by Roubiliac of Ray and Willoughby, standing on marble plinths on either side of the door, the same sculptor's Bacon and Newton facing them at the far end on similar plinths, and nine further busts of former members of the College – six by Roubiliac, two by Peter Scheemakers and one by John Bacon – placed on wood plinths at the ends of the cases. Another bust by Scheemakers of Edward Wortley Montagu stands on a bracket at the foot of the stairs, and nineteenth-century marbles by Thomas Woolner and others have been moved elsewhere.

Although these busts are almost all of eighteenth-century date, decoration of the Library with figure sculpture was evidently envisaged by Wren. In the event this was largely confined to the exterior, where Ketton stone figures of Divinity, Law, Physic and Mathematics were executed by Caius Gabriel Cibber in 1681 and placed in a central position on the balustrade facing Nevile's Court (figs. 52–5). A payment to Cibber of £80 for these was recorded in the accounts of Robert Grumbold, Wren's master-mason. The other sculptural element on the exterior is the pediment relief in the central arch of Ptolemy II receiving the Greek translation of the scriptures in the library at Alexandria. While the choice of this subject may well have been prompted by a knowledge of the classical sources, it is conceivable that Wren or a member of the College was familiar with the representation of this event on the ceiling of the Vatican Library.[3] In its figure style this is closely comparable to the relief carved by Cibber for the base of the Monument erected to celebrate the rebuilding of the City of London following the Great Fire and is probably connected with a payment of £38 12s. 4d. made on 23 April 1679 to 'ye Carver in London for cutting ye middle-pees in ye Midl arch for ston and other things'.[4]

The intention that figure sculpture, as well as the decorative carving of foliage and heraldry, should form a significant part of the interior is evident from both Wren's detailed and highly finished section and elevation of the interior and a sketch for the bookcases (figs. 33 and 43). According to the drawings submitted to Trinity, he envisaged that the end of each case was to be surmounted by a standing male figure, approximately $3\frac{1}{2}$ feet high, placed on a square plinth of about 1 foot. Although their form in the sketch suggests that they may have been conceived as a series of classical authors or philosophers, Wren gives no details in his accompanying letter of any particular iconographical scheme, simply stating that the 'statues will be a noble ornament, they are supposed of plaister, there are Flemish artists that doe

3 For the Vatican scene see A. Masson, *Le Décor des bibliothèques du moyen âge à la révolution* (Geneva, 1972), p. 41.

4 Trinity College, MS 0.4.46; the connection between this payment and the relief is made in Royal Commission on Historical Monuments, *City of Cambridge*, 2 (1959), p. 235. Somewhat surprisingly, the first mention of the relief in the Cambridge guidebooks occurs only in 1790. Although the inclusion of such a feature would seem to contradict Wren's statement that he had 'given noe other Frontispeice to the middle other than Statues, according to auncient example because in this case I find any thing else impertinent, the Entrances being endwaies', there is no evidence to suggest that this is a later insertion.

them cheap'.[5] It was also apparently undecided at this stage who should supply them, although as represented in the drawing they resemble the angels carved a few years later by Grinling Gibbons for the great organ case at St Paul's, designed by Wren and Gibbons.[6] In the event no plaster figures of this type were apparently executed, but in 1691 or 1692 a payment of £200 was made to 'Mr Gibbons' for an unspecified number of 'Bustoes', along with 'the Duke of Somersets Statue Coats of Arms and Cifers'.[7] A further payment of £1 was made to 'Mr Gibbon's men who set up the Busto's'. These were probably the two wood busts – of Ben Jonson and Anacreon – that are among those still on the cases (figs. 56 and 57). Although it is possible that they were part of a larger group, the others of which were replaced by the existing plaster busts in the mid eighteenth century, it is more likely that they were simply the beginning of an uncompleted scheme.[8]

The marble statue of the Duke of Somerset mentioned in the account is the only other figure sculpture in the interior that dates from the opening of the Library (fig. 58). This was placed in the right hand of two niches flanking the south window, and the accounts for 1691–3 include payments to Matthew Fitch 'for Scaffolding and cutting the Niches' and to Grumbold for 'Stone and Work for the Niches' and for 'drawing up and placing the statue'.[9] No such niches were, however, originally planned by Wren in his designs. The inclusion of the statue was presumably prompted by the extent of Somerset's benefactions, although it may well have been commissioned only after Somerset's election as Chancellor in March 1689.[10] The way in which it is accommodated rather awkwardly within the niche, however, suggests that it may have been originally conceived for some other location. Freestanding statues were in a few cases placed in the centre of libraries (as the statue of Codrington was to be at All Souls), but, given the problems already encountered with the structural stability of the floor, it is unlikely that this was planned for the Somerset.[11] It is possible, however, that the statue was commissioned initially to stand at Petworth, where Gibbons was working for Somerset, though no documentary evidence has been found to support this. Whatever the intended location, the difficulty with which it seems to have been accommodated may be said to register the increasingly marginal position of Somerset within the University.[12]

Apart from the Somerset statue, the only figure sculptures within the Library to date from the seventeenth century are the two busts. On the basis

5 *Wren Society* 5 (1928), p. 33.

6 D. Green, *Grinling Gibbons: his Work as carver and statuary* (1964), pp. 95–7, ills. 135–8.

7 Trinity College, MS 0.4.46, accounts December 1690–March 1691/2.

8 No mention of busts is made by Celia Fiennes in her account of the Library, cited by G. Beard, *The Work of Grinling Gibbons* (1989), p. 36.

9 Trinity College, MS 0.4.46.

10 M. Whinney (*Grinling Gibbons in Cambridge* (Cambridge, 1948), p. 7) suggests that Mr Bathurst's delivery in 1689 to the Duke of Somerset of a letter from the College may have been connected with this.

11 Continental examples of statues of patrons within libraries include that of Karl VI in the Hofbibliothek, Vienna (for which see F. Matsche, 'Die Hofbibliothek in Wien als Denkmal kaiserliche Kulturpolitik', in C.-P. Warncke (ed.), *Ikonographie der Bibliotheken, Wolfenbütteler Schriften zur Geschichte des Buchwesens* 17 (Wiesbaden, 1992), pp. 223–4). For the Codrington statue see M. Baker, 'Sir Henry Cheere and the response to the rococo in English sculpture', in *The Rococo in England*, ed. C. Hind (London, 1986), pp. 145–6.

12 For Somerset's position see J. Gascoigne, *Cambridge in the age of the Enlightenment* (Cambridge, 1989), pp. 89–91.

of the surviving evidence, it would seem that the sculptural decoration of the Library, though envisaged early on, was only undertaken on any considerable scale in the mid eighteenth century. Before examining the various busts acquired by the College at this period and the circumstances in which they were commissioned, it is necessary to look at the tradition of decorating libraries with sculpture and the way in which this had developed in eighteenth-century England.

When Wren was formulating his scheme for the library at Trinity College, both painted and sculptural portraits had already been long recognised as an established component of library furnishing. Portraits of dead and living writers and scholars had formed two of the categories of famous men represented in the celebrated collection gathered together by Giovio at Como.[13] Here these subjects were not placed in a library, but formed part of a far more extensive series of great men worthy of emulation. Like the many series of portraits of rulers, providing a visual representation of continuity through lineage, such groups of 'worthies' were to be found in many public spaces during the sixteenth and seventeenth centuries. However, as Justus Lipsius had already recognised in 1602, representations of authors were obviously particularly relevant in the setting of a library.[14] Gathering together the references made by classical authors to portraits in libraries, Lipsius had regretted that the practice had not been adopted in modern times. Their use in this way was advocated again in two influential French publications about the formation and organisation of libraries: Gabriel Naudé's *Advis pour dresser une bibliothèque* (1627) and Claude Clément's *Musei sive bibliothecae ... extructio ...* (1635).

According to Naudé, who cited antique precedents in Pliny and Suetonius of libraries decorated with 'likely statues of all the gallant men', it was desirable to include

good Copies drawn from such are as are most famous in the profession of Letters; that thereby a man may at once make judgement of the wit of authors by their Books, and by their bodies; figure, and physiognomy by these Pictures and Images, which joyn'd to the description which may have been made of their lives, may serve, in my opinion, as a puissant spurre to excite a generous and well-born Soul to follow their *track*, and to continue firm and stable in the wayes and beaten paths of some noble enterprise and resolution.[15]

13 For these early series of 'worthies' see F. Haskell, *History and its images* (New Haven and London, 1993), pp. 26–79, and E. Dwyer, 'André Thevet and Fulvio Orsini: the beginnings of the modern tradition of classical portrait iconography in France', *Art Bulletin* 75 (1993), pp. 467–80.
14 J. Lipsius, *De bibliothecis syntagma* (1602), cap. x. For Lipsius see G. Schmook, 'Justus Lipsius' "De Bibliothecis Syntagma"', *Handelingen van het Zesde Wetenschnappelijk Vlaamse Congres voor Boek- en Bibliotheekwezen Gent, 31 Maart 1940* (Antwerp, 1941), pp. 33–58.
15 This passage (p. 85) is quoted from John Evelyn's translation of 1661. The original reads: 'images et statues représentant au vif ... ceux qui ont esté les plus célèbres en la profession des lettres, pour juger en mesme temps de l'esprit des autheurs par leur livres et de leur corps, figure et physionomie ... pour exciter une âme généreuse et bien née à suivre leurs pistes'.

16 C. Clément, *Musei sive bibliothecae ... extructio ...* (1635).

17 As J. N. L. Myres has demonstrated (*Bodleian Library Record* (October 1950), pp. 82–90, (April 1952), pp. 30–51 and (October 1956), pp. 290–307, the scheme follows the list of authors in the *Chronologia scriptorum ecclesiasticorum* by Thomas James, Bodley's first librarian. For a detailed analysis of the Bodleian frieze, seen as 'the pictorial image of the Republic of Letters which Thomas Bodley wanted his library to serve', see M. R. A. Bullard, 'Talking Heads: the Bodleian frieze, its inspiration, sources, designer and significance', *Bodleian Library Record*, 14 (1994), pp. 461–500.

18 M. Grosley, *A Tour to London; or, New observations on England and its Inhabitants*, 1 (1772), p. 196. As the translator's preface states (p. x), Grosley had himself been involved in the commissioning of a set of worthies, having 'undertaken to embellish the saloon of the town-house of Troyes, with the marble busts of the illustrious natives of that city, executed by Mons. Vasse, the king's sculptor; who has already finished those of P. Pithou, P. le Comte, Passerat, Girardon, and Mignard'.

19 For Queen Caroline's Hermitage see J. Colton, 'Kent's Hermitage for Queen Caroline at Richmond', *Architectura* 2 (1974), pp. 181–90; for the library see H. M. Colvin *et al.*, *The history of the King's works*, 5 (1976), p. 242, pls. 30A and B.

20 M. Brownell, *Alexander Pope and the arts of Georgian England* (Oxford, 1978), pp. 333–4. For Pope's involvement in the ordering of busts from Roubiliac for his friend Ralph Allen, probably for the library at Prior Park, see also *The correspondence of Alexander Pope*, ed. G. Sherburn, 4 (Oxford, 1956), pp. 253, 353–4, 360. Another celebrated private library with busts was that of Dr Richard Mead, the interior of which was represented in the engraved frontispiece to M. Maty, *Authentic memoirs of the life of Richard Mead, M.D.* (1755); this is discussed in T. Friedman, *James Gibbs* (New Haven and London, 1984), p. 209.

Naudé does not give any detailed advice about the placing of busts, although perhaps Daniel Marot's design for a library showing them alternating with globes along the top of the presses may follow Naudé's thinking here. Clément, on the other hand, was rather more specific about their disposition, recommending that the 'bookcases ... are surmounted by statues of men distinguished in the discipline for which the bookcase is intended'.[16] This well-established tradition of using portraits of earlier authors could therefore be employed to articulate the relationship between ancient and modern authors, to represent a literary canon through images, and even to function as a visual key to the library's contents.

In England series of portraits were being prominently used in libraries by the early seventeenth century when Cotton's bookpresses were surmounted by busts of the Caesars, along with Faustina and Cleopatra. Far more extensive and more iconographically telling, however, was the series of 200 painted images of ancient authors, Church fathers, and modern writers and theologians that adorned the Bodleian.[17] But while painted images were relatively common from an early date, the incorporation of sculptural images on any scale occurred only in the eighteenth century. When Grosley visited England in 1765 he noted how many different types of interior, from 'the palaces of great noblemen' to the 'houses where people meet for public diversions', were 'adorned with figures painted and engraved, and with busts of all sizes, made of all sorts of materials, of Bacon, Shakespeare, Milton, Locke, Addison, Newton, and even Cromwell himself'.[18] But already by the 1730s ambitious series of historicising portrait busts were being employed in various locations. At Stowe the temple of British Worthies erected in accord with the Whig opposition politics of Lord Cobham juxtaposed busts of writers and philosophers, such as Newton, Bacon and Milton, with images of figures such as Queen Elizabeth, John Hampden and Sir John Barnard, who were seen as upholding English liberties in the active life of public affairs. In 1733 busts of Locke, Newton, Clarke, Boyle and Woolaston were carved for Queen Caroline's Hermitage at Richmond,[19] and two years later Rysbrack was commissioned to produce portraits of English monarchs that, according to William Kent's design, were to be placed on brackets between the arches of her new library. By the end of the decade Pope's library at Twickenham contained busts of Homer, Newton, Spenser, Dryden, Milton, Shakespeare, Inigo Jones and Palladio.[20] Sculptural portraits here took the place of the painted portraits of authors that were to be seen in many eighteenth-century libraries, among the most notable being those at Knole, Chesterfield House[21] or that of Lord Morton, in which the 'several faculties ... of science ... are represented by a basso-relievo in painting, which unites in several groupes the most eminent men in each faculty, both amongst the ancients and moderns'.[22]

By the mid eighteenth century sculptural portraits were becoming an increasingly prominent element within interiors, particularly libraries. It is therefore not surprising that they form an important part of those college libraries being fitted out in Oxford, Cambridge and Dublin at this period. The commissioning of the busts at Trinity was preceded by the production of extensive series of busts for two other major libraries, the Codrington Library at All Souls, Oxford (fig. 59), and the Long Room of the Old Library at Trinity College, Dublin (fig. 60). The Codrington interior had been finished in 1751, complete with a series of twenty-four plaster busts of former Fellows. These had been commissioned from John Cheere in January 1749/50 in accord with Gibbs's earlier advice to have only one gallery with its book-presses supporting 'a handsome pedestal ... for bustos, vases, or balls', and remain in their original positions.[23]

By this date most, if not all, of the marble busts were to be seen around the gallery of the Long Room in Dublin.[24] In 1743 a sum of £500 had been bequeathed by Dr Claudius Gilbert, the Vice-Provost, 'for the purchase of busts of men eminent for learning to adorn the library'. Some at least of these must have been in place by March 1749, when it was reported that Roubiliac's bust of Swift was 'to be placed in the College Library, among the heads of other men eminent for genius and learning'. Executed partly by Roubiliac and partly by Scheemakers, the thirteen marble busts acquired with Gilbert's bequest consisted of six ancients (Homer, Demosthenes, Socrates, Plato, Aristotle and Cicero), six moderns (Shakespeare, Milton, Bacon, Newton, Locke and Boyle) and two benefactors (Archbishop Usher and the 8th Earl of Pembroke). Unlike the All Souls series, the Dublin busts served not to illustrate the college's own past but rather to provide images that might, in Naudé's words, 'at once make judgement of the wit of authors by their Books, and by their bodies [and] ... excite a generous and well-born Soul to follow their *track*'.[25]

Although these two libraries provided the most extensive, as well as the most recently made, examples of library portrait sculpture when the Master

21 For Lord Chesterfield's library see D. Piper, 'The Chesterfield House library portraits', in R. Wellek and A. Ribiero (eds.), *Evidence in literary scholarship: essays in memory of James Marshall Osborn* (Oxford, 1979), pp. 179–95. The use of author portraits in libraries is discussed by D. Piper, 'The development of the British literary portrait up to Samuel Johnson', *Proceedings of the British Academy* 54, pp. 51–72.

22 Grosley, *A Tour to London*, I, pp. 197–8. As well as commenting that the 'hint of these several ornaments seems to have been suggested by the tombs of the ancients', Grosley lists the epic and dramatic poets, modern writers, historians and 'heroes of experimental philosophy'.

23 For the library's history see H. H. E. Craster, *The History of All Souls College Library*, ed. E. F. Jacob (1971), and J. S. G. Simmons, *A Note on the Codrington Library, All Souls College, Oxford* (Oxford, 1982); its place within the development of Oxford college libraries is discussed by J. Newman, 'Oxford libraries before 1800', *Archaeological Journal* 135 (1978), 248–57. Details of the commission given by Blackstone to Cheere are recorded in All Souls MS 401 (b), F. 180v, transcribed in T. Friedman and T. Clifford, *The man at Hyde Park Corner: sculpture by John Cheere 1709–1787* (Leeds, 1974), appendix B. Perhaps when referring to busts and balls Gibbs had in mind Marot's view with busts and globes.

24 The library and its portraits at Trinity College, Dublin are discussed by A. Crookshank, 'The Long Room', in *Treasures of the Library, Trinity College Dublin*, ed. P. Fox (Dublin, 1986), pp. 16–28. For fuller details of individual portraits see W. G. Strickland, *A descriptive catalogue of the pictures, busts and statues in Trinity College, Dublin and in the Provost's House* (Dublin, 1916), and A. Crookshank and D. Webb, *Paintings and sculptures in Trinity College, Dublin* (Dublin, 1990).

25   According to Horace Walpole (*Anecdotes of painting in England* (Strawberry Hill, 1765–71), 4, p. 99), Roubiliac owed the commission for 'half the busts at Trinity-college, Dublin' to a recommendation from Sir Edward Walpole. This reference was taken by Strickland and later writers as a confusion by Walpole of Trinity College, Dublin with Trinity College, Cambridge. Recent reconsideration of the series (M. Baker, 'The making of portrait busts in the mid eighteenth-century: Roubiliac, Scheemakers and Trinity College, Dublin', *Burlington Magazine* 137 (1995, forthcoming) has suggested that Walpole was correct in his attribution and that the busts of Aristotle, Plato, Socrates, Newton, Boyle and Bacon were executed by Roubiliac, possibly in collaboration with Scheemakers. The mention of Sir Edward Walpole, however, may have been a confusion of the Dublin commission with the Cambridge set, with which Sir Edward may indeed have been connected.

26   They appear in R. P. Claude du Molinet, *Le Cabinet de la Bibliothèque de Sainte-Geneviève* (Paris, 1692). For a discussion of the furnishing of this and other library interiors see P. Thornton, *Seventeenth-Century Interior Decoration in England and France* (New Haven and London, 1978), pp. 303–15.

27   For a rich and detailed account of the portraits in the Bibliothèque Sainte-Geneviève see A. Boinet, *Catalogue des œuvres d'art de la bibliothèque Sainte-Geneviève* (Paris, 1920; (reprint from *Mémoires de la Société de l'Histoire de Paris et d'Ile de France* 48 (1920); see also A. Boinet, 'Les Bustes de Coyzevox', *Gazette des Beaux-Arts*, 5e pér., 2 (1920), pp. 1–13, and 'Les Bustes de Caffiéri', *Gazette des Beaux-Arts*, 5e pér., 3 (1921), pp. 133–46.

28   Piganiol de la Force, *Description de Paris* (1765), 6, p. 92, cited by Masson, *Décor*, p. 144.

29   [Thomas] Salmon, *The foreigner's companion through the Universities of Cambridge and Oxford* (1748), p. 66; *Cantabrigia Depicta: a concise and accurate description of the University and Town of Cambridge* [1763], p. 85.

and Fellows of Trinity began to concern themselves with the provision of further busts for the Wren Library, the most impressive and possibly best-known series of library busts was to be found not in England or Ireland but in France. The Bibliothèque Sainte-Geneviève by the end of the seventeenth century contained no fewer than twenty-six busts, several of which are shown in engravings of 1692, placed on tapering plinths against the pilasters dividing the bookcases (fig. 61).[26] Although other French libraries were also decorated with busts, the Bibliothèque Sainte-Geneviève remained by far the most celebrated and widely known example, its collection of sculptural portraits growing steadily throughout the eighteenth century. Some of these were of ancients, others of the French royal house; but a considerable proportion were of relatively modern sitters. In some cases they were given by the sculptors – most notably those by Girardon and Caffieri – but many of this last category were donated by relatives or descendants of those commemorated.[27] The library thus became, according to Piganiol de la Force in 1765, 'une espèce de temple de mémoire où les parents et amis des hommes illustres en tout genres s'empressaient de déposer leurs portraits'.[28]

It was against this background that the Master, Robert Smith, began to supplement (or possibly replace) the wood busts produced earlier by Gibbons. The chronology and documentation of the busts is fragmentary, as only occasional references may be found in the Bursar's records to the setting of busts and no record survives of any gifts. A discussion of this renewed interest in the sculptural decoration of the interior should perhaps begin, however, with the plasters that were placed alongside the two wooden busts on top of the cases, so continuing an established arrangement. These were indeed set on what appear to be the square wooden plinths designed by Wren.

No mention is made of busts in the 1748 guidebook, and a letter from Elizabeth Montagu of July 1753, describing a plan to erect twenty-six busts, '13 in memory of the ancients 13 of the moderns ... to be cast in plaisters of Paris', indicates that they were at that date still not in place. However, they are unambiguously described in the edition of 1763. This repeats the account of the Library's interior from earlier guides but adds: 'The Tops of the Classes ... are adorned with beautiful Busts, on one side those of the most celebrated ancient Poets, Orators and Philosophers, and on the other the Moderns.'[29] Although no indication is given here about either sculptor or donor, information on the latter point is provided by the antiquarian William

Cole in a note he added to a passage transcribed from the *Cambridge Chronicle* for 1763 about the monument erected in the chapel to Dr Francis Hooper, the Vice-Master. According to Cole, the '*Doctor* gave in his Life Time many fine *Busts* in *Plaister of Paris* to be set on the *Classes* of the *College Library*'.[30]

The plasters given by Hooper were not individually modelled as new compositions but produced as multiples, the series consisting of subjects chosen from a range of such images available in different sizes from one of various 'plastermen' in mid-eighteenth-century London.[31] Rather than being new inventions by a single sculptor, they were cast from busts already executed by a variety of sculptors, albeit with various modifications. Those of Inigo Jones and John Locke, for example, were based on sculptures produced in the 1730s by Michael Rysbrack, which had already become established images, reproduced in various materials.[32] Similarly, the portrait of Dryden is based on Scheemakers' bust on the monument erected in Westminster Abbey by the Duchess of Buckingham in 1731.[33] The busts of classical authors were also in large part cast from a familiar repertoire of images. The Seneca, for example, was taken from a well-known head that had been erroneously identified with the Roman moralist in the sixteenth century and since then had become the standard image. However, not all these plasters were casts of conventional and long-established images, and a few at least may have been inventions of the eighteenth century, perhaps even by the 'plasterman' who supplied them. These include the Plato (fig. 62) among the ancients, and the Beaumont and Fletcher (fig. 63) among the moderns. Although the latter pair were based on two engraved author portraits that were reproduced together in numerous editions of their works, they are unfamiliar subjects as busts. Like the modifications made to the standard types, such as the addition of drapery around the truncation of the Inigo Jones, these perhaps represent the contribution of the 'plasterman' in his attempt to produce a full and consistent set of literary busts.

By far the best known and most successful of these 'plastermen' was John Cheere, who had produced the plaster busts for the Codrington Library and whose yard at Hyde Park Corner figured prominently in much contemporary satirical writing.[34] Cheere is certainly among the most likely suppliers of Hooper's busts, but he is not the only candidate. In 1747 there were evidently enough producers of such work for Thomas Campbell to devote a chapter to 'Those who work in Plaister of paris' in his *London Tradesman*. The possibility

30 This note was added by William Cole to a passage transcribed by him about Hooper's monument, discussed below (British Library, MS Add. 5834, f. 35r).

31 The subjects of the two sequences of plasters are listed in the appendix to this chapter.

32 For the marble version of the Jones executed for Lord Burlington, see M. Webb, *Michael Rysbrack sculptor* (1954), pp. 102–4; in the Trinity plaster this is modified, perhaps to harmonise with other busts, by the addition of a swathe of drapery around the truncation. The Locke is a version of the Rysbrack bust formerly in Queen Caroline's grotto, discussed above.

33 The documentation about the Dryden monument is assembled by I. Roscoe, 'Peter Scheemakers and classical sculpture in early eighteenth-century England', Ph.D. thesis, University of Leeds, 1990, p. 214.

34 For these references see Friedman and Clifford, *The man at Hyde Park Corner*, and M. Baker, 'Squabby Cupids and clumsy Graces: garden sculpture as luxury in eighteenth-century England', *Oxford Art Journal* 18 (forthcoming 1995).

of producing plaster multiples of author busts for private libraries had already been glimpsed by Lipsius in 1602, and by the early eighteenth century this market was being developed in England.[35] In 1736 the posthumous sale of the 'Eminent Statuary' Richard Dickenson included 'a great Number of Plaster Figures Bustoes etc of all sorts', and by 1741 one of Benjamin Rackstrow's advertisements was offering to 'all Lovers of their Country ... all sorts of bust, figures and Basso-Relievo's, either in Plaister or Metal, and ... several fine busts of the Ancient and Modern poets, Philosophers and Great Men'.[36]

Several of the Trinity plasters are known in versions that may be associated with John Cheere. The Addison (fig. 64), for example, is close to one of a series of smaller busts supplied by him for the Turner family at Kirkleatham and another plaster at Stourhead. The links between the Trinity examples and documented Cheeres (which are generally of a smaller size) may, however, be explained in terms of a common use of well-known originals. Furthermore, moulds for plasters of 'worthies' evidently circulated among different 'plastermen', and there are many points of connection between the Trinity plasters and busts produced in the late eighteenth century. Casts of Dryden, Milton and Locke corresponding closely in size and detail to the Trinity plasters but on socles of a type uncommon until the late eighteenth century are found at West Wycombe and Wimpole Hall – the latter being signed by P. Sarti of Dean Street – and all of the subjects in Hooper's set, including less common authors such as Beaumont and Fletcher and Sydenham, are indeed included, in various sizes, in the catalogue issued by Charles Harris, probably in the 1780s. Presumably the moulds used for the Trinity busts were taken over by these later suppliers, but it cannot be assumed that Cheere was the only possible source.

The Trinity plasters differ from busts documented as coming from Cheere's workshop in that they are set on square socles, conforming to the pattern employed earlier for the two wooden busts, rather than the distinctively shaped socles, with undulating fronts, characteristic of his productions. However, the inclusion among them of two particular images makes it very likely that they were supplied by him.[37] Firstly, the image of Sydenham – a rare figure in these plaster sets – corresponds closely to that among the plasters purchased from Cheere by All Souls. Secondly, a similarly large-size version of the Pope bust (figs. 65 and 66), adapted with many

35 Lipsius quoted Pliny's remarks about the novel practice of inventing imaginary likenesses for libraries (*Natural History* xxv. 2), adding 'Apellat *novitium, id est* Pollionis, *inventum*. ostendit mortuorum & è metallo plurimum fuisse: sed addo etiam è gypso, in privatis (pro cuiusque scilicet copia) Bibliothecis' (Lipsius, *De bibliothecis syntagma*, p. 30).

36 Dickenson's sale took place in 1736. For Rackstrow see R. Gunnis, *Dictionary of British sculptors* (1953), p. 314; for his trade card and scientific activities see A. Morton and J. Wess, *Public and private science* (Oxford, 1993), pp. 157–8.

37 Some recollection of the sources of the images as well as John Cheere's involvement may lie behind the confused reference in the 1790 guide to the Library having 'on the front of each class ... marble busts, by Roubiliac, Scheemakers, Sir Henry Cheere, &c. of the most celebrated ancient and modern poets, orators, philosophers etc.' (*A concise and accurate description of the University, town and county of Cambridge* (1790), p. 90).

modifications from Roubiliac's bust, is among the plasters once at Shardeloes, all of which are on typical Cheere socles.[38]

Enough sets of plaster busts of authors, set on library bookcases in the second half of the eighteenth century, survive to suggest that by this date they were not only being produced in considerable numbers but were made up of a relatively standard series of canonical authors.[39] Hooper's plasters, however, form one of the earliest and most extensive sets to survive. While they are not quite a standard, pre-determined group and some choice seems to have been exercised as to which authors were to be included, most of the subjects were familiar from other sculptural images, and the set might be seen as an illustration of the canon as it was formulated in mid-eighteenth-century Cambridge.

Although the marble busts by Roubiliac and Scheemakers, donated from 1751 onwards, also include some authors whose reputations might have been seen as equal to those represented on the cases above, the subjects here were chosen not as authors but as illustrious former members of the College (with two exceptions). What was being constructed here was not an illustrated canon but a visual history of the College's past. This, however, is to suggest a rather more coherent and carefully planned programme than the evidence can support.

Each bust is inscribed not only with the signature of the sculptor (on the bust itself) and the name of the sitter (on the socle) but also with the name of the donor and a date. The earliest portraits are those of Newton, Bacon, Willoughby and Ray, all by Roubiliac and dated 1751. Then follow five further busts by the same sculptor, those of Isaac Barrow and Richard Bentley dated 1756, and Baron Trevor, Lord Whitworth and Sir Robert Cotton dated 1757. Dating from the next year were busts of Roger Cotes and Robert Smith by Peter Scheemakers, who also executed the busts of James Jurin and Edward Wortley Montagu, both dated 1766. The latest eighteenth-century bust was John Bacon's portrait of the mathematician Anthony Shepherd, dated 1790 and bequeathed by the sitter in 1796, although he was not a member of the College.[40]

Although the abundance of inscriptions suggests that the chronology is clear, several pieces of documentary evidence about the process of commissioning raise questions about their various dates, the circumstances in which they were conceived and the settings for which they were intended. As Esdaile recognised, the guiding hand behind the acquisition of all these sculptures

38 For the Shardeloes busts (now at Aston Hall, Birmingham) and the Pope in particular see W. K. Wimsatt, *The portraits of Alexander Pope* (New Haven and London, 1963), pp. 255–7.

39 As well as the set from Kirkleatham, these include groups at Arniston, Temple Newsam, and Lamport Hall, for which see Friedman and Clifford, *The man at Hyde Park Corner*, p. 14. A less conventional set is placed within niches in Wyatt's library at Belton. Libraries, of course, were not the only location for such plasters, the stair and the hall being decorated with them.

40 For details of these inscriptions see the appendix to this chapter.

was the Master, Robert Smith, who was himself responsible for the commissioning and gift of Roubiliac's statue of Newton in the Chapel.[41] Smith's role and his plans for the decoration of the Library are vividly described in a letter of 25 July 1753 from Elizabeth Montagu to her husband, mentioning her conversation with the Master earlier that day:

> we then fell into discourse upon some embellishments and ornaments to be added to the fine library at Trinity College, there are to be 26 busts put up, 13 in memory of the ancients 13 of moderns. These are to be cast in plaister of Paris, but Mrs. Middleton talks of a fine Marble Busto of Dr. Middleton to be done by Roubilliac, which I think very proper as he was so eminent, there should be a public memorial of him, and as he was long [University] Librarian it is proper it should be in that place: there are to be likewise 48 portraits of considerable persons that have been of the College. I think Dr Smith is very right in all this, so fine a Temple of the Muses should be adorned with all the arts of the ingenious as well as the studious nine especially in an age that honors the polite arts more than severe science.[42]

From this it would seem that at the beginning of 1753 the plaster busts donated by Hooper, presumably prompted by Smith, were expected but had not yet arrived. Roubiliac was already involved, though not apparently on any of the busts mentioned above but in discussions about a bust of Conyers Middleton which was never in fact executed. No mention is made of other busts, and it is unclear whether the forty-eight 'portraits' of 'considerable persons' were painted or sculptural images. The way in which they are here apparently considered distinct from the 'bustoes' perhaps suggests that Smith had in mind a large series of relatively modest painted portraits rather than busts.

A number of painted portraits had already been introduced into the Library since its completion, Gibson's portrait of Sir Henry Puckering being purchased in 1702 (fig. 4) and that of Roger Gale being acquired in 1740.[43] During the next two decades there was to be an intensive development of the College's iconography, largely no doubt through Smith's successful attempts to persuade former members or friends of the College to commission or donate portraits of illustrious past members. Following Edmund Garforth's

41 Esdaile, *Louis François Roubiliac*, pp. 99–103.

42 Quoted by R. Blunt, *Times Literary Supplement*, 26 February 1925. See also E. J. Climenson. *Elizabeth Montagu the Queen of the Blue-stockings* (1906), pp. 35–6; a later letter (1756) reports that Dr Smith 'is much pleased with your present of Dr Barrow's bust to the Library' (p. 91). Although no bust of Conyers Middleton was produced, two versions of a 'medal of Dr Middleton' were included in Roubiliac's posthumous sale (12–15 May 1762, 1st day, lot 67, 2nd day, lot 27), and J. Mallet ('Some portrait medallions by Roubiliac', *Burlington Magazine* 104 (1962), pp. 153–8) has convincingly linked these with a bronze relief at present on loan to the Victoria and Albert Museum.

43 The Junior Bursar's accounts record payments of £21 10s. 0d. (with £4 for the frame) being made to Gibson for Puckering's picture in 1702. The Senior Bursar's accounts included a payment of £18 18s. 0d. to 'Dr Knight fr Bp Pearson's & Mr Gale's pictures' in 1740.

gift of Thomas Hudson's Bentley in 1749 and Sir Peter Burrel's donation of a half-length of Bacon in 1751, portraits of Newton, Bacon, Barrow, Cowley, Ray and Battely, were given in 1752, Dryden in 1753, Radcliffe in 1761 and Newton in 1766.[44] The donation of the marble busts, each from a different patron, but executed mainly by Roubiliac, was evidently part of a grander campaign by Smith that extended beyond the adornment of the Library.

It is possible that Smith was initially thinking in terms of painted portraits for the members of the College and sculpture only for the images of ancient and modern authors. This would be consistent with the sense of Mrs Montagu's letter but would seem to contradict the date of 1751 inscribed on four of the busts. The way in which they are inscribed, however, is not wholly consistent. Those of Newton (fig. 67) and Bacon (fig. 68) have their socles inscribed with the name of the donor, Daniel Lock, and the date 1751, while the signature of each of the two busts is followed by the '1751' too. Despite the fact that Mrs Montagu does not mention them, there is little reason to doubt that they were carved and given in that year. The portraits of Ray (fig. 69) and Willoughby (fig. 70) likewise have the date 1751 and the name of the donor, Edmund Garforth, on the socle, but the busts proper have a signature without date (fig. 71). Roubiliac seems to have been paid by Garforth only in June 1756, and a reference in the Minutes of the Trustees of the British Museum suggests that the bust of Ray at least had not been executed as late as January 1755. On 17 January leave was 'given to Mr Roubilliac at the request of the Revd Dr Smith, Master of Trinity College in Cambridge, to make a Draught from the picture of Mr John Ray [now in the National Portrait Gallery] ... in Order for the making of a Busto of him to be placed in the said College' (fig. 72).[45] The date so prominently recorded on the socles here would therefore appear to be the date when Garforth agreed to make his gift rather than the date when they were produced.

This may also have been the case with the bust of Edward Coke. In a letter of 1757 Richard Walker, the Vice-Master, asked Lord Leicester to donate to the College a bust of Lord Chief Justice Coke, adding:

Mr Roubilliac, our Sculptor, has lately made several Busts for us, is now at work upon more, and knows the size and situation, if your Lordship pleases to grant us this favour, we could send up to London the picture you gave us some years agoe for him to work by.[46]

44 These examples are taken from the list of paintings and sculpture in the guidebook of 1803.

45 Payment of £108 10s.10d. by 'Garforth's bill on Hoare' is recorded in Roubiliac's bank account at Drummond's Bank for 27 June 1756. (I am grateful to Dr Tessa Murdoch for kindly allowing me access to her copy of the account.) The granting of permission to Roubiliac to copy the Ray portrait is recorded in British Museum, Minutes of the Trustees General Meeting, vol. I, 17 January 1755. (I am grateful to Dr R. Robson for this reference.) The disparity in date between that on the plinth and the reference in the British Museum Minutes is discussed by A. Sherbo, 'Some early readers in the British Museum', *Transactions of the Cambridge Bibliographical Society* 6 (1972), p. 63 (kindly brought to my attention by Nigel Ramsay).

46 Letter of Richard Walker to the Earl of Leicester, Holkham House, cited by Esdaile, *Louis François Roubiliac*, p. VI.

It is probable that such a bust would have taken more than a year to produce; the marble of Sir Mark Pleydell, for example, had been commissioned by May 1755, when Pleydell sat, but was not delivered until February of the following year.[47] The date of 1757 on the socle of the Coke bust, with the signature unaccompanied by a date on the bust itself, would again appear to record the date of gift rather than of execution. The act of donation was what had to be recorded publicly and prominently rather than the act of making, and there might well be a significant disparity between the two. Although the first two of the Roubiliac busts were probably produced in 1751, some of the others may have been made rather later than the dates inscribed on them, and this has to be taken into account in any attempt to track the progress of the project.

As the documentary evidence quoted above makes clear, the commissioning of each of these busts involved a three-way transaction between Smith (or the Vice-Master Dr Richard Walker) on the part of the College, the donor and the sculptor. Smith evidently had clear views as to who might be represented in the College's portraits, and, as we shall see, his own intellectual and academic concerns were articulated through some of the commissioned portraits as well as his own donations and bequests. The combination of busts that were in the end executed was, however, determined by those who were persuaded to become donors. While all those represented were illustrious figures, the inclusion of many of them probably owed as much to family *pietas* as any grand iconographical scheme.

Although the connection of donors, sitters and the College is often clear, this is not so in all cases. The donor of Newton and Bacon, Daniel Lock, a scholar at Trinity in 1702, remains an obscure figure, despite the fact that he was commemorated in the Ante-Chapel by a monument by Roubiliac, on which he is described as being a lover of all the arts and shown surrounded by attributes showing his interests as a virtuoso.[48] His portrait by Hogarth (priv. coll., New York: fig. 75) shows him holding the plan of a house, and he is known from other sources as a successful architect.[49] Since he died intestate there is no will to provide evidence about his connections, although the William Lock named in the probate document may possibly have been the connoisseur and collector William Lock of Norbury.[50] More information is available about Edmund Garforth, who gave the Willoughby and Ray, as well as the portrait of Bentley in 1749. As Edmund Dring – he later changed his name to inherit from a Garforth relation – he had been admitted to Trinity

47 For the Pleydell bust see the catalogue entry in *Rococo* (Victoria and Albert Museum exhibition) (1984), p. 301, S33, and Baker, 'Squabby Cupids'.

48 For the monument see D. Bindman and M. Baker, *Roubiliac and eighteenth-century monument; sculpture as theatre* (New Haven and London, 1995), cat. no. 33. The statement by Esdaile (*Roubiliac's work*, p. 37) that Lock was an FRS is without foundation.

49 For the portrait see R. Paulson, *Hogarth* (1993), 3, pp. 291 and 503, although the suggestion here that he founded Lock's hospital is apparently erroneous. The evidence for his architectural activities is given in H. M. Colvin, *A biographical dictionary of British architects* (1978), p. 523.

50 Details of Lock's probate are in PRO Prob. 6/130 f. 113v; administration of his estate was granted to his brother William Lock. For William Lock of Norbury and his collecting activities see C. Avery, 'Bernardo Vechietti and the wax models of Giambologna', *Atti del I Congresso Internazionale sulla Ceroplastica nella Scienza e nell'Arte*, Florence, 1975 (Florence, 1977), pp. 461–76.

51 Cotton had been a member of Jesus College, rather than Trinity, although in early accounts he was confused with another Robert Cotton and so assumed to have been an undergraduate at Trinity. For the exhibition of Cotton's Roman stones at the foot of the Library staircase see pp. 101–2.

52 For Folkes's bust see *Rococo*, cat. no. 511. Folkes was linked with the St Martin's Lane circle as well as the Earl of Pembroke and others involved with the Royal Society. For the importance of the Royal Society in providing Roubiliac with a network of patrons early in his career see Bindman and Baker, *Roubiliac*.

53 Smith's bequests to Walpole are recorded in his will made on 6 May 1766 and a codicil of 8 August 1767 (PRO Prob. 11/938 ff. 323r–324v).

54 See n. 25 above.

55 This description was transcribed by William Cole (British Library, MS Add. 5834, f. 35r). Roubiliac's bank account at Drummond's Bank records payments of £63 on 15 September 1758 ('Hooper's bill on laidler') and £22 10s. od. on 27 November (Hooper's bill on Child). (I am grateful to Dr Tessa Murdoch for allowing me access to her copy of the account.) Seeing the monument itself in 1768, Cole commented that the 'Back part … is a pyramidal flat Stone of white Marble: had it been of black marble it would have shewn the bust to greater Perfection, which is very like the Original'.

as an undergraduate in 1720, with Smith as his tutor. Having been made a Fellow in 1726, he later moved to a living in York, where in 1750 he married Elizabeth Willoughby, a descendant of the naturalist. The choice of Willoughby and his associate Ray as subjects was presumably occasioned by this recent marriage, even if it also reflected Smith's interests and Garforth's own loyalty to the College. In several cases a bust was given by a direct descendant of the next generation – daughters in the case of both Bentley and Trevor, a nephew in Whitworth's – but the portraits of Cotton and Barrow were given by benefactors who had no family connection.[51]

During the 1750s the relationship between Roubiliac and the College must have been close, as is suggested by Walker's reference to 'Roubiliac our sculptor' in his 1757 letter to Leicester. How Roubiliac came to be chosen is unknown. It is conceivable that he became known to Smith through Martin Folkes, the President of the Royal Society, whose bust the sculptor executed in 1747,[52] but the link was perhaps more likely to have been made through Smith's 'worthy and honoured friend' Sir Edward Walpole, to whom the Master left a ring and £2,000 of stock.[53] Sir Edward Walpole is indeed named in Horace Walpole's account of Roubiliac as the person responsible for recommending the sculptor for some of the busts at Trinity College, Dublin, and the circumstances of these two sets of commissions seem to have been conflated here.[54]

As well as producing ten busts during the 1750s, Roubiliac was responsible for the statue of Newton given by Smith in 1755 (fig. 73), the monument to Daniel Lock (fig. 74) and the bust incorporated on the monument of Francis Hooper, signed by Roubiliac's assistant Nicholas Read (fig. 76). A note from the *Cambridge Chronicle* of 30 July 1763 about this last work recorded that 'The *Bust* was the Workmanship of the late famous *Roubilliac*, & the *whole Monument* was finished according to the *Doctor's own Direction* about *three years ago*', and the payments of £63 and £22 10s. od. made to Roubiliac in 1758 by a person named Hooper were probably connected with the bust.[55] The 1763 reference (although known only from Cole's transcription) indicates that the monument was erected in Roubiliac's lifetime, although all other monuments signed independently by Read were executed after his master's death in 1762. It also leaves unexplained how the College used the funds left by Hooper at his death in 1763 for the 'Erecting of an Obelisk or some other kind of Monument in memory of those who regardless of their own interest have by raising this New Fabrick set so shining an example and so generously contributed to the good of Posterity'.[56]

Given this sustained patronage of Roubiliac, the commissions to his rival Peter Scheemakers require some explanation. While the choice of Scheemakers might seem reasonable for the busts of James Jurin (fig. 77) and Edward Wortley Montagu (fig. 78) in 1766, produced after Roubiliac's death, it is more difficult to understand why Smith should have gone to him for the portrait of Cotes (fig. 79) or the College for the bust of Smith himself in 1758 (fig. 80).[57] The most probable explanation is that at this date Roubiliac and his workshop were engaged in making no fewer than three major monuments for Westminster Abbey. Smith's commissioning of Scheemakers may not have been limited to portrait busts. Among his gifts to the College was, according to the guide of 1803, a 'beautiful statue of Edward VI [which] graces the centre of the Hall [of the Master's Lodge], cast in plaster of Paris, under the direction and at the expence of Dr Robert Smith, master, 1767'.[58] This no longer survives, and the sculptor is not named in the guide. The will made by Smith in 1764, however, specifies that his 'statue of Edward the 6th by Scheemakers' should 'remain in the Master's Lodge', along with 'the picture of Sir Isaac Newton by Vanderbank, the Busto of Galileo by Carcini, and the picture of Galileo by Ramsay who painted the Head from an original by Giusto in the Grand Duke's Palace at Florence'. The statue of Edward VI had been executed by Gibbons for the Royal Exchange, and it is possible that Smith arranged for a cast to be made from this.[59] It is likely that Smith's plaster was a cast of the figure carved by Scheemakers in 1737 for St Thomas's Hospital (fig. 81).[60]

Although the extent of the College's patronage of Scheemakers is in this way uncertain, there can be no doubt about the significance of the commissions given to Roubiliac during the 1750s in terms of his business practice, the growth of his reputation and his self-presentation as an artist over this period. In at least two cases the commissioning of a bust for Trinity may have led to other work. The year after Eliab Harvey gave the Cotton to the College, his elderly mother, Elizabeth Harvey, probably under his guidance, commissioned from Roubiliac the monument to her and her husband at Hempstead, and in the early 1760s the sculptor was working on at least two busts for Lord Leicester.[61] Important though the commissions for the Trinity busts were for Roubiliac, they were not conceived as a coherent group and must be understood in the

56 PRO Prob. 11/890 ff. 381r–382r. Hooper's will also lays down the requirements for the English oration to be given in the Chapel 'on a subject entirely relative to the English Nation or History ... to celebrate the nature and Excellence of the Constitution and present happy Establishment of our Church and State as now fixed upon the sound Principles of the Revolution'.

57 For an account of these busts and Scheemakers's practice at this period see Roscoe, 'Peter Scheemakers'.

58 *A guide through the University of Cambridge* (1803), p.103.

59 Other sculptural images of Edward VI include that by Gibbons for the Royal Exchange (Gunnis, *Dictionary*, p.168), Cartwright's statue at St Thomas's Hospital (*ibid.*, p.87) and Rackstrow's 'figure of Edward VI' purchased by the Ironmongers' Company in 1751 (*ibid.*, p.314). For the Ramsay portrait of Galileo see A. Smart, *Allan Ramsay* (London and New Haven, 1992), p.127.

60 For Rackstrow's figure see Gunnis, *Dictionary*, p.314. The statue at St Thomas's and its sources are discussed in Roscoe, 'Peter Scheemakers'.

61 For the Harvey monument see Bindman and Baker, *Roubiliac*, cat. no. 38. Models for works executed for Lord Leicester, along with an uncompleted bust, were included in Roubiliac's posthumous sale, 12–15 May 1762 (1st day, lot 87, 2nd day, lot 27, 3rd day, lots 21 and 90, 4th day lots 55–7) and are discussed by Esdaile, *Louis François Roubiliac*.

context of the sculptor's other work, as far as both his business practice and his workshop procedures were concerned.

As the surviving documentary evidence for both the Ray and Coke portraits shows, the starting point for one of Roubiliac's busts was often an earlier painted portrait. None of these portraits was of course done from the life, and all involve the use of conventions familiar in earlier representations, either painted or sculptural. One of their most interesting aspects is the way in which Roubiliac modified and inflected these conventions so as to construct unusually animated and vivid images. Busts such as the Cotton or the Coke were evidently executed as new compositions, invented in response to a commission from the donor and the College and making use of earlier images with the ostensible aim of achieving an accurate and true likeness. But this was not so with all the Trinity marbles. The busts of Newton and Bacon given by Lock were not new inventions but versions of portraits already executed for other patrons. The Bacon had already been included among the busts for the Long Room in Dublin (fig. 60) and a plaster version was also supplied, perhaps around this date, to the Earl of Pembroke at Wilton. The marble Newton is a version of one of Roubiliac's earliest commissions. The terracotta model (now in the Royal Greenwich Observatory, Cambridge; fig. 82) was 'made under the eyes of Mr Conduit and several of Sir Isaac Newton's particular friends, by Roubiliac, from many pictures and other Busts',[62] and the earliest version of the marble was purchased by a Mr Freeman 'with the intention of making a Present of it to the [Royal] Society' in April 1738.[63] A further marble was also produced for Dublin. Even when the head was modelled on the basis of a painted portrait, the bust as a whole was not necessarily a completely new composition. Although, for example, Roubiliac used the portrait in Sloane's collection for the image of Ray, the lower part of the bust conforms exactly in the arrangement of its drapery to a pattern already used for the portraits of two contemporary sitters, Jonathan Tyers (fig. 83) and Henry Streatfield. Even when the different images are juxtaposed, however, the repeated format is not immediately obvious on account of the vivid treatment of the face and hair.

To understand how Roubiliac came to formulate his compositions and produce some of his busts in this way it is necessary to examine the evidence provided by both the posthumous sale catalogue and the surviving terracottas and plasters, particularly those purchased from the 1762 sale by Matthew

62 As recorded in the Royal Society's Minutes of Council, VII, pp. 230–1, 18 August 1785, when the bust was bequeathed by John Belchier. Regarded by Esdaile (*Louis François Roubiliac*, p. 20) as a plaster cast, the terracotta was identified as a terracotta model by Hugh Tait (*British Museum Quarterly* (1965), news supplement, pp. 1–3).

63 Royal Society, *Journal Book*, XVII, pp. 231–2, 13 April 1738. On 19 June 1738 (*Minutes of Council*, III) approval was given for the payment to Roubiliac of £2 7s. 0d. for a 'pedestal', presumably the present socle carved with a cartouche incorporat-ing a diagram from the *Principia*.

Maty and given to the British Museum. Among the 'Busts of Great Men and Authors being Casts and Models of the late Mr. Roubilliac' were not only various classical and modern writers and figures from British history, including Charles I and Cromwell, but also 'Ray, Willoughby, Dr Barrow, and Dr. Bentley, original models in *Terra Cotta*, from which the marble Busts in Trinity College Cambridge were executed' (figs. 84–7).[64] Thanking Maty for his 'considerable donation', the Trustees asked that he 'place them in his department in such a manner as he thinks proper with suitable inscriptions', so making possible a reconfiguration of the Trinity busts in another library context, albeit supplemented with other worthies. The significance of these models in the present discussion, however, is that they allow us to examine the technical processes that lay behind the production of at least some of the Trinity portraits. From examination of the Ray it is clear that the head is modelled but the bust proper was cast from moulds – presumably those also used for the terracottas of Tyers and Streatfield – the mould lines being removed before firing when the clay was in a leather-hard state. This empirical evidence is complemented by that of the sale catalogue, in which a number of versions of the same subject are recorded, suggesting that the production and sale of multiples was a sig-nificant part of Roubiliac's business. Some of these multiples, including a version of one of the Trinity subjects, were drawn by the sculptor Nollekens, either at Roubiliac's sale or before this in his workshop. A workshop practice in which moulds and casting were used for the making of models as well as multiples in terracotta and plaster would therefore seem to lie behind the production of at least some of the Trinity portrait busts.

Such procedures would seem most obviously applicable to those busts that were donated in the first half of the 1750s, but not exclusively so. The portrait of Lord Trevor (fig. 89), for example, was given in 1757 but employs a bust type that had been used for earlier portraits of Andrew Fountaine and others. There none the less seems to be some distinction between the busts of Newton, Bacon, Willoughby and Ray and those of Cotton (figs. 90, 94), Coke (fig. 91) and Whitworth (fig. 92). The differences lie not only in the fact that the latter group do not appear to involve a reuse of existing types but also in their format and greater scale. It is as if the later images were conceived (by both sculptor and patron, perhaps) as more ambitious works. Instead of having a format with a truncation with incurved sides, of the sort commonly used on

64 British Museum, Trustees General Meeting Minutes, II, p. 420.

126

earlier busts by Roubiliac, these portraits are more expansive in their out-
lines, prompting the viewer to read on to them more dramatic and complex
narratives. Perhaps this is what Chantrey had in mind when he commented
that they were not so much like portrait busts as the upper parts of statues.

The distinction noted here may also be interpreted in terms of Roubiliac's
move towards the making of increasingly bolder claims about his own status
as an artist as well as the execution of sculptures that demand to be seen as
works of art in their own right. It was indeed during this period that unusually
detailed accounts of his monuments begin to appear, employing a critical
language appropriate to the assessment of aesthetic qualities. The Trinity
busts produced during the second half of the 1750s are in accord with this,
not only in their form but also in the way their surfaces are finished. Although
the planes of the Newton are more subtly carved than those of any contemporary English portrait bust, the surfaces of the Cotton or the Bentley (fig. 93)
are given still more virtuoso treatment. Such carving predicated close and
detailed viewing by an audience – or at least some members of it – that
regarded such busts as works of art in their own right and not merely as
sculptures with a public function.

While Rysbrack made similarly careful use of a variety of earlier visual
sources for his bust of Shakespeare, intended for James West's Gothic hall
at Alscot Park, the resulting marble, highly finished as it is, remains very
much an historicising portrait in a way that Roubiliac's Cotton is not.[65]
Many historicising busts by other sculptors seem to fit well into a sequence of
such images, but despite the first impression of the busts as they are now
arranged in the Wren Library, this does not apply to many of the Roubiliac
portraits. Through their animation of pose and expression, as well as their
format, the accidents of individual likeness are emphasised at the expense
of group identity.[66] Rather than following a standard format, the distinctive-
ness of each of these portraits as a self-contained composition encourages the
viewer to understand it not as part of a sequence but as a focus for a narrative
based on that sitter's biography.

Such distinctions between the various groups of Roubiliac busts, and
between Roubiliac's portraits and those of other sculptors, may be understood
partly in terms of changing attitudes to sculpture and Roubiliac's exploitation
of this in his promotion of himself as an artist. But they may also be interpreted
in terms of settings and viewing conditions. The evidence for the positions in

65   The bust is now in Birmingham City
Art Gallery. For a discussion of the sources
employed see Webb, *Michael Rysbrack*,
pp. 117–19.
66   For recent discussions of portraiture
conventions and group identity see M. Pointon,
Hanging the head (New Haven, 1993), and
R. Brilliant, *Portraiture* (1991).

which the marbles were set at different dates is fragmentary and at points contradictory. The setting of the two pairs given by Lock and Garforth respectively is, however, unambiguous. Included in the description of the Library in the 1763 Cambridge guidebook is a reference to '4 beautiful Busts on marble Terms, two at each end, of the celebrated *Ray, Willoughby, Bacon,* and *Newton*', and mention of them in their present position – the Bacon and Newton at the south end and the other two at the north end – continues to be made in later descriptions. Account was evidently taken of their intended situation when they were still in the workshop, as the Ray has the inscription about Garforth's donation not on the front but on the (viewer's) right-hand side, while the Willoughby has it on the left, so that both would be clearly visible to the visitor passing through the entrance which they flank (fig. 71). Each pair is placed on matching marble plinths, though the way in which those used for Bacon and Newton differ in design from those supporting Ray and Willoughby suggests again that they were conceived as two pairs rather than as a set of four.

No mention is made in the 1763 guide of any busts in the Library other than these four marbles and the twenty-six plasters. By 1803 the 'bust of that early favourite of science, Roger Cotes' had been placed alongside an antique statue of Aesculapius in 'the physical class at the upper end', and it probably remained there since it is mentioned in Ackermann's *Cambridge* in 1815.[67] A payment of nineteen guineas had already been made in 1757 for the 'Carriage of Dr Barrow and Dr Bentley's busts & setting them up in the library', but there is no further reference to indicate that these two busts remained in the Library.[68] In Ackermann's view of 1815 (fig. 10) one of the two busts at the south end is represented, but this view shows no busts on plinths at the ends of the cases, although the busts on the cases are there.

Although the lack of references in the guidebooks before this date is hardly conclusive proof that some of the others were not included, it seems likely that the only marble busts displayed on a permanent basis within the Library in the eighteenth century were the four on marble plinths, divided into pairs placed at the two ends, and possibly the portrait of Cotes set back in one of the bays. Six further busts are shown placed at the ends of the cases on matching tapering plinths in a print (fig. 97) included in J. and H. S. Storer's *Delineations of Trinity College, Cambridge,* published soon after 1832, but the first description of the Library to mention the busts of Cotton, Coke, Trevor and Whitworth is that of 1843.[69] It would appear that those now on wood

67 *A guide through the University of Cambridge* [1803], pp. 96–7; R. Ackermann, *A History of the University of Cambridge* (1815). Although the book was published in 1815, some of the prints are dated 1814.

68 Junior Bursar's accounts, 1757. Mrs Montagu's letter of 1756 (quoted above, n. 42) indicates that she thought that the bust was for the Library.

69 J. and H. S. Storer, *Delineations of Trinity College, Cambridge* [after 1832].

70 J. Wilson, *Memorabilia Cantabrigiae* (1803), p. 257.

plinths at the ends of the cases were brought in during the 1830s, possibly as part of a reorganisation that involved the making of the bookcases designed by Cockerell. Unfortunately, however, neither the accounts of the various interiors in the eighteenth-century guides nor the list of pictures included first in the guide of 1803 make any mention of portrait busts being placed elsewhere. The one exception is Wilson in 1803, who concludes his description of the Hall by stating that 'Under the pictures on the one side are the busts of the most celebrated of the ancient poets, orators, and philosophers; and, on the other, the moderns.'[70] This might be dismissed as the misplacing of a passage used in earlier guides about the plasters in the Library, but busts on brackets immediately beneath the full-length painted portraits are shown in Ackermann's 1815 view of the Hall (fig. 95). These busts are only represented in a schematic way and their subjects cannot be identified. It is possible that they included some of the Roubiliac portraits, although it seems somewhat improbable that such highly finished, large-scale marbles would have been placed in such a position.

While their precise location remains uncertain, it is likely that most of the larger and more ambitious of the Roubiliac busts were originally elsewhere in the College and that in mentioning to Lord Leicester that Roubiliac knew of their 'size and situation' Walker had in mind a setting other than the Library. A variety of settings would indeed help to explain the busts' disparity in size, format and conventions. The thinking behind Smith's scheme also becomes more apparent. The larger busts were images of illustrious figures of the College's past in various fields, commissioned, albeit by descendants or relations on Smith's prompting, to form part of a College iconography in painted and sculptural form. In this respect Smith's plans were comparable to (and possibly prompted) those of the Fellows of Emmanuel, including Richard Hurd, who in 1755 wrote to Sir Edward Littleton suggesting that

> the 50 pounds you so kindly intend the College ... might perhaps be best laid out in a Bust of one of the Worthies of the Society, suppose Dr Cudworth, Bp Hall, Sir W Temple or Abp Sandcroft, as you like best, to be placed in the Gallery ... It would be an elegant way of Employing this Sum and might prove the beginning of a fine collection of such things, which others might be helped to carry on by your example.[71]

The busts commissioned for the Library were evidently envisaged as a far more distinctive scheme, arising from Smith's particular academic interests.

71 Letter of 19 February 1755 from Hurd to Littleton, Staffordshire Record Office, D 1413/1.

129

72 According to the Senior Bursar's accounts, a payment of £105 was made to Cipriani in 1773; his drawing is now in the Fitzwilliam Museum (see fig. 14). Peckitt was paid £315, and this is recorded, along with a description of the window, in his Account Book in York City Art Gallery, for which see J. T. Brighton, 'William Peckitt's Commission Book', *Walpole Society* (1988), p. 395.

73 PRO Prob. 11/938 ff. 323r–324v.

74 *Cantabrigia depicta* [1776], p. 84. In the 1803 account (*A guide through the University of Cambridge*, p. 96) the narrative is developed further through the figure of Bacon with his book being interpreted 'as if preparing to register the reward about to be bestowed on Sir Isaac'.

75 The position of Bacon within the lineage and iconography of experimental science was established visually through the inclusion of his bust in the frontispiece of Thomas Sprat's *History of the Royal Society of London* (1667). By 1769, when busts of Newton and Bacon were placed together at Wilton House (see appendix to this chapter, B1), the pairing of the two was already well established.

76 [W. Heberden,] *Strictures upon the discipline of the University of Cambridge* (1792), pp. 46–7, cited by Gascoigne, *Cambridge in the age of the Enlightenment*, p. 12.

77 This process is analysed by Gascoigne, *Cambridge in the age of the Enlightenment* (particularly in the introduction), on which the following paragraphs are based.

78 *Ibid.*, p. 155.

The subjects of the five busts recorded as being in the Library during the eighteenth century were all eminent scientists, and even the two – Bentley and Barrow – whose busts may have been there at one point could be claimed to have a place in the development of the physical sciences – the 'new Philosophy' – in Cambridge at the end of the seventeenth century. This scheme was continued consistently even after Smith's death in the imagery of the window, designed by Cipriani and executed by the York glass painter William Peckitt in 1774, with funds bequeathed to the College by Smith (fig. 13).[72] The window was commissioned in accordance with Smith's will bequeathing the £2,000 to the 'master and Seniors' for 'such publick Uses or Ornaments in the College as they think proper; only desiring that the Window in the South End of the College Library be glazed with the best painted glass'.[73] In it 'Sir *Isaac Newton* and Lord Chancellor *Bacon*, the two distinguished Members of this Society, are presented to the King by the Muse of the Place; his Majesty attended and admired by the *British Minerva*, is giving the Laurel Chaplet to Sir *Isaac*, who is explaining the sphere. Lord *Bacon* in his Chancellor's Robes, is seated in the Attitude of Study.'[74] The iconography of the window is in this way linked (fig. 96) with the two busts below it, and in repeating a well-established pairing that symbolised experimental science, so reinforced the scientific emphasis of Smith's additions to the Library's decoration.[75]

By the 1750s the research activity of Newton's time had ceased, allowing Heberden to comment more generally that the resident Fellows of the University were incrusted with the 'corroding rust of inactivity'.[76] But, while the earlier experimental advances could not be matched, the mid eighteenth century was significant as a period in which Newtonianism and natural philosophy became integrated into a reformed curriculum at Cambridge and the 'holy alliance' between Newtonian science and Anglican theology found institutional expression in the Whig University.[77] Trinity was at the centre of these developments and, in Gascoigne's words, 'formed a catalyst for the cultivation of scientific activity within the university as a whole'.[78] Bentley's role was especially significant. Through his Boyle lectures and the provision of preliminary reading that was less difficult than works like the *Principia*, he succeeded in making Newton's work far more accessible and establishing the 'new Philosophy' as an important element within the Cambridge curriculum. This was continued by Roger Cotes, James Jurin and Smith himself. As well as being

Bentley's protégé, successor as Master and supporter – he described Bentley as Trinity's 'second founder' – Smith built on Bentley's attempts to promote and popularise the study of Newtonian natural philosophy through the publication of works such as the *Opticks* and *Harmonia mensurarum*, an edition of the papers of his cousin Cotes.

Smith's choice of subjects for the Library needs to be interpreted in relation to these concerns. In one sense the prominence given to the images of Newton and Bacon may be seen as an attempt to make the most of the College's illustrious scientific past at a period when research in the experimental sciences, like undergraduate numbers, was at a low ebb, just as the inclusion of Ray and Willoughby might be associated with the not wholly successful attempts made by Richard Walker (who might indeed have suggested the commissioning of the busts) to re-establish botanical studies through his foundation of the University's Botanic Garden. But Smith's additions to the imagery of the Library and the Chapel are better understood as the visual equivalent to his popularising of experimental science through the publication of accessible textbooks. The place of science within the Cambridge curriculum was being consolidated not only through the publication of these works but also through the presence of scientists' images in the library where they were read.

By the 1830s the place of science within the curriculum was being discussed in a different way, and the division of the portrait busts between the Library and other parts of the College would not have been charged with the meaning that it probably had in the 1750s. It is not surprising, therefore, that when the College's portraits were redistributed at this period, probably as a consequence of architectural changes, the eighteenth-century sculptural portraits were brought together in the Library. From this date onwards the sculptural scheme was not merely less focused than that envisaged by Smith, being expanded to include (as in Dublin) 'men eminent for learning', but was modified to constitute, like the Codrington Library at All Souls, a gallery of the most illustrious figures from the College's own past. When the portraits were reconfigured in this way, it must have seemed quite appropriate in 1845 to integrate Thorvaldsen's statue of Byron within this visual construction of an institutional history.[79]

Far from being the coherent ensemble that it might at first sight appear, the portraiture in the Wren Library is made up of different groups of images,

79 For the Byron statue see J. Murdoch and A. Burton, *Byron* (Victoria and Albert Museum exhibition) (1974), p. 123.

brought together at different times as the Library changed its role and the College redefined its own past in the light of current concerns. The early arrangement consisted of the painted portraits of those whose book collections were given to the Library along with two wood busts from a planned, but apparently incomplete, set of classical and modern authors. During the 1750s this set was completed by the plasters given by Dr Hooper and the College's commitment to science emphasised by the introduction of some of the marble busts and, in 1774, Smith's window. Although the guide of 1790 could claim that the 'portraits of learned members are such and so many that no college can equal', this remark applied to images distributed throughout the College. Only in the 1830s was it possible to recognise this by visiting the Library alone. Although the Wren Library has rightly been seen as the model for numerous later libraries in so many respects, its remarkable sculptural portraits represent the culmination, as much as the beginning, of a rich and complex tradition of library portrait sculpture.

Appendix

In the following entries, 'l.' and 'r.' refer to the viewer's left and right, not the sitter's. 'Support' refers to the section of marble at the back of the bust, carved from the same block.

A PLASTER BUSTS OF ANCIENT AND MODERN AUTHORS

East side (from the north end)
1. Homer; 2. Democritus; 3. Demosthenes; 4. Socrates; 5. Julius Caesar; 6. Marcus Aurelius; 7. Horace; 8. Cicero; 9. Brutus; 10. Seneca; 11. Virgil; 12. Anacreon [wood]; 13. Plato; [14. Hooper; similar to, but not cast from, Roubiliac's bust on Hooper's monument; possibly a version of the bust formerly in the Combination Room, mentioned under c.4 below].

West side (from the north end)
15. Shakespeare; 16. Spenser; 17. Ben Jonson [wood]; 18. Beaumont; 19. Fletcher; 20. Inigo Jones; 21. Sydenham; 22. Milton; 23. Dryden; 24. Locke; 25. Tillotson; 27. Addison; [28. Porson; a later addition cast from Chantrey's marble].

B MARBLE BUSTS OF CONTEMPORARIES AND MODERN WORTHIES
(listed in order of date)

1 Francis Bacon. By L. F. Roubiliac
Inscribed: 'BACON' (front of socle); 'VISCOUNT / S.T ALBANS' (l. side of socle); 'LORD / CHANCELLOR' (r. side of socle); 'Ex Dono / Danielis Lock / Hujus Collegij AM' (r.h. of support); 'L. F. Roubiliac / Sculpit 1751.' (l.h. of support).

Other versions: unsigned marble, Trinity College, Dublin; terracotta, coll. Earl of Pembroke, Wilton House, probably that described in 1779 (James Kennedy, *A new description of pictures, statues and bustos ... in the Earl of Pembroke's house at Wilton* (Salisbury, 1779) p. 64) as being on chimney piece in the New Dining Room with a bust of Newton.

2 Isaac Newton. By L. F. Roubiliac
Inscribed: 'NEWTON' (front of socle); 'L. F. Roubiliac / Sculp.it 1751' (l.h. of support); 'Ex Dono / Danielis Lock / Hujus Collegij A M' (r.h. of support).

Other versions: terracotta made for John Conduitt before 1737, Royal Greenwich Observatory, Cambridge; marble, Royal Society, London; marble, Trinity College, Dublin; plaster, coll. Earl of Pembroke, Wilton House.

3 John Ray. By L. F. Roubiliac
Inscribed 'JOA.S RAY.' (front of socle); '1751 / POSUIT / EDM. GARFORTH A.M.' (r. side of socle); 'L. F. Roubiliac Sc.t' (l.h. of support); 'L. F. Roubiliac Sc.t' (r.h. of support).

A possible explanation for the presence of two 'signatures' may be that the first was inscribed on the left side before the position of the bust was determined; when it was established that the portrait would be placed on the left side of the door, the second 'signature' on the right might then have been added so that the viewer would be aware of the sculptor's name. The payment of £108 10s. 10d. made to Roubiliac by Garforth in June 1756 (see n. 45) was probably for the busts of Ray and Willoughby, together with their marble plinths. The basis for the image was the oil painting formerly in Hans Sloane's collection (now National Portrait Gallery), copied by Roubiliac in 1755. The drapery pattern had been employed by Roubiliac for the terracotta busts of Jonathan Tyers and Henry Streatfield.

Other versions: terracotta model, British Museum; terracotta, Saffron Walden Museum; terracotta on London art market and included in Sotheby's sale, 17 November 1970, lot 130; a plaster in the Victoria and Albert Museum

(1788–1892) appears to have been cast from the marble and is not an eighteenth-century multiple.

4 *Francis Willoughby. By L. F. Roubiliac*

Inscribed 'FR.US WILLOUGHBY' (front of socle); '1751 / POSUIT EDM. GARFORTH A.M.' (l. side of socle); 'L. F. Roubiliac. Sc.t' (l.h. of support).

Other versions: terracotta model, British Museum.

5 *Isaac Barrow. By L. F. Roubiliac*

Inscribed: 'BARROW / Pos.it Edv. Montagu Armig. / MDCCLVI.' (front of socle); '1756' (r. side of socle); 'L. F. Roubiliac Sc.t' (l.h. of support); 'L. F. Roubiliac.' (r.h. of support).

Other versions: unfired clay model, British Museum.

6 *Richard Bentley. By L. F. Roubiliac*

Inscribed: 'BENTLEY / Pos.nt Bentleii Filiae / MDCCLVI.' (front of socle); '1756' (l. side of socle); 'L. F. Roubiliac' (l.h. of support).

Other versions: unfired clay model, British Museum; plaster, Lambeth Palace.

7 *Robert Cotton. By L. F. Roubiliac*

Inscribed: 'ROB. COTTON / Baronettus. / Posuit Eliab Harvey. / 1757.' (front of socle); '1757' (l. side of socle); 'L. F. Roubiliac' (l.h. of support).

Other versions: terracotta model, British Museum (acquired in 1924, with a provenance from the Harvey family).

8 *Edward Coke. By L. F. Roubiliac*

Inscribed: 'E. COKE / Summus Judex. / Posuit Comes Leicestriae. / 1757.' (front of socle); '1757' (r. side of socle); 'L. F. Roubiliac' (r.h. of support).

9 *Thomas, Baron Trevor. By L. F. Roubiliac*

Inscribed: 'TH.S BARO TREVOR / Posuit ELIZABETHA FILIA, / CAR: Duc: MARLB: conjux / MDCCLVII.' (front of socle); 'L. F. Roubiliac / Sculpit. 1757' (r.h. of support).

The same drapery pattern was employed by Roubiliac for the busts of Sir Andrew Fountaine (Wilton House), Aristotle (Trinity College, Dublin) and Thomas Winnington (on his monument at Stanford, Worcestershire).

10 *Charles, Lord Whitworth. By L. F. Roubiliac*

Inscribed: 'C. WHITWORTH. / Baro de Galway / Dono Dedit. / RI: WHITWORTH Nepos.' (front of socle); 'L. F. Roubiliac Sculpit: 1757' (l.h. of support).

Other versions: drawing by Nollekens of a bust with a differently shaped socle, Harris Museum, Preston.

11 Roger Cotes. By Peter Scheemakers
Inscribed: 'ROGERUS COTES / Posuit ROBERTUS SMITH Magister Collegi / 1758.' (front of socle); 'P. Scheemakers F.t' (r. side of socle); 'P. Scheemakers / Fecit 1758.' (r.h. of support).

12 Robert Smith. By Peter Scheemakers
Inscribed: 'ROBERTUS SMITH S.T.P. / COLLEGÎ S.TRINITATIS / APUD CANTABRIGIENSES / MAGISTER: / PRAESENTI TIBI MATUROS LARGIMUR HONORES / A.D. 1758. Aetat. 68' (front of socle); 'P Scheemakers / Fecit: 1758' (l. side of support).

    Other versions: cast recorded in Scheemakers' sale of 6 June 1771, lot 20 (info. Ingrid Roscoe).

13 James Jurin. By Peter Scheemakers
Inscribed: 'IACOBUS. IURIN. M.D. / IACOBUS. IURIN. F. POSUIT.' (front of socle); '1766' (r. side of socle); 'P. Scheemakers / F.t' (r. side of support).

    Donated by Jurin's son, James.

14 Edward Wortley Montagu. By Peter Scheemakers
Inscribed: 'EDV. WORTLEY / MONTAGU' (front of socle); 'P. Scheemakers Ft, 1766' (r. side of socle).

    A payment to 'Mr Schamakers' of £42 9s. 0d. for this bust was recorded in the Senior Bursar's 1767 accounts, a further payment of £10 10s. 0d. being made in the next year for the bracket on which it stands at the foot of the stairs. The way in which the back of the bust was finished roughly with the point suggests that an architectural setting against a wall was always envisaged. According to the 1790 *Description* (*A concise and accurate description of the University, town and county of Cambridge* (1790), p. 90), the bust was purchased with money given by Montagu's daughter, to accompany the marble inscription already bequeathed by her father.

15 Anthony Shepherd. By John Bacon
Inscribed: 'ANTHONIUS SHEPHERD, S.T.P. / PROFESSOR PLUMIANUS, / 1760–1796.' (front of socle); 'IPSE LEGAVIT, / 1796.' (l. side of socle); 'J. Bacon R.A. / sculp.t 1790' (r. side of the support at back).

C OTHER EIGHTEENTH-CENTURY SCULPTURAL PORTRAITS

The following list records other sculptural portraits that are (or were) elsewhere in the College during the eighteenth century.

1 Sir Isaac Newton. Ante-Chapel

Inscribed: 'NEWTON / Qui genus humanum ingenio superavit.'; 'Posuit Robertus Smith S.T.P. / Collegij hujus S.Trinitatis Magister. / MDCCLV.'; 'L.F. Roubiliac inv.it et sc.it'.

This is the most ambitious and important of all of Smith's contributions to the College's iconography. For the circumstances of the commission, first mentioned in a letter of Mr Montagu to his wife in July 1753, see K. A. Esdaile, *The life and works of Louis François Roubiliac* (1928), pp. 101–3. A plaster death mask in the Library has a label linking it with the statue and stating that it had been given by Roubiliac to his 'pupil', Nicholas Read.

2 Daniel Lock. Ante-Chapel

Signed on the bottom edge of the tablet and documented by the reference in the sculptor's posthumous sale catalogue to 'A design for a monument for D. Lock, Esq:' (2nd day, 13 May 1762, lot 72). The same drapery pattern had already been used by Roubiliac for the portrait of Swift at Trinity College, Dublin. For a more detailed account see D. Bindman and M. Baker, *Roubiliac and the eighteenth-century monument; sculpture as theatre* (New Haven and London, 1995), cat. no. 34.

3 Francis Hooper. Ante-Chapel

Although the monument is signed 'N. Read int et sct', the *Cambridge Chronicle* reference quoted by Cole (see p. 123 above) makes clear that the bust was executed by Roubiliac in Hooper's lifetime. It also suggests that the 'whole monument' was completed before Roubiliac's death, although in the absence of such evidence, it might have been assumed that the monument was erected later by Read, who continued Roubiliac's business for a short time following the latter's death.

4 Francis Hooper. Formerly in the Combination Room

The 1803 *Guide* (p. 105) includes among the portraits in the Combination Room a 'bust of Dr Richard [*sic*] Hooper, the builder of this room &c over the door'. This may have been a version of either the Roubiliac bust on the monument or the plaster in the library set.

5 *Edward VI. Formerly in the hall of the Master's Lodge*

Recorded in Robert Smith's will as a 'statue of Edward the 6th by Scheemakers' that should 'remain in the Master's Lodge', this was described in the 1803 *Guide* (p. 104) as a 'beautiful statue of Edward VI ... cast in plaster of Paris, under the direction and at the expence of Dr Robert Smith, master, 1767'. Now lost, this was probably a version of Scheemakers's statue for St Thomas's Hospital. It might conceivably have been that the 'figure of *Edward VI*, ditto [i.e. model]' was recorded as lot 20 of Scheemakers's sale on 1 March 1756 (info. Ingrid Roscoe), but the statement that it was cast at Smith's direction suggests otherwise. Its position in 1790 in the 'centre of the Hall' in any case suggests that this was a full-size figure.

6 *Galileo. Formerly in the dining parlour of the Master's Lodge*

Described in the 1803 *Guide* (p. 104) as 'Galilei Archetypum, Carcini fecit, Robert Smith posuit, 1759'. It is uncertain whether this was a bust or a painting, but it is possible that the unknown 'Carcini' is a misreading of the sculptor Agostino Carlini, working in London from the mid 1750s. Neither this nor any other versions, however, are mentioned in any of the documentation relating to Carlini, for which see M. Trusted, '"A man of talent": Agostino Carlini', *Burlington Magazine*, 134 (1992), pp. 776–84 and 135 (1993), pp. 190–201.

52 *Divinity*. Ketton stone. By
Caius Gabriel Cibber. 1681.

53 *Law.* Ketton stone. By
Caius Gabriel Cibber. 1681.

54 *Physic*. Ketton stone. By
Caius Gabriel Cibber. 1681.

55 *Mathematics*. Ketton stone.
By Caius Gabriel Cibber. 1681.

56 *Ben Jonson.* Wood.
By Grinling Gibbons (?)

57 *Anacreon*. By Grinling
Gibbons (?).

58 *The Duke of Somerset.* Marble.
By Grinling Gibbons. *c.* 1690–3.

59 Interior of the Codrington Library, All Souls College, Oxford. Engraving. After James Malton.

60   Interior of the Long Room, Trinity College, Dublin. Engraving. From James Malton, *A picturesque and descriptive view of the city of Dublin* [1797].

61 Interior of the Bibliothèque Sainte-Geneviève, Paris. Engraving by François Erliger, 1689. From
R. P. Claude du Molinet, *Le Cabinet de la bibliothèque de Sainte Geneviève* (Paris, 1692).

62 *Plato*. Plaster. By
John Cheere. *c.* 1755–60.

63 *John Fletcher*. Plaster.
By John Cheere. *c.* 1755–60.

64 *Joseph Addison.* Plaster.
By John Cheere. *c.* 1755–60.

65 *Alexander Pope*. Plaster.
By John Cheere. *c*. 1755–60.

66 *Alexander Pope.* Plaster. By
John Cheere. *c.* 1755. Aston Hall,
Birmingham.

67 *Sir Isaac Newton.*
Marble. By Louis François
Roubiliac. 1751.

68 *Francis Bacon*. Marble.
By Louis François Roubiliac.
1751.

69 *John Ray*. Marble. By Louis
François Roubiliac. 1755 (?).

70 *Francis Willoughby*. Marble.
By Louis François Roubiliac.

71 *John Ray*, on the original plinth.
Marble. By Louis François Roubiliac.
1755 (?).

72 *John Ray*. Oil on canvas. By an unidentified artist. Late seventeenth century. National Portrait Gallery.

73 *Sir Isaac Newton*. Marble.
By Louis François Roubiliac.
1755. Trinity College Chapel.

74 Monument to Daniel Lock. Marble. By Louis François Roubiliac. About 1755. Trinity College Chapel.

75 *Daniel Lock*. By William Hogarth. *c.* 1732–5. Private collection, New York.

76 Monument to Francis
Hooper. Marble. Bust by
Louis François Roubiliac.
Trinity College Chapel.

IACOBUS. IURIN. M. D.
IACOBUS. IURIN. F. POSUIT.

77 *James Jurin*. Marble. By
Peter Scheemakers. 1766.

78 *Edward Wortley Montagu.* By Peter Scheemakers. 1766.

79 *Roger Cotes*. Marble. By
Peter Scheemakers. 1758.

80 *Robert Smith*. Marble.
By Peter Scheemakers. 1758.

81 *Edward VI*. Bronze. By Peter Scheemakers.
1737. St Thomas's Hospital, London.

82 *Sir Isaac Newton*. Terracotta. By Louis
François Roubiliac. 1738. Royal Greenwich
Observatory, Cambridge.

83 *Jonathan Tyers*.
Terracotta. By Louis
François Roubiliac.
c. 1740–5 (?). Victoria
and Albert Museum.

84 *John Ray*. Terracotta.
By Louis François Roubiliac.
1755 (?). British Museum.

85 *Francis Willoughby*. Terracotta. By Louis François Roubiliac. 1755 (?). British Museum.

86 *Isaac Barrow*. Unfired clay. By Louis François Roubiliac. 1756 (?). British Museum.

87 *Richard Bentley*. Unfired clay. By Louis François Roubiliac. 1756. British Museum.

BARROW

Pos.^{tr} dv. Montagu Armig.
MDCCLVI.

ISAAC BARROW MASTER
1650-1677 Roubiliac

88 *Isaac Barrow.* Marble. By
Louis François Roubiliac. 1756.

89 *Thomas, Baron Trevor.* Marble.
By Louis François Roubiliac. 1757.

ROB.COTTON
Baronettus.

Posuit Eliab Harvey.
1757.

90 *Sir Robert Cotton.* Marble. By Louis François Roubiliac. 1757.

91 *Edward Coke*. Marble. By
Louis François Roubiliac. 1757.

92 *Charles, Lord Whitworth.*
Marble. By Louis François
Roubiliac. 1757.

93 *Richard Bentley*. Marble. By
Louis François Roubiliac. 1757.

94 *Sir Robert Cotton* (detail). Marble. By Louis François Roubiliac. 1757.

95 Interior of the Hall, Trinity College. Aquatint. After A. Pugin. From [William Combe] *A history of the University of Cambridge* (London: R. Ackermann, 1815).

96 The south end of the Wren Library, with the Cipriani window and the busts of Bacon and Newton.

97 Interior of the Wren Library. Engraving. From J. and H. S. Storer, *Delineations of Trinity College, Cambridge* (Cambridge, after 1832).

POSTSCRIPT

David McKitterick

This book has been concerned with a period beginning in the reign of Charles II and ending in the first years of that of Queen Victoria. During the late seventeenth century, the country, and within it the University and the colleges of Cambridge, sought stability following the upheavals of the mid-century. This stability was to be severely tested following the Glorious Revolution of 1688, as members of the University were once more obliged to parade their loyalties in public, and to protest allegiance to the new monarchy. Not everyone swore allegiance to the new King and Queen, and not everyone who did so meant the same thing. But for the majority, and for the University as a whole, the new regime brought outward stability that was to remain for two centuries. No less severely, economic circumstances in the last decades of the seventeenth century were unfavourable; and by 1700 the internal affairs of Trinity College itself were in plain need of reform. Bentley's new broom was not to everyone's liking, and it was one that he cheerfully wielded with little consultation whenever (often mistakenly) he thought it possible to do so. In important respects, the last years of the seventeenth century were those of Newton and his circle; but they were also years of crisis for the College, University and country alike.

In the second quarter of the nineteenth century, the closing years of this book, the University likewise faced a crisis, albeit of a different kind, but again not unrelated to political opinion in the country at large. Numbers of students were increasing, but the subjects they should study, and the manner whereby they should be taught and examined, were each subject of debate. Between the end of the Napoleonic wars in 1815, and the 1840s, the number of degrees granted at Cambridge more than doubled, to almost six hundred in 1840. The proportionate rise in the numbers of Bachelors of Arts alone, to 339, was even greater during the same period. The proportion of those who matriculated and also took a degree likewise increased.[1] There was a new

1 These figures are taken from V. A. Huber, *The English universities: an abridged translation*, ed. with additional matter by Francis W. Newman, 3 vols. (1843), 2, part 2, pp. 503–8.

educational seriousness, as well as a greater university population. More fundamentally, in the 1830s Parliament began to take an interest in the University's affairs to an extent that it had not since the mid seventeenth century. In 1834, the religious tests that had on the whole restricted members of the University to the Church of England were questioned; and in 1837 it was proposed in the House of Lords that a parliamentary committee of enquiry should be formed to examine Oxford and Cambridge more generally. Though religious tests were not in fact to be abolished until 1871,[2] the days of the *ancien régime* were clearly approaching their end.

But the University was also taking stock of itself. Every year, the customary annual commemorations of benefactors provided opportunities to search in the past for lessons applicable to the present. In 1827, the congregation gathered in Trinity's Chapel observed the hundredth anniversary of the death of Newton; and in the following year William Whewell reminded the congregation (mistakenly) that they celebrated the two hundredth anniversary of the birth of John Ray.[3] In December 1832, Adam Sedgwick's sermon at the annual commemoration became, within a year, a much-expanded *Discourse on the studies of the University of Cambridge*. At liberty to select from the past as he wished, Sedgwick was vehement in his tribute to Newton, countering it with an outspoken attack on the falsities and misconceptions of current teaching. His task was made to seem the more urgent in the light of recent geological discoveries and opinion: 'such dreams of cosmogony as I believe find no parallel in the recent history of continental Europe'.[4] History, scientific observation and reform in the curriculum seemed to march hand in hand. The foundation of the Cambridge Antiquarian Society and of the Cambridge Camden Society, both in 1839, were two formal, widely shared and more mundane manifestations of this historical spirit. In Trinity, and in Cambridge at large, anxiety to document the past and put it in order were marked in 1842 by two events: for the College, the publication of Bentley's correspondence, and for Cambridge as a whole, the first volume of C. H. Cooper's *Annals of Cambridge*, in which University and town alike were brought under scrutiny. Historical researches and current criticism (this time from abroad) came together again in the following year, in the English translation of V. A. Huber's history and assessment of English universities (1843), introduced by a reformer from Oxford, Francis W. Newman.[5] Not for the last time, the University sought guidance for the future by taking a critical look at its past.

2 D. A. Winstanley, *Early Victorian Cambridge* (Cambridge, 1940), pp. 83–96; D. A. Winstanley, *Later Victorian Cambridge* (Cambridge, 1947), pp. 36–90.
3 William Whewell, *Sermons preached in the chapel of Trinity College, Cambridge* (1847), p. 328. But Ray was born in 1627, not 1628: see, for a history of this error, Charles E. Raven, *John Ray, naturalist: his life and works* (Cambridge, 1942), p. 1.
4 Adam Sedgwick, *A discourse on the studies of the University of Cambridge* (1833), p. 108.
5 See n. 1 above. Huber's work originally appeared as *Die englischen Universitäten* in 1840.

In such an environment, and in the generation that produced Pugin, architectural decisions easily became charged not only with aesthetic or historical arguments, but also with overtones even of moral values.[6] But by the time that Pugin's *Contrasts* was published, Trinity had already taken its decision as to how to proceed with New Court, the first buildings to be set next to Wren's library. It had rejected a pallid and unconvincing proposal by William Wilkins for a neo-classical block that made no attempt to meet the challenge of Wren's design, and instead settled upon Wilkins's alternative suggestion of Gothic revival.[7] The decision to choose a Gothic rather than a classical style was to prove a landmark in Cambridge architecture, confirmed by Rickman's New Court at St John's. Thus the two largest colleges set an example that others found it convenient to follow.

But while Wren's work had in these years little influence on provision for accommodation, he found a champion in C. R. Cockerell. More than any other individual, Cockerell was responsible for the re-evaluation of Wren as an historic figure, and therefore of his buildings as historical achievements. The change in status, a subtle one in some respects, was to be most fully acknowledged by the decision in the 1850s to replace the flat ceiling that Maria Edgeworth (and no doubt others) had found so dull[8] with a design more akin to Wren's known original intentions. In 1838 Cockerell executed a large watercolour *Tribute to the memory of Sir Christopher Wren*, giving pride of place to the ecclesiastical buildings but also including the Wren Library.[9] His lectures to the Royal Academy in the 1840s paid further tribute.[10] But for Cambridge, there was a further, and much greater, reminder in Cockerell's design for the new University Library, of which the north range was erected in 1837–44. Cockerell's new building has never been completed; but in the tradition it shares with the Wren Library at Trinity there was also an irony. In 1675, the previous occasion when the University had considered the complete rebuilding of its library, one result of the inconclusive discussions had (according to tradition) been Isaac Barrow's determination to build a new library for his own college. Now, in the 1840s, as the University again faced the same question, but this time proceeded a little with a project, it was to a consequence of those previous discussions that members of the University could look if they wished. The only local building comparable with Cockerell's new University Library was the Wren Library.

In the course of one and a half centuries, bordered by periods in which the functions and foundations of colleges and University alike were questioned,

6 A.W. N. Pugin, *Contrasts* (1836; 2nd edn, 1841). Pugin concentrated most of his fire, here and elsewhere, on ecclesiastical buildings; but he had secular buildings also in mind: 'When Protestantism did anything *of itself*, it was ten times worse than their [i.e. Roman Catholics'] extravagances, since it embodied the same wretched pagan ideas, without either the scale or richness of the foreign architecture of the same period. Queen's College, Oxford; the new quadrangle of Christ's Church; Radcliffe Library; St. Paul's Cathedral, London, and many other buildings of the same class, are utter departures from Catholic architecture, and meagre imitations of Italian paganism. It is most fortunate for English architecture, that during the greatest rage for classic art, the desire for church building was nearly extinct, in consequence of Protestant ascendancy. Hence many of our finest monuments remained comparatively safe in their neglect, while all the furor for the new style was diverted into mansions, palaces, and erections for luxury and temporal splendour' (*Contrasts* (1841), p. 57).

7 R. W. Liscombe, *William Wilkins, 1778–1839* (Cambridge, 1980), with a reproduction of the neoclassical proposal, pl. 64.

8 *The life and letters of Maria Edgeworth*, ed. Augustus J. C. Hare, 2 vols. (1894), 1, p. 200.

9 Reproduced in David Watkin, *The life and work of C. R. Cockerell* (1974), pl. 9.

10 The manuscript of parts of one series of these lectures is now Trinity College MS R.2.1; but see also the reports in *The Builder* during these years.

the Wren Library became established in the appearance and purpose by which, to a very great extent, it survives today. Visually, with the notable exceptions of Thorvaldsen's statue of Byron (introduced in 1845) and the trabeated ceiling (itself an adaptation of Wren's original design) of 1850–1, there has been little change. But thanks not only to further benefactors, but also to different expectations of the libraries of Cambridge as a result of university reforms in teaching, and new impetus in the mid nineteenth century for research in the humanities and sciences alike, the collections of books and manuscripts expanded at an unprecedented rate in the mid and late nineteenth century. In the 1890s separate provision was made in an adjoining new building for modern books. Notwithstanding these expansions, commonplaces of the Victorian world, many of the principles of the modern library were in place by 1840. By then, the shelves designed by Wren were full. The demarcations of bibliographical study, with their concomitant emphasis on rarity, and consequent dependence on great libraries, had marked the College's manuscripts and early printed books, most of them at that stage acquired during the previous century and a half, as one of the most important collections in the country. It remained for the next generation to reconcile several demands: from readers keen to use the earlier collections; for space required for further similar gifts (some themselves of great riches); and for the requirements of undergraduate teaching as it diversified beyond all recognition during the remainder of the century. By the time that the College finally built a new reading-room with space for the great increases in numbers of books during the nineteenth century, using space to the north of Nevile's Court, Barrow's vision for the Library in 1675 had lasted for more than two hundred years.

APPENDIX

Letter by Sir Christopher Wren

To accompany his drawings, Wren prepared a letter, probably to Isaac Barrow himself, with an explanation of some of the principles he had followed in proposing the designs. Like most of Barrow's other papers, the copy of this letter sent to him has not survived; but Wren retained the draft for his own use, and this is set out below. The drawings referred to are reproduced as figs. 32–4 in the present book. The letter (now in All Souls, Wren papers 1.44) is not dated, but clearly falls later than the proposal for a rotunda. The first page is reproduced in *Wren Society* 5, pl. XXII.

Sir,

A building of that consideration you goe about deserues good care in the designe and able workemen to performe it; & that he who takes the generall management upon him may haue a prospect of the whole, and make all parts inside & outside corresponde well together. To this end I haue comprised the whole designe in 6 Figures.

Fig I.

[fig. 32] Shewes halfe the Groundplot of the substruction Cloister & first Flightes of the Staircases. I haue chosen middle pillars & a double porticoe & lightes outward rather then a middle wall, as being the same expence, more gracefull, & according to the manner of the auncients who made double walkes (with three rowes of pillars or two rowes and a wall) about the forum.

Fig II

[fig. 32] Shewes half the groundplot of the upper floor, the entrances from the stairecases, & the disposition of the shelues, both along the walls & breaking out from the walls, wch. must needes proue very convenient & gracefull, & the best way for the Students will be to haue a litle square table in each Celle

142

with 2 chaires. The necessity of bringing windowes and dores to answer to the old building leaues two squarer places at the endes & 4 lesser Celles not to study in but to be shut up with some neat Lattice dores for archiues.

Fig III

[fig. 32] Shewes the face of the building next the court with the pavillions for the stairecases & the sections of the old buildings where they joyne to the new. I chose a double order rather then a single, because a single order must either haue been mutilated in its members or haue been very <chargable *deleted*> expensiue, & if performed would not have agreed with the lownesse of the porches wch. would haue been too darke & the solids too grosse for the openings. I haue given the appearance of arches as the order required fair & lofty: but I haue layd the floor of the Library upon the impostes, wch. answar to the pillars in the cloister, & the levells of the old floores, & haue filled the Arches with relieues of stone, <where if you please you may *deleted*> of wch. I have seen the effect abroad in good building, & I assure you where porches are lowe with flat ceilings is infinitely more gracefull then lowe arches would be & is much more <agre *deleted*> open & pleasant, nor need the mason feare the performance because the Arch discharges the weight & I shall direct him in a firme manner of executing the designe. By this contrivance the windowes of the Library rise high & giue place for the deskes against the walls, & being high may be afforded to be large & being wide may haue stone mullions & the glasse pointed, which after all inventions is the only durable way in our Climate for a publique building, where care must be had that snowe driue not in. I have given noe other <ornament *deleted*> Frontispeice to the midle then Statues according to auncient example, because in this case I find any thing else impertinent, the Entrances being endwaies & the roofe not suiting it. This may be don if you please, you may make the three middle Arches with 3 qtr columnes & the rest with pilasters of a third <or 4th *deleted*> of their <module *deleted*> Diameter, wch. will saue some charge in stone, but it is best as it is designed.

Fig IV

[fig. 33] Shewes halfe the outside of the building next the River wch. I designe after a plainer manner to be performed most with Ashler, the three portalls one against each cloister & <anothe *deleted*> one in the middle <giue it grace

enough *deleted>* & the pavillions for the Staires give it grace enough for the viewes that way.

Fig: v

[fig. 33] Shewes half the Section the longest way & discovers the insides of the Staircase, the porticoe belowe the Library, the disposition of the shelues, the side dores from the old building, the division of the ceeling, & the roofe. The Staires are soe carried, they [are] made of marble or hard stone, with Iron rayles, & if the middle ally of the Library were paved with small marbles, you would much consult for the quiet of the place, & for the cleanesse of the bookes from dust, the Celles may be floored with wainscote. I haue added thin pilasters to the walles, wch. are <supposed to be *deleted>* easily performed in rendering upon brickworke. The cornices divide the ceeling into three rowes of large square pannells answering the pilasters wch. will prooue the best fret because in a long roome it giues the most agreeable perspective. I made the pavillions of the Staires soe as I might not loose my end Lightes & least the Lightes next the old buildings should be cut of within. I would advise to loose the 2 last roomes in the garrets & lay a covering of lead upon the 2d story, wch. may be ordered not to be discovered <without *deleted>* in the Court, the stone worke continuing.

Fig vi.

[fig. 34] Giues the transverse section through the middle Arche with the thicknesses of the walles the manner of the roofe & the insides to be compared with the other designes. I haue given the auncient forme of roofe wch. the experience of all ages hath found the surest, noe other is to be trusted without doubling the thicknesses of the walles. The statues will be a noble ornament they are supposed of plaister, there are Flemish artists that doe them cheape.

I suppose you haue good masons, how ever I would willingly take a farther paines to giue all the mouldings in great, wee are scrupulous in small matters & you must pardon us, the Architects are as great pedants as Criticks or Heralds. And therfore if you approue the designes, let <copies be taken of them *deleted>* the mason take his measures as much as is necessary for the present setting out of the worke & be pleased to transmit them to me again & I shall copy out partes of them at large, more proper for the use of the workemen & giue you a carefull estimate of the charge, & returne you again the originall designes, for in the handes of the workemen they will soon be soe defaced that they will not be able from them to pursue the worke to a conclusion. I haue made a Cursory estimate & it is not that at wch. you will stumble as not exceeding the charge proposed.

[no signature]

Index

Institutions at Cambridge are listed under their names; those elsewhere are gathered under their appropriate cities or other locations.